THE CENTENNIAL JOURNAL

National Bar Association Centennial Commission
Publisher

Editor

Patricia Moore Rosier, Esquire

Assistant Editor

Rosalind Ray, Esquire

Contributing Editors

Evett Simmons, Esquire
Debra Matlock, Esquire
Monique English
Yardyne Day
Ozzie Jenkins
Graphics – Oswego Newman
Devon Dillon

Dedication

This book is dedicated to all the lawyers, past and present whose diligence, hard work and determination have embodied the mission and work of the National Bar Association.

Acknowledgements

We acknowledge and give special thanks for the assistance and support of the following: Attorneys Patricia Rosier, Evett Simmons, Ben Crump, Frank Seales, Andrea Evans, John Crump, Rosalind Ray, Ricky Anderson, Debra Matlock, Kim Keenan, Algenita Scott Davis, U. Lawrence Boze, Paulette Brown, Arthenia Joyner, Vanita Banks, Belinda Stith, Michael Rosier and the NBI as well as all sponsors and supporters of this publication.

Table of Contents

Preface

As we commemorate the centennial of the National Bar Association, this volume stands as both a celebration and a testament—a celebration of a hundred years of courage, advocacy, and relentless pursuit of justice, and a testament to the extraordinary individuals and institutions that shaped, challenged, and redefined the legal landscape for African Americans and communities of color across the United States and beyond.

From its inception in 1925, the National Bar Association has served not only as a professional home for Black attorneys, judges, law professors, and students, but also as a beacon of justice and equity in the face of discrimination, exclusion, and systemic inequality. The stories and achievements chronicled within these pages offer a window into the unwavering spirit of our founders, the transformative work of our local and international affiliates, and the dynamic legacy of our trailblazing leaders.

This book brings together voices, victories, and visions—of bar associations established in defiance of exclusion, of landmark legal battles fought in courtrooms and communities, of international bridges built through shared justice values, and of groundbreaking educational programs like the Crump Law Camp that continue to grow future leaders in the profession.

It also honors the sacrifices and milestones of individuals whose names may never grace a law review but whose service, mentorship, and passion have left indelible marks on the profession and the fight for civil rights.

To all who read this—whether practitioner, student, scholar, or community member—may this record serve as inspiration and call to action. The work of justice is far from over. As we reflect on a century of bold leadership and transformative change, let us move forward with renewed commitment, ever guided by the mission of the National Bar Association: to promote equal justice under law and to ensure that the legal system is a force for inclusion, empowerment, and progress.

In solidarity and service,
The National Bar Association Centennial Commission

OFFICIAL LETTERS

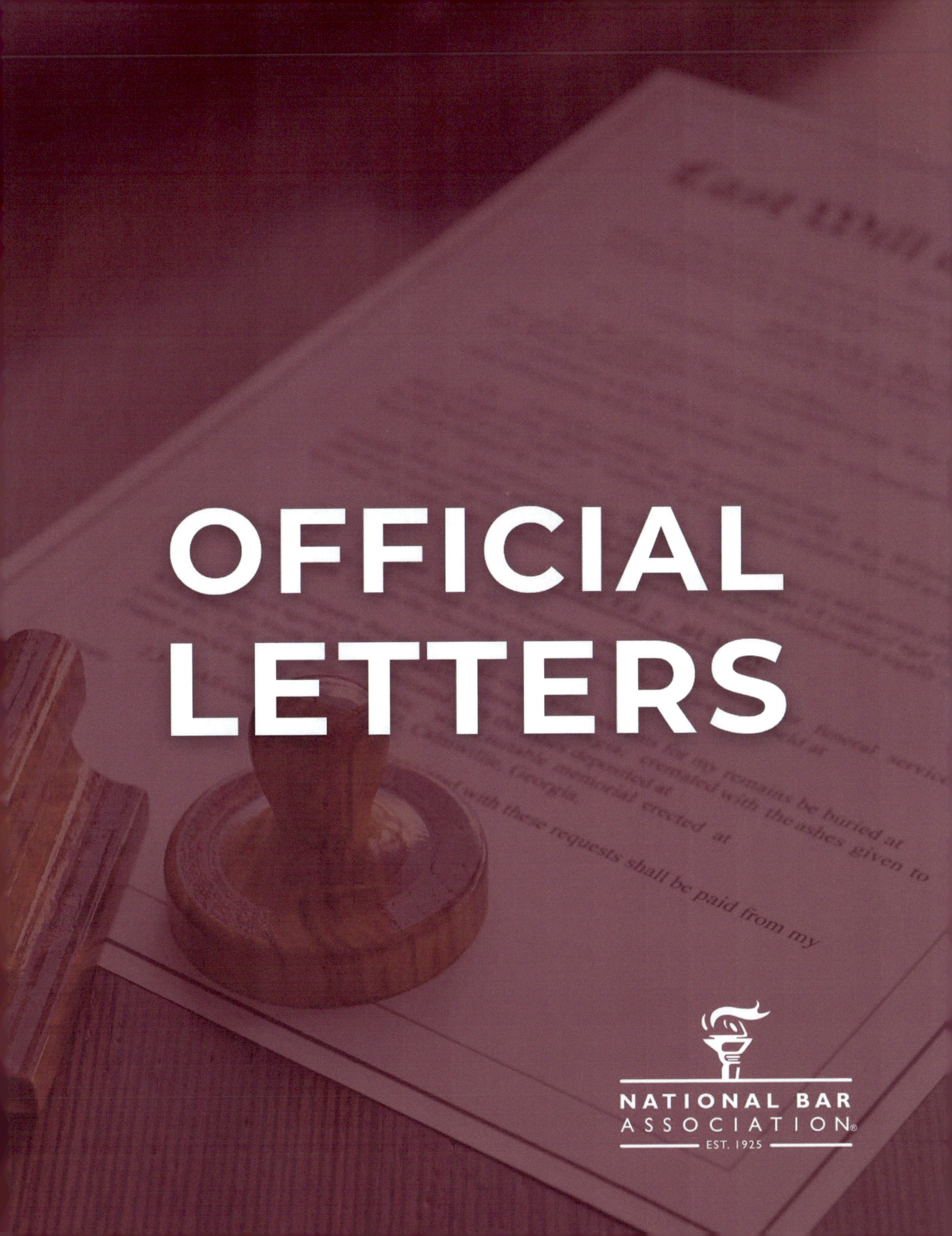

NATIONAL BAR ASSOCIATION
EST. 1925

THE NATIONAL BAR ASSOCIATION EST 1925 100 YEARS
IGNITING JUSTICE FOR 100 YEARS

July 26, 2025

On behalf of the National Bar Association ("NBA") and our Centennial Celebration Commission ("Centennial Commission"), I extend my deepest thanks and appreciation to you for purchasing a copy of The Centennial Journal. Your support honors our past, strengthens our present, and helps secure the future of the NBA as we commemorate 100 years of Black legal excellence and leadership.

This limited-edition commemorative journal is more than just a keepsake—it is a reflection of the rich legacy, trailblazing achievements, and unyielding commitment to justice that define the NBA. Your purchase directly supports the important work of our Centennial Commission, which has planned and executed a year of powerful events, reflections, and initiatives worthy of our historic milestone.

I especially want to recognize and thank the outstanding leadership of our Centennial Commission Co-Chairs, all of whom are esteemed Past Presidents of the NBA:

- Evett L. Simmons
- Sen. Arthenia Joyner
- Paulette Brown
- Keith Watters

Their vision, dedication, and strategic guidance have been instrumental in bringing the Centennial Celebration to life with both purpose and pride. I also extend heartfelt thanks to every member of the Centennial Commission, whose collective efforts have ensured that this year will be remembered for generations to come. We are grateful for your partnership in this historic journey. With your support, we will continue to amplify the voices of Black lawyers, uplift the next generation of leaders, and boldly carry forward the mission of the National Bar Association for the next 100 years and beyond.

Thank you again for your generosity and commitment.

Wiley S. Adams

Wiley S. Adams
Centennial President
National Bar Association

July 26, 2025

Dear NBA Members and Stakeholders:

What a privilege it has been for me to serve as Chair of the NBA Centennial Celebration Commission. I was also privileged to serve as Chair of the NBA's Seventy-Fifth Anniversary. It was an honor to have three Past Presidents serving as my Co-Chairs: Honorable Arthenia Joyner, Paulette Brown and Keith Watters. We were pleased to lead a Commission that worked together to bring you a series of programs, activities, art, and other events to remind us of the importance of our great association.

I must especially thank Paulette Brown, who led programming; Patricia Rosier who led the efforts to bring this Table Top Book to life; Frank Seales, who has been our lifesaver regarding the collection of funds; Vanita Banks, who led our technology efforts; Anne-Marie Clarke and Ellen Douglass, who led our efforts to showcase our Affiliates; Henry Hamilton, who made our Midyear shine; Cenceria Edwards, who has provided us with fantastic newsletter as editor; Arthenia Joyner, who has led our awards efforts; Kim Keenan, who assisted in securing our Rendering; Algenita Davis, who is leading our archive efforts; Iris Green, who has assisted in fundraising; Sonya Hoskins and Kevin Judd, who also worked on our Midyear programming; Zenobia Waters and Elizabeth Winfield, who have worked to bring new lawyers into the NBA; Monique Edwards, Antoinette Barksdale, our NBA Officers and staff who have stepped up to the plate; and many others who have shown your support to make this Centennial special.

I also want to thank our sponsors who purchased ads for this effort of love. Many of you are members of the NBA and want to showcase your Division, Section or a Member who has left us. Without you, there would be no Tabletop Book.

When you read this Book, we hope that you will fall in love again with the NBA. We hope you will see yourself as a part of the NBA's future. We are only as great as our weakest link. Yet, there is strength in numbers and as we grow, we will have a legacy to leave behind. With God's blessings and your support, we will have a building housing our archives for those attending the NBA's Two Hundred Year convention to see what we have accomplished.

With gratitude,

Evett L. Simmons

A Letter from President-Elect Ashley L. Upkins

In Honor of the National Bar Association's Centennial

As we stand on the threshold of a new century for the National Bar Association, I am humbled, honored, and profoundly inspired to offe my congratulations on 100 years of legal excellence, unshakable resolve, and relentless advocacy.

On August 1, 1925, the National Bar Association was born out of exclusion and necessity, built by visionaries who dared to create space where none existed. Its founding purpose to "advance the science of jurisprudence, uphold the honor of the legal profession, promote social intercourse among members of the American Bar, and protect the civil and political rights of all citizens" was not just aspirational. It was radical, necessary, and rooted in a fierce belief in justice.

This year, I have the extraordinary honor of being sworn in as President on the very day of our founding, August 1st. That moment is deeply symbolic. It reminds us not only of how far we have come, but also of the urgency and responsibility we now carry into our second century. The timing is not accidental. It is sacred. As we celebrate the legacy of those who laid the foundation, we must also ignite the path forward.

The NBA has opened doors that were once sealed shut, preparing generations of African American attorneys to serve with distinction in courtrooms, boardrooms, legislatures, and law schools across this nation. Yet, as access has increased, so too has the temptation to forget the price that was paid. Many now walk through doors that others built and believe the struggle is behind us. But history has taught us: progress is not permanent, and freedom is never free.

In the face of today's challenges, we are witnessing the rise of a new era of resistance. We are entering what I call the Second Civil Rights Movement. And just as before, the National Bar Association must stand at the front lines, unwavering and unapologetic in our mission.

This is our charge...not for recognition, but for liberation. The future of justice in America still depends on Black lawyers willing to fight for it. I do not carry this responsibility alone. I carry it with the spirits of our foremothers and forefathers beside me. I carry it with you.

To the National Bar Association: thank you for shaping me, for teaching me, for making it possible for a little Black girl from Tennessee to grow, to serve, and now, on the day of our founding, to lead. As we look ahead, let this be a moment of recommitment. Let us double down on our purpose. Let us remain bold in our pursuit. Because freedom and justice are inextricably bound, and because FREEDOM and JUSTICE cannot wait.

Congratulations on a century of courage!

With gratitude and resolve,
Ashley L. Upkins
President-Elect, National Bar Association

CORY A. BOOKER
NEW JERSEY

UNITED STATES SENATE
WASHINGTON, D. C. 20510

The National Bar Association
1816 12th Street NW

4th Floor
Washington, DC 20009

Dear Friends,

It is a pleasure to extend my warmest greetings and congratulations as you gather to celebrate 100 years of the National Bar Association.

Since its founding in 1925, the National Bar Association (NBA) has served as a pillar of opportunity, professionalism, and support for countless African American attorneys. For a century, the NBA has played a significant role in advancing the science of jurisprudence and protecting the civil rights of all Americans. Your participation in landmark Supreme Court cases such as Brown v. Board of Education, Gomillion v. Lightfoot, and Chambers v. Florida was crucial to creating a more equitable and inclusive nation. Your network of attorneys has provided protection for the crucial underpinnings of our country's Constitution and have had a profound impact on the history of the United States.

Again, congratulations on this incredible milestone, and thank you for all that you continue to do to bend the moral arc of our country toward justice. I look forward to celebrating your continued

Sincerely,

Cory A. Booker
United States Senator

RAPHAEL WARNOCK
GEORGIA

HOUSE OF REPRESENTATIVES
WASHINGTON, D. C. 20515

National Bar Association
1816 12th St. NW
4th Floor

Washington, D.C. 20009
333 East Walton Street

Dear Esteemed Member of the National Bar Association.

It is my distinct pleasure to congratulate the National Bar Association on their 100th anniversary and national conference.

The National Bar Association has been a stalwart ally in the fight for justice, equality, and fairness in America. I commend your commitment to empowering Black legal professionals across the nation. I am immensely grateful for the leaders, volunteers, and members of that make the advocacy possible. Reaching your 100th anniversary as an organization is no small feat, and such an impressive milestone would not be possible without the many dedicated individuals.

Please accept my most sincere wishes for a fulfilling and enlightening national conference, and congratulations again on significant milestone.
Keep the faith, and keep looking up.

Sincerely.

Reverend Raphael Warnock
United States Senator

ANGELA ALSOBROOKS
MARYLAND

COMMITTEES:
BANKING, HOUSING, AND URBAN AFFAIRS
ENVIRONMENT AND PUBLIC WORKS
HEALTH, EDUCATION, LABOR, AND PENSIONS
SPECIAL COMMITTEE ON AGING

United States Senate
WASHINGTON, DC 20510

May 22, 2025

Greetings National Bar Association members,

I am delighted to extend my warm congratulations to the National Bar Association (NBA) and its members on reaching 100 years of providing legal guidance and services to so many individuals from all walks of life!

I believe NBA founders, George H. Woodson, S. Joe Brown, Gertrude E. Rush, James B. Morris, Charles P. Howard, Sr., Wendell E. Green, C. Francis Straford, Jesse N. Baker, William H. Haynes, George C. Adams, Charles H. Calloway and L. Amasa Knox are looking down and saying "job well done." The NBA members have been great stewards of these Founders' legacies.

As the NBA embarks on its next 100 years, know that your strides toward justice and equality will continue to be appreciated by so many all over the world.

The impact the National Bar Association has had on jurists across this nation is critical. Many members of the NBA have served as staunch advocates for the underserved, their keen sense of justice and respect for our democracy has left its mark on our communities.

I am delighted to offer the National Bar Association and its members my congratulations and best wishes for their continued success!

Sincerely,

Angela D. Alsobrooks

Angela D. Alsobrooks
United States Senator for Maryland

HAKEEM S. JEFFRIES
8TH DISTRICT, NEW YORK
DEMOCRATIC LEADER

Congress of the United States
House of Representatives
Washington, DC 20515

WASHINGTON OFFICE:
2267 RAYBURN HOUSE OFFICE BUILDING
WASHINGTON, DC 20515
(202) 225-5936

DEMOCRATIC LEADERS OFFICE:
U.S. CAPITOL, H-204
WASHINGTON, DC 20515
(202) 225-4700

DISTRICT OFFICES:
CENTRAL BROOKLYN OFFICE:
55 HANSON PLACE, SUITE 603
BROOKLYN, NY 11217
(718) 237-2211

SOUTH BROOKLYN OFFICE:
445 NEPTUNE AVENUE, FIRST FLOOR
BROOKLYN, NY 11224
(718) 373-0033

JEFFRIES.HOUSE.GOV

July 26, 2025

Dear Friends,

Please accept my warmest greetings on the occasion of the National Bar Association's 100th Anniversary. I am honored to recognize the National Bar Association (NBA) for its century-long commitment to advancing justice and equity as the nation's oldest and largest national association of predominantly African American lawyers, judges, law professors, and law students. The NBA's network includes more than 67, 000 members who serve as champions of legal excellence and community advocacy.

The Association's expansive reach is evident in its 80+ chapters across the United States and its affiliations with legal organizations in Canada, the United Kingdom, Africa, Morocco, and the Caribbean. As a pillar of strength, the NBA fosters an inclusive, trusted and welcoming space that enriches the legal profession and enhances the vitality of our communities.

As the Representative of the 8th Congressional District, I thank you for your commitment to service and invaluable contributions. Best wishes for a memorable and joyful 100th anniversary celebration.

Sincerely,

HAKEEM JEFFRIES
Member of Congress

HOUSE OF REPRESENTATIVES
WASHINGTON, D.C. 20515

JAMES E. CLYBURN
SIX CONGRESSIONAL DISTRICT
SOUTH CAROLINA

June 3, 2025

Dear Members of the National Bar Association,

I would like to extend my heartfelt congratulations on your 100th anniversary. This remarkable milestone is a testament to the enduring legacy of excellence, advocacy, and leadership that has been cultivated within this association.

Since its founding in 1925, the National Bar Association has stood as a steadfast champion for justice and civil liberties for all citizens. Throughout the ebbs and flows of history, the association continues the pursuit of improving the administration ofjustice. As the nation's oldest and largest network of predominantly African American lawyers and judges, your resilience and dedication continue to inspire and uplift the next generation of those entering the legal profession.

I offer my sincerest congratulations on reaching this centennial anniversary.

With kindest regards,

Sincerely,

James E. Clyburn
Member of Congress

June 6, 2025

Congratulations to the

NATIONAL BAR ASSOCIATION®

EST. 1925

I am pleased to congratulate the National Bar Association (NBA) on the momentous occasion of your 100th Anniversary Celebration.

The mission of the NBA since its founding has always been clear and urgent: to advance equal justice under the law and protect the human and civil rights of Black Americans.

A century later, the NBA continues to stand as a powerful force for justice. Thanks in part to your members' advocacy, landmark civil rights legislation has transformed the legal and social landscape of our nation. And yet, many of the same struggles persist – reminding us that the work is far from finished.

With over 80 chapters throughout the United States, the NBA is our nation's oldest and largest association of predominantly African American lawyers, judges, law professors, and law students. At a time when fundamental rights and protections are once again under threat, your work remains as essential as ever.

I commend the NBA for its enduring strength and unwavering commitment to the law. I look forward to seeing your continued leadership in the vital legal battles that lie ahead.

Sincerely yours,

Maxine Waters

Maxine Waters
Member of Congress
43rd District, California

Jonathan L. Jackson
1st District, Illinois

Committee on Foreign Affairs
Subcommittee on Africa

Committee on Agriculture
Nutrition, Foreign Agriculture, and Horticulture

Commodity Markets, Digital Assets, and Rural Development

CONGRESS OF THE UNITED STATES
HOUSE OF REPRESENTATIVES
WASHINGTON, DC 20515

Washington
1641 Longworth House Office Building
Washington, D.C. 20515-1301
(202) 225-4372

Chicago
11750 S. Western Avenue
Chicago, IL 60643-2400
(773) 779-2400

National Bar Association
1816 12th St. NW, 4th Floor
Washington, DC. 20009

Dear Members of the National Bar Association,

As the U.S. House Representative for Illinois' First Congressional District, I extend my deepest gratitude to the National Bar Association for your unwavering commitment to justice, equity, and the rule of law.

Your enduring advocacy and leadership legacy has profoundly shaped the legal profession and the broader communities you serve. The National Bar Association stands as a beacon of justice, championing the rights of those too often overlooked by our legal system. Your commitment to advancing civil rights, expanding access to legal representation, and upholding the highest standards of professional excellence continues to inspire generations.

Your work strengthens our communities in my district and across the nation. It underscores the vital need for greater African American representation in the legal profession. You are building a more just, equitable, and inclusive society for all by mentoring future leaders and breaking down systemic barriers. Thank you for everything you do.

The relationship between my office and the National Bar Association is of utmost importance, and I want to reassure you of my unwavering commitment to our shared priorities. Whether protecting voting rights, increasing access to quality legal representation, or ensuring that our legal institutions reflect the diversity of the people they serve, I am committed to working alongside you. Please know that my office stands ready to support and amplify your vital work. I look forward to the opportunities ahead as we continue the fight for justice together.

Very truly yours,

Jonathan L. Jackson
Member of Congress

JonathanJackson.House.Gov

KWEISI MFUME
7TH DISTRICT OF MARYLAND

CONGRESS OF THE UNITED STATES
HOUSE OF REPRESENTATIVES
WASHINGTON, D.C. 20515

July 26, 2025

Dear Members of The NationalBar Association, I would like to extend warm wishes to you all as you gather in Chicago at this Centennial Convention to celebrate this major milestone. This esteemed gathering marks 100 years of the National Bar Association advancing the science of jurisprudence, honoring the legal profession, and protecting the individual, civil, and political rights of all citizens.

When this great organization was founded 100 years ago, it consisted of a dozen trailblazing Black attorneys sitting around a table in Des Moines, Iowa - today, the National Bar Association boasts more than 80 chapters and a network over 67,000 strong, the oldest and largest association of mostly African American lawyers, judges, legal experts, and law students in the United States. The NBA's annual convention has grown into one of our nation's preeminent platforms for forging professional relationships, discussing the day's most pressing legal, social, and economic issues, and engaging in opportunities for professional and career development. I will also be forever grateful for the support the National Bar Association provided to the NAACP during my time as President of the organization.

The 2025 theme of "Honoring Our Past, While Preparing for Our Future" could hardly be more appropriate for the landscape we now navigate - one shaped by attacks on the value of diversity and on the very foundations of our legal system. It both acknowledges the historic accomplishments of the National Bar Association, while also recognizing the difficult work that remains to be done to achieve a more perfect union. The path forward will demand the same courage and conviction that has defined the NBA for a century.

Congratulations, again, for years of effective advocacy and on the successful organization of this critically important gathering. I am proud to stand with you as you celebrate 100 years of Black excellence in the legal profession.

Sincerely,

Kweisi Mfume
Member of Congress

MEMBER OF CONGRESS

National Bar Association
1816 12th St. NW
4th Floor

Washington, DC 20009

Dear National Bar Association Members and Guests:

It is with great pleasure that I offer congratulations as you celebrate the 100th Anniversary of the National Bar Association (NBA).

For a century, the NBA has been one of our nation's leading advocates for equality across legal professions and the judiciary. The NBA has also been a constant presence in the struggle to expand equal protections under the law, from the early stages of the Civil Rights movement to new battles that are currently being waged. In this perilous time for our nation, where advancements that previous generations gained have come under assault, it is critical that organizations like the NBA, that possess critical expertise, continue to lead the way.

As you celebrate this milestone, it is my hope that the significance of this milestone will afford your membership the opportunity to reflect on the last century of progress and refocus the organization to continue serving as a support system for law students, professors, lawyers and judges for many years to come.

Very Truly Yours,

Robert C. "Bobby" Scott
Member of Congress

HOUSE OF REPRESENTATIVES
WASHINGTON, D. C. 20515

AL GREEN
9TH CONGRESSIONAL DISTRICT
HOUSTON, TEXAS

May 23, 2025

Dear National Bar Association,

I am pleased to congratulate the National Bar Association on reaching the significant milestone of 100 years of dedicated service to our nation. On behalf of the constituents of the Ninth Congressional District of Texas, I commend the organization for its unwavering commitment to excellence and justice.

The National Bar Association, as the oldest and largest national association of predominantly African American lawyers, judges, law professors, and law students, has played a vital role in advancing the science of jurisprudence, upholding the honor of the legal profession, and safeguarding the civil and political rights of all citizens. The steadfast contributions to our society over the past century have been courageous and invaluable.

I look forward to continuing to work with the National Bar Association on future endeavors and to continue to serve you well as a Member of Congress. Best wishes to all for a momentous occasion.

Sincerely,

Al Green
Member of Congress

Scion of the Enslaved Africans-
Sacrificed to Make America Great

Progenitor of August and August 20th
as Slavery Remembrance Month and Day

JASMINE CROCKETT
30TH DISTRICT, TEXAS

VICE RANKING MEMBER
HOUSE COMMITTEE ON
OVERSIGHT AND
GOVERNMENT REFORM

RANKING MEMBER
SUBCOMMITTEE ON OVERSIGHT
HOUSE COMMITTEE ON
THE JUDICIARY

Congress of the United States
House of Representatives
Washington, DC 20515–4330

WASHINGTON OFFICE:
1616 LONGWORTH HOUSE OFFICE BUILDING
WASHINGTON, DC 20515–4330
(202) 225–8885

DISTRICT OFFICE:
1825 MARKET CENTER BOULEVARD #440
DALLAS, TX 75207
(214) 922–8885

June 5, 2025

Dear National Bar Association,

As the Congresswoman for Texas' 30th Congressional District, it is my great pleasure to extend heartfelt greetings to you as you commemorate your 100th anniversary and national conference.

For a century, the National Bar Association has been at the forefront of the fight for justice, standing firm in its commitment to advocacy and equity. No matter the issue, this esteemed organization has consistently provided a voice for our most vulnerable neighbors and played a pivotal role in shaping and mentoring the next generation of legal professionals.

While the road ahead will no doubt present new challenges, I remain confident that with your continued leadership-and through strong partnerships with elected officials and community stakeholders-we will continue to make meaningful progress.

Congratulations again on 100 years of service, advocacy, and impact. I look forward to your continued contributions and stand ready to partner with you in the years to come. If my office can ever be of assistance, please don't hesitate to reach out.

Sincerely,

Jasmine Crockett
Member of Congress

HOUSE OF REPRESENTATIVES
WASHINGTON, D.C. 20515

ELEANOR HOLMES NORTON
DISTRICT OF COLUMBIA

July 26,2025

GREETINGS!

Welcome to all of you attending the National Bar Association (NBA) Conference, as you celebrate your 100th Anniversary. This annual event is a celebration of cultural brilliance and educational advancement.

As you celebrate this milestone, I hope this anniversary provides an opportunity to reflect on your significant achievements.

I applaud the National Bar Association, under the leadership of President Wiley Adams, for making positive change within the legal profession. The District of Columbia is privileged to have the NBA based in our city.

My best wishes for an outstanding conference and continued success in your important work!

Sincerely,

Eleanor H. Norton

Eleanor Holmes Norton

JOHN LEWIS

July 26, 2014

Dear Friends:

I welcome you to Atlanta. I am delighted you have chosen our beautiful city for the 89th annual convention of the National Bar Association. I hope this letter finds you all in good spirits.

Fifty years ago, I locked arms and marched with millions of others to ensure that every person can reap the fruits of justice. Along the way, hundreds of lawyers and judges helped us break down Jim Crow barriers, integrating buses and schools and paving the way for the march from Selma to Montgomery.

Today, we face new threats to those principles. The theme for this convention, Standing Our Ground for Justice, reflects what we all must do to not go back to the past.

Justice Thurgood Marshall once said, "The legal system can force open doors and sometimes even knock down walls. But it cannot build bridges. That job belongs to you and me." It is hard work to speak up and speak out, especially when fighting injustice. But I have every confidence the fine members of this Association will find the courage to do just that, just as they have for decades.

Please continue your hard work promoting justice across America. Keep the faith!

Best wishes,

John Lewis
Member of Congress

JULIANA STRATTON
LIEUTENANT GOVERNOR
STATE OF ILLINOIS

June 5, 2025

Dear National Bar Association Members and Guests,

I am pleased to join you in celebrating the National Bar Association's 100th Anniversary Centennial Journal – congratulations on this important milestone!

In 1925, when the NBA was founded, Black lawyers were not welcome to join the American Bar Association. Refusing to be ignored or left behind, twelve Black lawyers convened in Iowa to create a space that was both safe and welcoming for other Black lawyers who shared a commitment to upholding the law. In the century since your founding, the NBA has built a diverse network of resources, encouraged lawyers to work collaboratively, and promoted the importance of an equal judicial system. In doing so, you have helped expand the broader legal community and strengthened protections for the rights of all Americans.

As you take time to reflect on the NBA's historic impacts, I encourage you to consider how your own story will be woven into the Association's legacy. Think back to what inspired you to join this esteemed organization and take stock of what keeps you engaged in your work on the hardest days. By welcoming the voices of those who went unheard for too long, you have strengthened our judicial system for all.

Congratulations again on your 100th anniversary and thank you for being part of our nation's story!

Respectfully,

Juliana Stratton
Lieutenant Governor
State of Illinois

CITY OF DES MOINES
OFFICE OF THE MAYOR

Members of the National Bar Association,

As the Mayor of Des Moines, I want to congratulate you all on the centennial anniversary of the National Bar Association. Des Moines proudly serves as the birthplace of the association, dating back to 1925 when it was founded.

Gertrude E. Rush was the first African American female lawyer in Iowa. Gertrude E. Rush was also the only female co-founder of the National Bar Association which now boasts over 65,000 members globally. Her legacy impacts both the National Bar Association and the City of Des Moines and will continue to be celebrated.

All of you continue to live out the legacy of Gertrude E. Rush as members of the National Bar Association. A century of existence would not be possible without the involvement of dedicated and prestigious legal professionals like yourselves.

Once again, I want to congratulate you all on this significant milestone. A centennial celebration is something to be proud of, and all of us at the City of Des Moines are proud to call our city the homeland of the National Bar Association.

Sincerely,

Connie Boesen

Mayor Connie Boesen
City of Des Moines

Congratulations

National Bar Association 100th Anniversary

July 26, 2025

As Mayor of Washington, DC, I am pleased to extend congratulations to the National Bar Association on the milestone occasion of your 100th Anniversary.

Founded in 1925 during the height of the Jim Crow era by a group of Black lawyers, the National Bar Association (NBA) is the nation's oldest and largest national association of predominantly African American lawyers, judges, law professors, and law students. Long championing equality in the practice of law, the NBA's work stems from heavy discrimination and rejection from most bar associations of the time, and your establishment soon became a powerful vehicle of change. Members of this esteemed organization helped bring about justice in several landmark cases surrounding civil rights and were essential in helping to lay the groundwork for significant legislation during the Civil Rights Movement. This impactful network of Black law professionals has since grown immensely to include more than 60,000 members spanning 80 chapters worldwide, thus remaining steadfast in your commitment to advocate for civil and political rights protections for all US citizens.

From uplifting local communities through volunteer efforts and youth programming, to providing professional development for membership, the NBA has served as a source of collective support for a century now. Thank you for making a difference, and for always amplifying the voices of those who often go unheard. I offer my most sincere gratitude to the NBA for all the progress made, and for all the progress future generations of law professionals will make thanks to your humble beginnings and decades of vital work.

Once again, I am proud to join the more than 700,000 residents of Washington, DC in congratulating the National Bar Association on your 100th anniversary—I can't wait to celebrate many more!

Muriel Bowser
Mayor, Washington, DC

NAACP

Derrick Johnson
President and Chief Executive Officer

Leon W. Russell
Chairman National Board of Directors

May 30, 2025

Re: Recognition of 100 Years of Excellence

On behalf of the National Association for the Advancement of Colored People (NAACP), I congratulate the National Bar Association (NBA) on the centennial of its founding. As you know, when the NBA was founded, "separate but equal" was the law of the land. Professional organizations were permitted to discriminate on the basis of race, and the largest bar association excluded Black lawyers from its membership. What some might have seen as a hurdle, the NBA's founders saw as an opportunity for Black lawyers to gather, fellowship, learn, and build careers. With a network of more than 67,000 members, the NBA is a force for equity and excellence.

As the oldest and largest civil rights organization in the United States, the NAACP has worked with members of the NBA, who have provided countless hours of legal services. NBA members and the NAACP have stood together to fight for, and preserve the rights of, Black Americans. Furthermore, the NBA has consistently taken a strong stance against racist and oppressive policies, including the 2025 immigration policy that grants preferential refugee status to white South Africans and the 2025 White House policy targeting legal professionals.

As set forth in the Memoranda of Understanding between the NAACP and the NBA, the NAACP and the NBA "share common priorities and interests in ensuring the political, educational, social, and economic equality of rights of all persons and eliminating race-based discrimination." Our organizations have worked together to formulate strategies to provide legal protections against voter intimidation and to build a sustained infrastructure by leveraging our respective advocates and activists.

The NBA is just as relevant and needed as it was when it was founded in 1925. The NAACP celebrates the NBA's milestone year. We rejoice in the NBA's success, and we look forward to the continuation of our long and historic collaboration.

Sincerely,

Derrick Johnson
President and CEO

National Association *for the* Advancement *of* Colored People
4805 Mt Hope Drive • Baltimore MD 21215-3297 • 410.580.5777 • 877.622.2798 • **naacp.org**

100 YEARS OF POWER, PURPOSE, & PROGRESS

Honoring the National Bar Association's Centennial Legacy

The National Urban League proudly salutes the National Bar Association on 100 years of unwavering service, groundbreaking advocacy, and leadership in the fight for justice.

For a century, the NBA has been a pillar in the pursuit of civil rights, the advancement of Black legal professionals, and the protection of our communities through the rule of law.

As President and CEO of the National Urban League and a proud member of the National Bar Association, Marc H. Morial joins the Urban League Movement in celebrating this historic milestone. We look forward to the next century of continued partnership and a shared commitment to equity, empowerment, and justice for all.

Marc H. Morial
President & CEO,
National Urban League

JOIN THE MOVEMENT & STAY CONNECTED!

NUL.ORG

Follow us on social @naturbanleague

National
Urban League

OFFICE OF THE ATTORNEY GENERAL
STATE OF ILLINOIS

KWAME RAOUL
ATTORNEY GENERAL

May 2,2025

National Bar Association
1816 12th St. NW, 4th Floor
Washington, DC 20009

Dear National Bar Association Members:

As Attorney General of Illinois, I offer my most heartfelt congratulations to the National Bar Association (the NBA) on 100 years of faithful leadership and service to African-Americans in the legal profession.

Over the last century, we have certainly made strides in our pursuit of justice and equality, but we have also encountered setbacks. Even the youngest members of our esteemed profession are bearing witness to significant changes in our nation's legal landscape. As only the second African-American Attorney General of Illinois, I can state unequivocally that progress is not a passé objective. It is an ongoing necessity.

I applaud the NBA's longstanding commitment to solidarity and proficiency in the Bar. Moreover, I am thankful for your tenacity in advancing the interests, relevance, and rights of African Americans in the legal profession and at large. Now more than ever, we need legal associations that value inclusivity and are unafraid to challenge injustice.

Again, congratulations on this historic milestone. I wish you a memorable celebration and many more years of continued success.

Very truly yours,

Kwame Raoul
ATTORNEY GENERAL

CHICAGO OFFICE
5051W.CHICAGO AVE.
CHICAGO, IL 60651
773.750.0866 OFFICE
773.786.0256 FAX
repford@lashawnford.com

CAPITOL OFFICE
239-ESTRATTON BUILDING
SPRINGFIELD, IL 62706
217.782.5962 OFFICE
217.557.4502 FAX

La Shawn K. Ford
State
Representative
8th District

The National Bar Association

On behalf of Illinois 8th District Office, I would like to congratulate The National Bar Association on its 100th Anniversary celebration.

Since 1925, the NBA thrives with a framework for administering justice and truth-seeking for individuals with its network of experts. Their emphasis on representation is interwoven with the Nation's democratic model that works to exercise due process with representation and with respect to established laws.

This important milestone resonates with the culture of the organization's history. For example, its work during the Civil Rights era that birthed the Civil Rights Act, the Voting Rights Act, and the Fair Housing Act to its members' continued presence in the Legal sector. For one hundred years, the organization has held a high regard for implementing social and political changes, so the rights of individuals are protected.

I am proud of The National Bar Association and its impeccable record of sustainability throughout the years. I join them in celebrating their history of upholding laws and working to implement their articles of incorporation that reads: "advance the science of jurisprudence, uphold the honor of the legal profession, promote social intercourse among the members of the American Bar, and protect the civil and political rights of all citizens of the several states and the United States."

As Illinois' 8th District Representative, I wish the Association many more years of excellence in leadership.

Sincerely,

La Shawn K. Ford
State Representative-Eighth District

COVINGTON

BEIJING BOSTON BRUSSELS DUBAI FRANKFURT
JOHANNESBURG LONDON LOS ANGELES NEW YORK
PALO ALTO SAN FRANCISCO SEOUL SHANGHAI WASHINGTON

Eric H. Holder, Jr.

Covington & Burling LLP
One CityCenter
850 Tenth Street, NW
Washington, DC 20001-4956
T +1 202 662 6000

By Electronic Mail **June 5, 2025**

National Bar Association
1816 12th St. NW 4th
Floor Washington, D.C.
20009

Esteemed Members of the National Bar Association:

It is with great pleasure and enormous pride that I congratulate you on one hundred years of steadfast work towards justice, equality and the rule of law. It is a privilege to be part of an institution that has become the embodiment of the profession's conscience. The National Bar Association's work demonstrates what it means to answer inequity with action, turn compassion into enduring infrastructure and meet individual need with life altering commitment.

While we gather to celebrate this momentous occasion, we also recognize that this is a moment in our nation's history of existential consequence. It is a time that calls each of us, and all our institutions, to demonstrate real commitment to those values that, at our best, have defined the country and the legal profession. We cannot be observers or supplicants in this moment, and we need not speculate about the uncertain future that lies ahead — because the history of the National Bar Association makes clear we have the power to shape it.

If we are to honor truly those who came before us, we cannot afford to look away. The further we drift from fact and truth, the more liable we become to repeat the worst parts of our past: where the existence of injustice was denied, where repression was normalized and where silence was equated with acceptance.

We will not go quietly. We are a proud and resourceful people in a consequential profession. Our unique capabilities mean we also have unique responsibilities to hold to account those in power — through the courts, by protecting our electoral system, by using our influence in boardrooms and by leading in our own communities.

COVINGTON

While the twelve founding members could not have foreseen what we would be facing and fighting one hundred years later, it is with their conviction and their fortitude that we must continue this important work.

Mighty are the shoulders upon which we stand.

In celebration,

Eric H. Holder, Jr.
82nd Attorney General of the United States

From the desk of Donna Brazile

Celebrating 100 Years of the National Bar Association.
A Milestone in Advocacy and Justice

Happy 100th anniversary to the National Bar Association!

Since its founding in 1925, the National Bar Association has stood as a beacon of advocacy for underrepresented communities, tirelessly working to uphold the principles of fairness and inclusion in the legal system.

The Association and its members have played an important role in our civil rights journey. It provided a platform and safe space for traditionally underrepresented legal professionals to collaborate, grow, and make a meaningful impact. Its members have shaped laws, influenced policies, and inspired future generations through their unwavering commitment to justice.

As we celebrate this remarkable milestone, we honor the legacy of those who laid the foundation for this institution and acknowledge the profound contributions of its members, past and present. This centennial is not only a reflection of achievements but also a reminder of the ongoing work needed to ensure equality and justice for all.

Congratulations to the National Bar Association on this historic occasion. Here's to the next century of transformative leadership and progress in the legal community!

Sincerely, Donna Brazile

1816 12th Street NW, Suite 410
Washington, DC 20009
Barbara Arnwine, Esq., Founder & President
WWW.TJCOALITION.ORG

June 9, 2025

Dear Members of the National Bar Association,

"In the end, we will remember not the words of our enemies, but the silence of our friends." — Dr. Martin Luther King, Jr.

This powerful reminder calls on all of us—especially those in the legal profession—to uphold the rule of law with courage and conviction. In light of recent attacks on the integrity of our courts and the intimidation of major law firms, it is especially important to honor the trailblazers and members of the National Bar Association as we celebrate 100 years of leadership and service.

The honorable Congressman John Lewis once urged us to "get in good trouble, necessary trouble, and help redeem the soul of America." In these challenging times—marked by unconstitutional actions and the cruelty of mass deportation—we are reminded of the vital role the National Bar Association plays in defending the civil rights and dignity of all people.

Congratulations on this historic milestone. We are proud to stand with you in what may be the most important fight of this century.

Sincerely,

Barbara Arnwine, Esq. & Daryl Jones, Esq.

Barbara Arnwine, Esq. & Daryl Jones, Esq.

HISTORY SECTION

NATIONAL BAR ASSOCIATION®
EST. 1925

The History of the National Bar Association

CHARLES H. CALLOWAY

The National Bar Association was founded when segregation and discrimination based on race were permissible under the law, including the "separate but equal" jurisprudence of Plessy v. Ferguson (1896). There was no effective organization of lawyers promoting equal justice under the law and protecting Black Americans' human and civil rights.

Because Black lawyers were excluded from membership in the American Bar Association ("ABA") and most local majority bar associations across the country, 12 black lawyers met in Des Moines, Iowa, on August 1, 1925, to spearhead the establishment of a national network of black lawyers committed to the pursuit of equal justice under law. They founded the National Bar Association.

These 12 NBA founders were George H. Woodson, S. Joe Brown, Gertrude E. Rush, James B. Morris, Charles P. Howard, Sr., Wendell E. Green, C. Francis Stradford, Jesse N. Baker, William H. Haynes, George C. Adams, Charles H. Calloway, and L. Amasa Knox.

The purpose of the NBA, as stated in its articles of incorporation, was to "advance the science of jurisprudence, uphold the honor of the legal profession, promote social intercourse among the members of the American Bar, and protect the civil and political rights of all citizens of the several states and the United States."

Black lawyers affiliated with the NBA became the legal voices and advocates for Black people in the courts and other forums.

Leaders and members of the NBA took this nation from the Jim Crow jurisprudence of Plessy v. Ferguson to landmark cases such as Chambers v Florida (1940) (criminal justice), Smith v. Allwright (1944) (voting), Morgan v. Virginia (1946) (transportation), Shelley v. Kraemer (1948) (housing), Sweatt v. Painter (1950) (college admissions), Brown v. Board of Education (1954) (public schools), and Gomillion v. Lightfoot (1960) (racial gerrymandering).

The work of the National Bar Association and its members provided the underpinnings for major civil rights legislation, such as the Civil Rights Act of 1964, the Voting Rights Act of 1965, and the Fair Housing Act of 1968.

Today, the National Bar Association is the nation's oldest and largest national association of predominantly African-American lawyers, judges, law professors, and law students, with a network of over 67,000. The NBA has over 80 chapters throughout the United States and has affiliations with lawyer organizations in Canada, the United Kingdom, Africa, Morocco, and the Caribbean.

George C. Adams

Samuel Joe Baker

Charles Henry Calloway

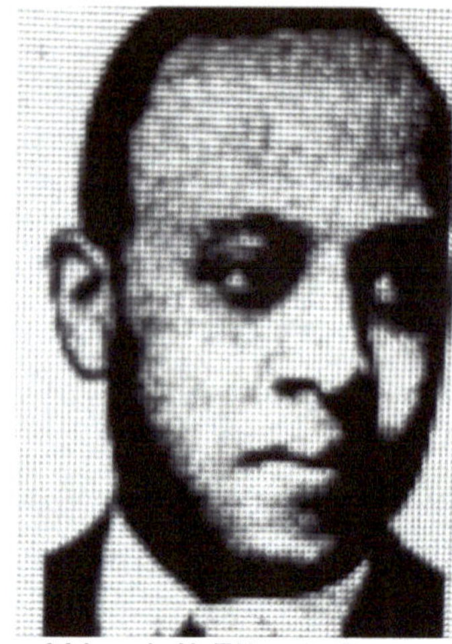
Wendell Elbert Green

Charles Howard

NATIONAL BAR ASSOCIATION®
EST. 1925

L. Amasa Knox

C. Francis Stradford

George Woodson

Gertrude Rush

James B. Morris

20s - Founding and Incorporation (1925)

The National Bar Association was founded out of the Greenville Movement and the Convention of the Iowa Colored Bar Association.

30s - Facing the Struggle (1930 - 1937)

The National Bar Association was concerned about private and municipal law libraries excluding black lawyers from their premises because of race.

40s - Membership Grows (1940 - 1947)

The National Bar Association attempted to establish "free legal clinics in all cities with a colored population of 5,000 or more."

50s - The Fight for Education (1950 - 1954)

Sweatt v. Painter ~ Encouraged by their victory in Gaines' case, the NAACP continued to attack legally sanctioned racial discrimination in higher education.

60s - Defining Decade (1960-1968)

NBA Journal and News was launched, later replaced by the NBA Bulletin. Key events included the 1963 March on Washington, the 1965 Voting Rights Act, and the 1968 founding of the National Conference of Black Lawyers by 17 lawyers seeking a new direction.

70s - Affirmative Action (1971 - 1978)

Flowers was ordained as a Methodist minister in 1971. The Women's Division of the NBA was approved in October.

80s - Membership Grows (1971 - 1978)

Arnette R. Hubbard assumed leadership, making her the first woman president of a major bar association.

90s - End of an Era (1992)

NBA submitted comments to the proposed "incubator" program described by the Federal Communications Commission (FCC) in its Memorandum Opinion and Order and Further Notice of Proposed Rule Making, FCC 92-361, released September 4, 1992.

2000s - A New Millennium (2000 - 2014)

Barack Obama, is sworn in as the 44th President, and the first black president in the United States

HISTORIC MILESTONES

1925-FOUNDING THE NBA

- The National Bar Association was incorporated on August 1, 1925, in Des Moines, Iowa, by 12 Black lawyers, aiming to promote equal justice under law and protect civil rights.

1937-FIRST BLACK FEDERAL JUDGE

- William Henry Hastie was appointed as the first Black federal judge, marking a significant advancement for African-American legal professionals.

1950-SWEATT V. PAINTER

- The U.S. Supreme Court ruled that racial segregation in graduate schools was unconstitutional, a landmark case argued by NBA members that helped dismantle the "Separate but Equal" doctrine in education.

1954-BROWN V. BOARD OF EDUCATION

- The U.S. Supreme Court unanimously declared segregation in public schools unconstitutional, a historic victory spearheaded by NBA members, including Thurgood Marshall.

1965-VOTING RIGHTS ACT

- The NBA played a critical role in supporting the passage of the Voting Rights Act, a cornerstone of the Civil Rights Movement that prohibited racial discrimination in voting.

1967

- Thurgood Marshall becomes the first African-American Supreme Court Justice.

1971-NBA JUDICIAL COUNCIL ESTABLISHED

1972

- The NBA officially approved the establishment of the Women Lawyers Division, promoting the inclusion and leadership of African-American women in the legal profession.

1978-NBA PRESIDENT DELIVERS TESTIMONY AT THE UNITED NATIONS

- Junius Williams was the first NBA President to speak at the United Nations on behalf Of justice for the people of Zimbabwe, Southern Africa. The NBA's position paper examining a fraudulent constitution purporting to give freedom to the black Africans Was accepted by the General Assembly as an official United Nations document.

1979-NBA HELD THE FIRST NATIONAL CONFERENCE ON "BLACK ON BACK" CRIME

- Under the leadership of NBA President Robert Harris, the NBA held the first ever National Conference on "Black on Black" crime and the first ever National Conference on Health and Law.

1981- NBA ELECTS FIRST WOMAN PRESIDENT

- Arnette R. Hubbard became the first woman president of the NBA, making her the first woman to lead a major bar association in the U.S.

1982-NATIONAL BAR INSTITUTE ESTABLISHED

1982-NBA PUBLISHES LAW JOURNAL

- Under NBA President Warren Hope Dawson, the NBA established the NBA Law

1985-NBA PRESIDENT ARRESTED IN PROTEST AGAINST APARTHEID

- The first NBA Treasurer and NBA president, Arthenia Joyner, was arrested at the South African Embassy in Washington, D.C., protesting the Regan Administration's position on apartheid in South Africa.

1986-NBA HALL OF FAME ESTABLISHED

- Under the leadership of NBA President Fred Gray, Sr., the NBA established its Hall of Fame to honor lawyers who had been licensed doe 40 years or more and made significant contributions to justice.

1991-NBA INTERNATIONAL AFFILIATES MEETING ESTABLISHED

- Under the leadership of NBA President Algenita Scott Davis and Vice President Ernestine Sapp, the NBA International Meeting was established.

1994-NBA MONITORS SOUTH AFRICA'S ELECTION

- Past President Paulette Brown leads a delegation of lawyers and judges to South Africa to monitor the first democratic election resulting in Nelson Mandela becoming President.

1995-NBA PRESIDENT APPOINTS VISION 2000 COMMISSION

- Under the leadership of President H.T. Smith and Chair, Evett Simmons, the NBA established the Vision 2000 Commission to conduct a self-assessment and develop ideas to improve the NBA in anticipation of its 75th Anniversary. From this came the Leadership Development Institute, the Walk for Justice, and Campaign 2000, a financial campaign to raise one million dollars.

1996-NBA WEBSITE AND ONLINE PRESCENCE ESTABLISHED

- Under the leadership of President Keith Watters, the NBA established its website and online presence.

1997-NBA LEGISLATIVE DIVISION AND HEMAN SWEATT LUNCHEON

- Under the leadership of NBA President U. Lawrence Boze', the NBA Legislative Division was founded, the Ronald Harmon Brown International Award of Merit was created and the first Heman Sweatt Luncheon was convened.

1997- NBA LED DELEGATION TO EAST AFRICA

- NBA President Randy Jones led the first delegation of NBA members to East Africa (Kenya and Tanzania), where NBA members attended the United Nations International Criminal Tribunal for Rwanda (ICTR) in Arusha, Tanzania and monitored the proceedings against persons responsible for the 1994 Rwandan genocide.

1998-NBA BRIDGES THE DIGITAL DIVIDE, ADVANCES ENVIRONMENTAL JUSTICE AND FOSTERS GLOBAL CONNECTION

- Under the leadership of NBA President Beverly McQueary-Smith, the NBA inaugurated a 'COMPUTERS IN OUR COMMUNITITES ACTION PLAN" donating computers to schools, churches and community centers to highlight the digital divide; inaugurated a "Corporate Green action Plan", planting trees to highlight the impact and synergistic consequences of environmental pollution on black and brown communities, and led a pilgrimage to the Holy Land-Israel and Jordan.

1998-THE NBA ESTABLISHES THE SMALL FIRMS & SOLO PRACTITIONERS DIVISION

2000-NBA LAUNCHES DR, MARTIN LUTHER KING, JR,. DRUM MAJOR FOR JUSTICE ADVOCACY COMPETITION

- Under the leadership of President Harold Pope, the NBA launched this competition at its 75th Annual Convention, fostering a new generation of advocates for justice.

2000- NBA CELEBRATES ITS 75TH ANNIVERSARY

2000-THE NBA SUBMITTED AN AMICUS BRIEF IN THE U.S. SUPREME COURT IN THE CASE OF BUSH V GORE, FOLLOWING THE PRESIDENTIAL ELECTION DEBACLE

2001-THE NBA LAW CAMP WAS ESTABLISHED UNDER THE LEADERSHIP OF PRESIDENT EVETT SIMMONS

2001-PRESIDENT MICHAEL ROSIER CONTINUES TO LEAD THE NBA'S PROGRAMS AND EVENTS IN SPITE OF THE SEPTEMBER 11 TERRORIST ATTACKS AND ITS AFTERMATH

2003-NBA PAST PRESIDENT DENNIS ARCHER BECOMES THE FIRST AFRICAN-AMERICAN PRESIDENT OF THE AMERICAN BAR ASSOCIATION

2003-2004- NBA TESTIFIED TO SUCCESSFULLY RENAME BWI AIRPORT TO BWI THURGOOD MARSHALL AIRPORT

- NBA President Kim Keenan organized the largest election protection effort to date including all the bars of color, raised over $1M, created the Cora T. Walker Corporate Partnership Award, the Johnnie Cochran Legends Award, and testified to successfully rename BWI Airport to BWI Thurgood Marshall airport.

2007-NBA PARTNERS WITH DRAKE TO HOUSE ITS ARCHIVES

- Under the leadership of NBA President Linnes Finney, Jr., historical documents were dedicated and deposited at Drake Law School in Des Moines Iowa.

2008-ELECTION OF BARACK OBAMA AS PRESIDENT OF THE UNITED STATES

- The first African-American President of the United States , was celebrated by the NBA as a monumental moment in the fight for equality and justice.

2010-NBA CREATES INITIATIVE TO FIGHT THE SCHOOL-TO-PRISON PIPELINE

- NBA President Demetrius Shelton led an initiative to build a pipeline to the profession, exposed and combatted the then emerging and disturbing trend that became known as, "The School-to-Prison Pipeline". The NBA also published a booklet, "How The Law Treats You Differently At Eighteen".

2010-NBA ADVANCES POLICIES IMPACTING AFRICAN-AMERICAN COMMUNITIES

- NBA President Mavis Thompson published and presented White Papers on issues that were critical and particular to African Americans, including foreclosures and hate crimes. The NBA also gave advice and counsel to the Congressional Black Caucus that contributed to the passage of the Affordable Care Act.

2012-PRESIDENT AND FUTURE PRESIDENT MAKE HISTORY REPRESENTING THE FAMILY OF TRAYVON MARTIN

- President Daryl Parks and future Ben Crump represent the family of seventeen year old Trayvon Martin, whose murder by a self-appointed vigilante, spared a national debate regarding the "Stand Your Ground" laws.

2013-NBA PRESIDENTS MICHAEL ROSIER AND PATRICIA ROSIER BECOME THE FIRST MARRIED COUPLE TO BE ELECTED NBA PRESIDENTS

2013-NBA IN PARTNERSHIP WITH THE AMERICAN CONSTITUTION SOCIETYM ESTABLISHES THE CONSTITUTION DAY PROJECT

- Under the leadership of President Patricia Rosier, the NBA launches its Constitution Day Project, in partnership with the American Constitution Society. The Project teaches school-age children about the U.S. Constitution on the federally recognized Constitution Day on September 17 annually. To date, this Project has reached over 500,000 children.

2015-NBA PAST PRESIDENT PAULETTE BROWN BECOMES THE FIRST AFRICAN-AMERICAN WOMAN PRESIDENT OF THE AMERICAN BAR ASSOCIATION

2016-2017-NBA TACKLES ECONOMIC EMPOWERMENT FOR THE AFRICAN AMERICAN COMMUNITY

- Under the leadership of NBA President Kevin D. Judd, the NBA focused on Economic Empowerment for the African- American community and tackled the widespread pandemic of police brutality thru advocacy and the law.

2019-MONUMENT HONORING NBA FOUNDERS IS DEDICATED IN DES MOINES, IOWA

2020-2021-NBA PRESIDENTS ALFREDA ROBINSON AND TRICIA (CK) HOFFLER LEAD THE NBA THROUGH THE COVID-19 PANDEMIC

2021-NBA MEMBER KAMALA HARRIS BECOMES THE FIRST WOMAN AND FIRST AFRICAN AMERICAN VICE-PRESIDENT OF THE UNITED STATES

2021-NBA PAST PRESIDENT REGINALD TURNER BECOMES PRESIDENT OF THE AMERICAN BAR ASSOCIATION

2021-NBA PRESIDENT MEETS WITH AFRICAN LEADERS

- Under the leadership of NBA President Carlos Moore, the NBA advocated for justice domestically and internationally, including traveling to and meeting with the Presidents of Ghana and Guyana.

2022-NBA WOMEN LAWYERS DIVISION CELEBRATES ITS 50TH ANNIVERSARY

2024-NBA LEADS ELECTION PROTECTION EFFORT

- Under the leadership of President Wiley S. Adams, the NBA leads national Election Protection Initiative, and in collaboration with the Transformative Justice Coalition, hosts three command centers in Atlanta, Georgia, Milwaukee, Wisconsin and Washington, D.C.

2025-NBA DEDICATES FIRST GRAVE MARKER FOR NBA FOUNDER GERTRUDE RUSH IN DES MOINES, IOWA

Corporation Record, No. 36

29551

ARTICLES OF INCORPORATION
OF THE
THE NATIONAL BAR ASSOCIATION.

Fee .60.

Filed for record July 29, 1926
At 3:05 P. M.

Mrs. E. O. Fleur Recorder
P. J. Griffin Deputy

---0O0---

We the undersigned members of the National Bar Assocation together with our associates do hereby form ourselves into a Corporation not for pecuniary profit, under theprovisions of Chapter 389 of the Code of Iowa, 1924 and adopt for our government the following:

Article I. Name

The name of this corporation shall be the National Bar Association.

Article II. Object.

The object of this association shall be to advance the science of jurisprudence uphold the honor of the legal profession, promote social intercourse among the members of the American Bar, and protect the civil and political rights of all citizens of the several states and of the United States.

Article III. Location

The principal place of business of this corporation shall be at Des Moines, Polk County, Iowa.

Article IV. Membership.

The membership of this association shallconsist of all who are now or shallhereafter, be admitted to membership in the National Bar Associatin, in accordance with the Constitution and By-laws of said association, as they now exist or as they shall hereafter be amended.

Article V. Officers.

The officers of this association for the first year shall be a President, a Vice President, a Secretary, Assistant Secretary, a Treasurer and seven Regional Directors, who shall constitute the Board of Directors to conduct the affairs of the corporation and be elected annually in accordance with the provisions of the Constitution and By-laws of this association and who for the first year shall be:

President, Geo. H. Woodson, Des Moines, Iowa; Vice President, C. H. Calloway, Kansas City, Mo.; Gustave B. Aldrich, Tacoma, Wash. director, 1st Region; David B. Henderson, Kansas City, Kans., Director 2nd Region; W. T. Francis, St. Paul, Minn. director, 3rd Region; I. Amasa Knox, Kansas City, Mo.; director 4th Region; Wm. H. Haynes, Chicago, Director 5th Region; W. C. Mathews, Boston, Mass.; Director 6th Region; and D. Hamilton Jackson, Christainstead, St. Croix, Virgin Islands, U. S. A. director 7th Region.

Article VI. Meetings

The annual meeting for the election of officers and the transaction of such other business as come within the purpose of this organization shall be held on the first Thursday in August at such place as shall be agreed upon at the previous annual meeting, except that in case of an emergency the Board of Directors may remove the meeting to such otherplace as they may agree upon; but the president may call a special meeting in the manner provided in the Constitution of the Association.

Article VII. Amendment

These Articles may be amended by the vote of three fourths of the members present and voting at any annual meeting, provided a copy of the proposed amendment shall have been filed with the secretary at least thirty days, prior to the date of said meeting and copy thereof mailed to the last known address of each member in good standing not less than ten days prior to the date of said meeting.

George H. Woodson, Des Moines Ia.
S. Joe Brown Des Moines,
Chas. P. Howard Des Moines, Ia.

DAY REGISTER—AUG. 2, 1925.

STRANGER ATTACKS IOWA CITY MAN AT NIGHT WITH KNIFE

Iowa City, Ia., Aug. 1 (Special). —When Orlas Cox reached for a match at the request of a man who stepped from the shadows near the cavalry barns here, early in the morning, he was suddenly attacked and severely injured by a knife in the stranger's hand.

Cox, who is on his way to recovery at his home, says he has no idea as to the identity or motives of his attacker.

Police who took the injured man to his residence, were unable to trace the mysterious assailant.

Arrested for Issuing False Check for $68

Burdette V. Marchant, who rented a touring car from the Bruce Rent-a-Ford company here over two weeks ago and failed to return it until yesterday, was arrested yesterday afternoon on a charge of issuing a false check for $68 under the name J. W. Marchant to the Rent-a-Ford company. He is being held in the city jail pending an investigation of the case.

Mason City's New Chief.

Mason City, Ia., Aug. 1. (Special)—Frank Sanford, member of the police department, was nominated chief of police today following a stormy session of the city council.

NEGRO ATTORNEYS FORM NATIONAL BAR ASSOCIAION

At the call of the Iowa State Negro Bar association, representative Negro lawyers from various sections of the United States met at the courthouse here yesterday and organized the National Bar association. Fifteen lawyers were present. Sixty others sent in telegrams or letters, asking that they be made charter members.

George H. Woodson of this city was chosen president of the national association. Other officers elected were: C. H. Galloway, Kansas City, Mo., vice president; Wendell Green, Chicago, secretary; Jesse N. Baker, Chicago, treasurer, and Gustave B. Aldrich, Tacoma, Wash., David E. Henderson, Kansas City, Kan., W. T. Francis, St. Paul, Minn., L. A. Knox, Kansas City, Mo., W. H. Haynes, Chicago, W. C. Matthews, Boston, and D. Hamilton Jackson, Christiansted, St. Croix, Virgin Islands, regional directors.

Members of the Iowa State Negro Bar association called the meeting because they felt the need of a national association where the Negro lawyers could work out the problems of the profession.

Chicago will be the meeting place for the 1926 national convention.

MR. CUPID BORROWS A MUSKET AND RAIDS HOME HERE

Cupid, who has visited the Faler home, 4128 North Union street, two Saturdays consecutively, used a musket in place of his trusty bow and arrow.

Bessie, 22 and Fern Faler, 18, marched to the altar July 25 and Aug. 1, respectively, each clinging to the arm of a Fort Des Moines soldier.

Bessie, who a week ago became Mrs. Einar Jackola, wife of Private Jackola, appeared with her husband in the office of County Clerk William Baldwin yesterday afternoon. After assisting in obtaining the license the couple witnessed the marriage of Fern to Private L. McHugh.

"Good-by folks," Mrs. Jackola said as she left the office. "We'll be back next Saturday. I have another sister who is 'strong' for the army."

C. E. Keeney Purchases Garage From Holsman

The purchase of the Iowa garage, Fifth street and Keosauqua way, by C. E. Keeney was announced yesterday. He bought the garage from J. A. Holsman, president of the Rent-A-Ford company. The consideration was not made public.

Mr. Keeney is also owner of the Hotel Savery garage, 421 Fourth street.

Who's Who Among Negro Lawyers

Published by
THE NATIONAL BAR ASSOCIATION
1945

WHO'S WHO
Among Negro Lawyers

Compiled and edited by
Sadie T. M. Alexander, Secretary of the
THE NATIONAL BAR ASSOCIATION

WHO'S WHO
Among Negro Lawyers

NATIONAL BAR ASSOCIATION

Organized 1923

OFFICERS

Charles W. Anderson, Jr., President
632 W. Walnut St., Louisville, Ky.

Perry B. Jackson, 1st Vice-President
Prospect-fourth Bldg., Cleveland, Ohio

J. R. Booker, 2nd Vice-President
Century Bldg., Little Rock, Ark.

Austin T. Walden, 3rd Vice-President
Herndon Bldg., Atlanta, Georgia

Sadie T. M. Alexander, Secretary
40 S. 19th St., Phila., Pa.

L. Marian Poe, Ass't Secretary
628-25th Street, Newport News, Va.

William Y. Garvin, Treasurer
217 W. 125th St., New York, N. Y.

Sidney R. Redmond, Editor
National Bar Journal
2103a Market St., St. Louis, Mo.

*A member of N B A, but no biographical information was su
M. S. denotes member of N B A serving in the military service.

Professional Sections and Divisions

Please check the sections and divisions that you are interested in.

	Section / Division	Fee
☐	Government Lawyers Division	$10.00
☐	Judicial Council Division	$100.00
☐	Law Professors Division	$10.00
☐	Law Students Division	No Charge
☐	Small Firms & Solo Practitioners Division	$25.00
☐	Women Lawyers Division	$15.00
☐	Young Lawyers Division	$10.00
☐	Administrative Lawyers	$10.00
☐	Arbitration	$15.00
☐	Bankruptcy Law	$20.00
☐	Civil Rights	$15.00
☐	Civil Trial Advocacy	$25.00
☐	Commercial Law	$25.00
☐	Criminal Law & Juvenile Justice	$10.00
☐	Energy and Environment Law	$10.00
☐	Entertainment and Sports Law	$10.00
☐	Family Law	$15.00
☐	Institutional/Corporate Law	$10.00
☐	Intellectual Property Law	$10.00
☐	International Law	$20.00
☐	Labor Law	$25.00
☐	Medical Law	$10.00
☐	Military Law	$15.00
☐	Partners in Majority Law Firms	$25.00
☐	Real Estate and Probate Law	$25.00
☐	Small Business Development	$5.00
☐	Tax Law	$20.00

Class Of Membership

Check one		Amount
☐	Student membership	No fee
☐	Associate membership	$50.00
☐	Admitted to practice less than 5 years	$75.00
☐	Admitted to practice more than 5 years	$150.00
☐	Life membership	$2250.00
☐	Subscribing life membership	$2250.00

Publications:

NBA members are kept abreast of developments in law-related areas through the

NBA Magazine

NBA Magazine is the most widely circulated legal publication focusing on African American attorneys in the U.S. NBA also publishes newsletters from its various sections and divisions.

Membership Directory:

The Directory is another important service of the association designed to increase networking and case referrals among African American attorneys. The Directory is also an important tool for private industry and governments in locating African American lawyers. When completed, the 1995 directory will be the largest and most comprehensive publication of African American attorneys in the world. The directory will contain more than 18,000 individual names in alphabetical and geographical listings with key codes identifying the types of practice and areas of law of each member.

Judicial Nominations:

The Judicial Nomination Selection Committee of the NBA is active in the nomination and selection of judges throughout the U.S.

Legislative Action:

The NBA is active in legislative affairs by participating in congressional hearings and drafting of legislation. Recently the NBA testified on the crime bill, Judicial Reform, Health Care, and other bills before Congress.

**For NBA Members
Law is More than a Career
...It's A Commitment**

Since - 1925

The National Bar Association

Making a Difference Then and Now

Join Today!

TODAY

people of African origin are faced with new and emerging challenges. These challenges come in the face of a developing new world order, which holds opportunities and promise for social, political and economic change, as well as national and international peace. This change which is forced by the reorganization of the Soviet Union is redirecting the world from how we once knew it. The deployment of new technologies and the search for new market places is bringing the people and cultures of the world closer together.

As people of a common origin, we believe that Black lawyers world-wide can take advantage of these times to ensure that progress and development reach our communities and nations. By networking, exchanging resources

President Bill Clinton

"The National Bar Association can help you maximize your career growth potential"

and coming together to learn more about each other, we can penetrate the forces that once prohibited us. This new opportunity can be beneficial to all of us.

The National Bar Association can help you maximize your career growth potential by participating in the NBA through its section activities, seminars, publications and Continuing Legal Education (CLE) programs.

The NBA provides numerous opportunities for its members to strengthen their legal skills and influence the highest levels of government. Members can also enhance their individual practices through networking activities, including CLE programs and inclusion in our membership directories and referral program.

As a member of the NBA you can take advantage of the comprehensive benefits package. The package includes access to credit union membership, group insurance, car rental discounts, travel services, group discount purchasing and the NBA gold MasterCard.

The NBA has demonstrated, through its many accomplishments, a commitment to its members' growth as well as to the advancement of the Black community.

National Bar Association
1225 11th Street, N.W
Washington, DC 2000
(202) 842-3900

Special Projects:

Black Elderly Legal Assistance Support Project

The National Bar Association (NBA) Black Elderly Legal Assistance Support Project (BELASP) is working to improve the availability and delivery of legal services to elderly Black Americans. Since its inception in 1986, BELASP has conducted a variety of programs designed to improve the Black elderly's access to legal assistance. BELASP has provided many training and continuing legal education seminars for lawyers, including Saving *The Home and Defending Against Fraud and Scams*.

The Commercial Law Section Corporate Counsel Conference

For the past seven years, the National Bar Association has sought through its Commercial Law Section to showcase the expertise and talents of NBA member attorneys, and develop networks between NBA member firms and national and international corporations. More than 150 NBA member firms spanning the US and Canada attend the conference along with 75 general counsels representing some 50 corporations and government agencies.

National Minority Bar Leadership Summit

National Bar Association hosted the first ever Minority Bar Leadership Summit aimed at developing a networking relationship among the leading minority bar associations nationwide. The conference is now an annual meeting of the leaders and officers of the four national minority bar associations which include the National Bar Association (NBA), the Hispanic National Bar Association (HNBA), the National Asian Pacific American Bar Association (NAPABA) and the Native American Bar Association (NABA). The group is now known as the **Coalition of Bar Associations of Color**.

Additional Benefits:

Computerized Legal Research

The NBA offers its members Lexis, the world's most comprehensive legal research tool.

Credit Card

NBA members can qualify for a "gold" Mastercard with up to a $10,000 credit line.

UPS Shipping Discounts

NBA can provide members a special discount rate which reduces the rate of overnight shipping. The program can be used for both personal and business mailing.

Travel Service

Through [illegible] Travel, members get a toll free "Bargain Finder Plus" search program for all domestic and special international rates, discount rental car program, individual cruise rebates and free flight insurance of $[illegible] all with two day priority mail delivery service.

1st Annual ARTHENIA JOYNER *Prayer* BREAKFAST

SUNDAY, JULY 17, 2016
8:00 AM - 9:30 AM

NATIONAL BAR ASSOCIATION®
EST 1925

NBA Prayer Breakfast History

In 1970, during the National Bar Association Convention at the Roosevelt Hotel in New York City, the Honorable Vince Monroe Townsend, from Los Angeles, California, led the discussion with several lawyers to have prayer on a Sunday before the day's events began. The group included now past president and former State Senator Arthenia Joyner, who along with a handful of her fellow attorney-attendees, agreed that faith and prayer were important in the lives of NBA lawyers. They secured a small conference room, each ordered their own meal, and had prayer. This informal tradition continued for many years until 1985 when, during her presidency, Joyner established the Inaugural NBA prayer breakfast at the 60th convention in Chicago.

The NBA's first prayer breakfast was an impactful and memorable event. It set a beautiful precedence, with Judge Shelvin Louise Marie Hall serving as its first chair, her father, the late Rev. Shelvin J. Hall serving as the first master of ceremonies, and the Rev. Jerry Blakemore Esq., Deputy Governor of Illinois serving as the first keynote speaker. In 2015, under the leadership of past president Pamela Meanes, the NBA passed a resolution to name the event The Arthenia Joyner prayer breakfast in honor of Joyner's longstanding dedication to faith as a foundation to success in the law and in life.

Now, forty years since its inception, the prayer breakfast remains an integral part of the NBA experience, signaling the start of the convention and providing music, inspiration, and a positive message for its attendees.

Program

SUNDAY, JULY 17, 2016
8:00 AM - 9:30 AM

FRANK SEALES, CHAIR

Call to Service	Lynn Whitfield
Invocation	Rev. Lee Clayton Goodman
Scripture Reading	Juan Thomas
Occasion	Arthenia Joyner
Introduction of Yolanda Adams	Ricky Anderson
Song of Preparation	Yolanda Adams
Preached Word	Yolanda Adams
Breakfast is Served	
Song of Praise	Yolanda Adams
Closing Remarks	President Benjamin Crump National Bar Association
Benediction	Rev. Lee Clayton Goodman

Charles Hamilton Houston was a prominent African American lawyer, educator, and civil rights activist who played a pivotal role in dismantling racial segregation in the United States and establishing the presence of the National Bar Association in Washington, DC. Born on September 3, 1895, in Washington, D.C., Houston grew up in a middle-class family that valued education and hard work. His father was a lawyer, which influenced his decision to pursue a career in law,

Houston attended Amherst College, where he graduated as valedictorian in 1915. After serving in World War 1, he enrolled at Harvard Law School, becoming the first African American editor of the Harvard Law Review. He earned his law degree In 1922 and later completed a Doctor of Juridical Science degree.

Houston was Dean of Howard University School of Law, where he transformed the institution into a rigorous training ground for future civil rights lawyers. He emphasized the importance of using the law as a tool for social change and Instilled this philosophy in his students, including Thurgood Marshall, who would later become the first African American Supreme Court Justice.

Houston is best known for his strategic legal work with the National Association for the Advancement of Colored People (NAACP). He devised a plan to challenge the "separate but equal" doctrine established by Plessy v. Ferguson (i896), focusing on inequalities in education. His efforts laid the groundwork for the landmark Brown v. Board of Education decision in 1954, which declared racial segregation in public schools unconstitutional.

Throughout his career, Houston faced significant challenges and discrimination, yet he remained steadfast in his commitment to justice and equality. He passed away on April 22, 1950, but his legacy endures through the countless individuals he inspired and the profound impact he had on civil rights law in America.

Our Collective IMPACT

No. 00-949

In the Supreme Court of the United States

October Term, 2000

George W. Bush and Richard Cheney,
Petitioners,
v.
Albert Gore, Jr. et al.,
Respondents.

On Writ of Certiorari to the Supreme Court of Florida

BRIEF *AMICUS CURIAE* OF THE NATIONAL BAR ASSOCIATION IN SUPPORT OF RESPONDENTS

Evett L. Simmons
President
National Bar Association
1225 11th Street N.W.
Washington, D.C. 20001
(202) 842-3900

David Earl Honig
3636 16th St. N.W.
Suite B-366
Washington, D.C. 20010
(202) 332-7005
Counsel of Record

Attorneys for Amicus Curiae

-i-

TABLE OF CONTENTS

Respectfully submitted,

David Earl Honig
3636 16th St. N.W.
Suite B-366
Washington, D.C. 20010
(202) 332-7005
Counsel of Record*

Evett L. Simmons
President
National Bar Association
1225 11th Street N.W.
Washington, D.C. 20001
(202) 842-3900

Attorneys for Amicus Curiae

December 10, 2000

* *Amicus curiae* appreciates the valuable suggestions provided by Anita Hodgkiss and Thomasina Williams, Esqs., and research provided by Ayesha Nichols, Esq.

INTRODUCTION TO THE NATIONAL BAR ASSOCIATION

Because Black lawyers were excluded from membership in the American Bar Association ("ABA") and most local majority bar associations across the country and there was no effective organization of lawyers promoting equal justice under law and protecting the human and civil rights of Black Americans, twelve (12) black lawyers met in Des Moines, Iowa, on August 1, 1925, to spearhead the establishment of a national network of black lawyers committed to the pursuit of equal justice under law which was initially the Negro Bar Association and later renamed the National Bar Association (NBA).

These twelve (12) NBA incorporators were George H. Woodson, S. Joe Brown, Gertrude E. Rush, James B. Morris, Charles P. Howard, Sr., Wendell E. Green, C. Francis Stradford, Jesse N. Baker, William H. Haynes, George C. Adams, Charles H. Calloway, and L. Amasa Knox.

The NBA was founded when segregation and discrimination, based on race, were permissible under the law, including the "separate but equal" j urisprudence of Plessy v. Ferguson (1896).

With the stated purpose in its articles of incorporation to "advance the science of jurisprudence, uphold the honor of the legal profession, promote social intercourse among the members of the American Bar, and protect the civil and political rights of all citizens of the several states and of the United States," the NBA started on a path that is now one hundred (100) years old to be the legal voices and advocates for Black people in the courts and other forums.

In the 1930s, the NBA was concerned about private and municipal law libraries excluding black lawyers from their premises because of race. Throughout the decade, Sadie T. Mosell Alexander and her husband, NBA Past President Raymond Pace Alexander, initiated legal fights that began to open restaurants, hotels and movie theaters to blacks in Philadelphia. Ms. Alexander was the first black woman to graduate from the University of Pennsylvania's Law School, and then the first admitted to legal practice in Pennsylvania.

In 1937, William Henry Hastie was appointed the nation's first black federal judge.

In 1938 in the case of Missouri ex rel. Gaines v. Canada, the U.S. Supreme Court ruled that states providing higher education to white students must also provide equal educational opportunities to black students within the state. The Court held that Missouri's practice of denying blacks admission to its law school and offering scholarships to attend out-of-state law schools violated the Equal Protection Clause of the Fourteenth Amendment.

In the 1940s, the NBA attempted to establish “free legal clinics in all cities with a colored population of 5,000 or more.” Legal clinics, managed by a group of black lawyers, were established in twelve states. Contemporary poverty law and legal clinics can be traced to the legal aid movement initiated by the NBA.

In 1941, NBA Past President Alexander founded the National Bar Journal, which became a platform for black lawyers to challenge legal principles contrary to the interests of black Americans.

In 1947, NBA Past President W. Harold Flowers defended two black men who had been charged with first-degree murder for the deaths of two white men. His motion to quash the entire jury on the grounds that there had been no black jurors in nearly fifty years led to the placement of thirteen blacks on the prospective jurors' panel, with three eventually seated on the jury. The defendants were found guilty of lesser charges, making this the first time in Arkansas that a black man had not gone to the electric chair upon conviction in the death of a white man.

The 1950s were the fight for education. Encouraged by their victory in the Gaines case, the NAACP led by NBA members continued to attack legally sanctioned racial discrimination in higher education. In the case of Sweatt v. Painter, in 1946 a black man named Heman Sweatt applied to the University of Texas' "white" law school. Hoping that it would not have to admit Sweatt to the "white" law school if a "black" law school already existed elsewhere on the University's campus, the state hastily set up an underfunded "black" law school. Sweatt employed the services of Thurgood Marshall and the NAACP Legal Defense and Education Fund and sued to be admitted to the University's "white" law school.

He argued that the education that he was receiving in the "black" law school was not of the same academic caliber as the education that he would be receiving if he attended the "white" law school. When the case reached the U.S. Supreme Court in 1950, the Court unanimously agreed with him, citing as its reason the blatant inequalities between the University's law school (the school for whites) and the hastily erected school for blacks. In other words, the "black" law school was "separate," but not "equal." Today, starting with the presidency of NBA Past President U. Lawrence Boze, the NBA's luncheon at its Midyear Conference is named in honor of Heman Sweatt.

In 1954, Thurgood Marshall and the NAACP Legal Defense and Education Fund represented the plaintiffs before the U.S. Supreme Court in the famous case of Brown v. Board ofEducation concerning the issue of segregation in public schools. It was the name given to five separate cases that were heard. These cases were Brown v. Board of Education of Topeka, Briggs v. Elliot, Davis v. Board ofEducation ofPrince Edward County (VA.), Boiling v. Sharpe, and Gebhart v. Ethel. While the facts of each case were different, the main issue in each was the constitutionality of state-sponsored segregation in public schools.

Meeting to decide the case, the Justices of the Supreme Court realized that they were deeply divided over the issues raised. While most wanted to reverse Plessy and declare segregation in public schools to be unconstitutional, they had various reasons for doing so. Unable to come to a solution by the end of the Court's in June of 1953, the Court decided to rehear the case in December of 1953. During the intervening months, however. Chief Justice Fred Vinson died and was replaced by Gov. Earl Warren of California. After the case was reheard in 1953, Chief Justice Warren was able to do something that his predecessor had not. He brought all of the Justices to agree to support a unanimous decision declaring segregation in public schools unconstitutional. On May 14, 1954, he delivered the opinion of the Court, stating that "We conclude that in the field of public education the doctrine of separate but equal' has no place. Separate educational facilities are inherently unequal.. ."

In the 1960s, the NBA Journal and News was established and focused on news and pictures of the membership and the business meetings of the NBA. It was eventually replaced by the NBA Bulletin and now a virtual newsletter. In 1963, members of the NBA participated in the March on Washington for Jobs & Freedom, MLK's "I Have a Dream" Speech and the signing of the Voting Rights Act in 1965. The case of Gomillion v. Lightfoot was a landmark decision of the US Supreme Court doing away with racial gerrymandering by finding that an electoral district with boundaries created to disenfranchise African Americans violated the Fifteenth Amendment. NBA Past President Fred Gray was involved with this case.

The work of the NBA and its members provided the underpinnings for major civil rights legislation, such as, the Civil Rights Act of 1964, the Voting Rights Act of 1965, and the Fair Housing Act of 1968.

The 1970s were the age of affirmative action in the wake of Bakke v. Regents of the University of California in which the U.S. Supreme Court introduced the concept of "reverse discrimination." In the wake of Bakke v. Regents, the NBA organization addressed pressing issues laid bare by this momentous decision. The structure of the NBA was changing. In October of 1972, by determination of the female NBA members, the Women Lawyers Division was established. 1978 was named the "Year of Affirmative Action."

The 1980s were roaring for the NBA. In 1981, NBA Past President Amette R. Hubbard assumed leadership, making her the first woman president of a major bar association. In March of 1981, the first NBA Legislative Conference was held. Under the leadership of then President Hubbard, in May of 1982, the NBA named its Mid-Year dinner in honor of Gertrude E. Rush, the organization's only woman co-founder.

In 1984. the NBA created a limited liability company to purchase its official headquarters at 1225 11th Street, NW Washington, DC 20001.

In 1985 on Lawyers Against Apartheid Day, NBA Past President Arthenia Joyner was arrested in front of the South African Embassy in Washington, DC.

In 1986, the NBA Hall of Fame was inaugurated by then-President Fred D. Gray, Sr. to honor those lawyers who have been licensed to practice for 40 years or more and who have made significant contributions to the cause of justice. In 1988, the first black U.S. Supreme Court Justice Thurgood Marshall and former secretary of the NBA addressed the NBA at its annual convention.

The 1990s began the corporate and regulation years. In 1992, the NBA submitted comments to the proposed "incubator" program described by the Federal Communications Commissions (FCC) in its Memorandum Opinion and Order and Further Notice of Proposed Rule Making, FCC 92-361, released September 4, 1992. In that same year, comments were also submitted in response to the Notice of Proposal Policy Guidance issued by the United States Department of Education and published in the Federal Register on December 1, 1991.

In 1990, under the leadership of Thomas Duckenfield, the NBA held its first Wiley A. Branton Issues Symposium and Awards Luncheon in Little Rock, Arkansas where then Governor Bill Clinton and First Lady Hillary Clinton hosted the NBA Board of Governors. Recipients of the Wiley A. Branton Award have included Dr. Dorothy Heights and actress Lorraine Toussaint.

In 1991. under the leadership of NBA Past President Algenita Davis, the NBA began its international journey to collaborate with attorneys of color in other countries with the first continent being Africa.

In 1995, the NBA participated in the Million Man March, also known as the Holy Day of Atonement, which took place on October 16^^ in Washington, DC. The call to organize one million black men to stand up for their families, communities and to atone with one another came from the Honorable Minister Louis Farrakhan. Although Hon. Min. Farrakhan called for one million men, more than two million men from all over the nation showed up.

1995 also saw the creation of the Vision 2000 Campaign under the leadership of NBA Past President H.T. Smith to raise one million dollars through the National Bar Institute for the benefit of the NBA.

In 1996, the NBA submitted comments before the Federal Communications Commission (FCC) in the Matter of Streamlining Broadcast EEO Rules and Policies, Vacating the EEO Forfeiture Policy Statement and Amending Section 1.80 of the Commission's Rules to Include EEO Forfeiture Guidelines.

The 2000s started a new millennium and an awareness by the NBA that less than four percent of the lawyers in the United States were black. If the number of black lawyers is to increase in the United States, the NBA would have to take proactive steps to motivate black youth to consider law as a career. Under NBA Past President Harold Pope's leadership, the NBA's first annual Dr. Martin Luther King, Jr. Drum Major for Justice Advocacy Competition was held at its 75th Annual Convention in Washington, D.C.

Under the leadership of NBA Past President Evett Simmons, the NBA established the National Bar Association- Crump Law Camp. In 2001, thirty-two students between the ages of 14 and 17 came to Howard University to form the inaugural class of the Law Camp. Students stayed in Howard's dorms and classes were held at the law school. All the students participated in the Evett L. Simmons Mock Trial Competition.

In 2003, NBA Past President Dennis Archer becomes the first black president of the American Bar Association. He was followed by Robert Grey, in 2004-2005; Paulette Brown, who was also the first black woman ABA president in 2015-2016; and Reginald Turner in 2022-2023.

In 2008, Barack Obama, a lawyer, was sworn in as the 44th President, and the first black president in the United States. 2013 marked the 50th Anniversary of March on Washington for Jobs & Freedom.

In 2013 in the case oiShelby v. Holder, the Voting Rights Act suffered a major blow making it more difficult to vote.

2014 brought two more anniversaries: the 50th Anniversary of Brown v. Board of Education and the 50th Anniversary of the Civil Rights Act.

On July 17, 2016, under the leadership of NBA Past President Ben Crump, the NBA held its first Annual Arthenia Joyner Prayer Breakfast, which continues to be the launch for the annual convention.

On January 19, 2021, Kamala Harris was sworn in as the first woman and first black vice president of the United States.

On March 13, 2020, with the death of Breonna Taylor and July 15, 2020, with the death of George Floyd, this country saw a movement against police brutality. NBA Past President Ben Crump, who Rev. A1 Sharpten calls Black America's Attorney General, was a legal giant in the movement. NBA Past President Lonita Baker represented the family of Breonna Taylor as well. In January of 2022, Representative Hakeem Jeffries becomes the first black Minority Leader of the House of Representatives.

Alongside fellow civil rights leader Diane Nash, a founding member of the Student Nonviolent Coordinating Committee, on August 7, 2022, NBA Past President Fred Gray was awarded the Presidential Medal of Freedom by President Joe Biden.

In 2025, under the presidency of Wiley S. Adams, the NBA celebrates its 100'*' anniversary in Chicago, Illinois. The Chair of the NBA Centennial Commission is NBA Past President Evett Simmons, and the Co-Chairs are NBA Past Presidents Arthenia Joyner, Paulette Brown and Keith Watters. The six NBA Affiliates who reached their Centennial are the Iowa National Bar Association, the Cook County Bar Association, the Mound City Bar Association, the South Hampton Roads Bar Association, the Marion County Bar Association, and the Washinton Bar Association.

Today, the NBA is the nation's oldest and largest national association of predominantly African American lawyers, judges, law professors, and law students. The NBA has over eighty (80) chapters throughout the United States and has affiliations with lawyer organizations across the world including Canada, the United Kingdom, Africa, Morocco and the Caribbean.

On July 17. 2016, under the leadership of NBA Past President Ben Crump, the NBA held its first Annual Arthenia .Joyner Prayer Breakfast, which continues to he the launch for the annual convention.

On January 19,2021. Kamala Harris was sworn in as the first woman and first black vice president of the United States.

On March 13, 2020, with the death of Breonna Taylor and July 15. 2020. with the death of George Floyd, this country- saw a movement against police brutality, NBA Past President Ben Crump, who Rev. A1 Sharpten calls Black America's Attorney General. w as a legal giant in the movement. NBA Past President Lonita Baker represented the family oi Breonna Taylor- as well. In January of 2022. Representative Hakeem Jeffries becomes the first black Minority Leader of the House of Representatives.

Alongside fellow civ il rights leader Diane Nash, a founding member of the Student Nonviolent Coordinating Committee, on .August 7, 2022. NB.A Past President Fred Gray was awarded the Presidential Medal of freedom by President Joe Biden.

In 2025. under the presidency of Wiley S. .Adams, the NBA celebrates its 100th anniversary in Chicago. Illinois, The Chair of the NB.A Centennial Commission is NB.A Past President Evetl Simmons, and the Co-Chairs are NBA Past Presidents Arthenia Joyner. Paulette Brown and Keith Watters. The six NBA Affiliates who reached their Centennial are the Iowa National Bar Association, the Cook County Bar Association, the Mound City Bar Association the South Hampton Roads Bar Association, the Marion County Bar Association, and the Washinton Bar Association.

Today the NBA is the nation's oldest and largest national association of predominantly African American lawyers, judges, law professors, and law students. The NBA has over eighty (KO) chapters throughout the United States and has affiliations with lawyer organizations across the world including Canada, the United Kingdom. .Africa. Morocco and the Caribbean.

NBA Past President Fred Gray, Presidential Medal of Freedom Recipient, for whom the Hall of Fame is named

NBA Past President Dennis Archer, First Bl ABA President, Michigan Associate Suprer Court Justice and Mayor of Detroit

Legacy OF EXCELLENCE

Thanks to Nick Pittman for his work creating and implementing the 2025 National Bar Association's Listening & Engagement Tour with President Wiley Adams, NBA Past Presidents, Past & Present NBA Officers & NBA Members and Their Families!

Through the NBA's Listening and Engagement Tour, we showed up in San Francisco, California, Los Angeles, California, Houston, Texas, Washington, DC and many other Cities while encouraging NBA Members and their families and friends to stand up for justice and the rule of law in communities across the country. Many warriors came out to hear from lawyers and judges about what we can do to address the attacks on our freedoms and share strategies for resistance, prosperity and advocacy within the legal profession.

This movement cannot stop here. We look forward to seeing you in our communities working toward justice and equality and encouraging our youth to do the same!

CURRENT BOARD MEMBERS

NATIONAL BAR ASSOCIATION®
EST. 1925

WILEY ADAMS
President

ASHLEY UPKINS
President-Elect

CHARLYN STANBERRY
Vice President of Regions and Affiliates

JAMES CARTER
Vice President of Finance

NATIONAL BAR ASSOCIATION
EST. 1925

KIMBERLEY ANN WARD
Vice President of Sections and Divisions

J. WYNDAL GORDON
Vice President of Membership

YURI WALKER
Treasurer

DANIELLE PINKSTON
Secretary

VALERIA OBI
Board Member at Large

LAWANDA HODGES
Board Member at Large

TORRENCE PHILLIPS
Board Member at Large

SHUMIKA T. R. SOOKDEO
Board Member at Large

LAMONT BAILEY
Board Member at Large

HAMID SAAHIR
Board Member at Large

KIM CARTER
General Counsel

KEVIN D. JUDD
Parliamentarian

ANTONIO LEE
Chief of Staff

REGIONS

National Bar Association Regions

Region I
States: Maine, Massachusetts, New Hampshire, Puerto Rico, Rhode Island, & U.S. Virgin Islands
Regional Director: Miniard Culpepper

Region II
States: Connecticut, New York & Vermont
Regional Director: Jason Clark

Region III
States: Delaware, Pennsylvania, & New Jersey
Regional Director: Nilaja Ford

Region IV
States: Maryland, North Carolina, South Carolina, West Virginia & Virginia
Regional Director: Frank Morris

Region V
States: Louisiana, Mississippi, & Texas
Regional Director: Amber Hamilton Grogg

Region VI
States: Kentucky, Ohio, Michigan & Tennessee
Regional Director: Princess Woodard

Region VII
States: Indiana, Illinois, & Wisconsin
Regional Director: Danielle Pinkston

Region VIII
States: Arkansas, Iowa, Minnesota, Missouri, Nebraska, North Dakota & South Dakota
Regional Director: Chalana Scales Ferguson

Region IX
States: Alaska, Arizona, California, Hawaii, Idaho, Montana, Nevada, Oregon, Washington & Guam
Regional Director: Terrance Evans

Region X
States: Colorado, Kansas, New Mexico, Oklahoma, Utah, & Wyoming
Regional Director: Hon. Shauna Graves-Robertson

Region XI
States: Alabama, Florida, & Georgia
Regional Director: Roger Johnson

Region XII
States: Washington D.C.
Regional Director: Gilbert Orsini

*Note: This section is based on available information; not all NBA regions or affiliates submitted updates or historical details.

REGION NINE

NATIONAL BAR ASSOCIATION
EST. 1925

REGION IX

Region IX Director, Terrance J. Evans	Region IX Deputy Director, Yuri Walker
Region IX Treasurer, Judge Terry Wiley	Region IX Secretary, Amy Depuy

BERNARD JEFFERSON

HUGH GOODWIN

SANTA CLARA
BLACK LAWYERS

EST. 1981

CABL
CALIFORNIA ASSOCIATION OF
BLACK LAWYERS

From Left to Right, Region IX Secretary& YLD Chair Elect Amy Depuy; Earl B. Gilliam Bar Fondation Board Member & Region IX Member Connie Broussard; Region IX Past Director, NBA Past Vice President, and Current Region IX Treasurer, Terry Wiley; NBA Treasurer & Region IX Deputy Director, Yuri Walker; California Association of Black Lawyers ("CABL") Palimentarian & Region IX Member, Onyebuchi Okeke; Region IX Director, CABL Vice President North, and Past Charles Houston Bar Association ("CHBA") President, Terrance J. Evans; CHBA President & Region IX Member, Vincent L. Brown; Black Women Lawyers of Los Angeles Co-Founder and Region IX Member, Ann Lloyd; and Black Women Lawyers Associaiton of Los Angles Past President & Region IX Member, Honorable Judge Yvette Roland at the 47 Annual Langston Bar Association Gala in Beverly Hills.

A Message From The Director of Region IX of the National Bar Association

Region IX of the National Bar Association and all of our affiliates proudly celebrate the Centennial of the National Bar Association. At least two of our affiliates: Charles Houston Bar Association and the John M. Langston Bar Association have roots dating back more than 100 years. We look forward to the growth and success of the National Bar Association over the next 100 years.

Sincerely,

Terrance J. Evans

Terrance J. Evans,
Director of Region IX of the National Bar Association

The History of the Charles Houston Bar Association

The Charles Houston Bar Association (CHBA) was founded in 1955 as the Charles Houston Law Club. The group took its name to honor the groundbreaking lawyer and educator Charles Hamilton Houston. Houston was a remarkable constitutional lawyer and the key legal strategist in the early battles against racial discrimination in education, labor, and housing. He fervently believed that African-American lawyers should be "social engineers" who use the law to promote fundamental social change. Both his career and his life were devoted to this precept.

Law Club Beginnings

Between 1910 and 1940, there existed but a handful of Black lawyers practicing in the Bay Area of Northern California. This small group included Lawrence Sledge, McCants Stewart, John Drake, Edward Mabson, Leland Hawkins, and Annie Virginia Stephens Coker (California's first African American woman lawyer), among others. For the most part, neither law firms nor the government would hire them. So these lawyers set up their own private practices. Some, like attorney Tabytha Anderson, worked out of their homes. Others, like Frank Larche and John C. Henderson, managed a caseload around full time non-legal jobs. A few attorneys, like Oscar Hudson in San Francisco and H. Leonard Richardson in Oakland, for example, built up successful practices and acquired prominence in the community. When Charles Hamilton Houston would visit the Bay Area during national tours of the NAACP branches, he would stay at the Derby Street home of attorney H. Leonard Richardson in Berkeley, or with Walter A. Gordon, another prominent African American lawyer who, in 1958, was later appointed Judge of the Federal District Court of the Virgin Islands.

These early African American attorneys faced overt racism on all fronts. The legal community itself was unwilling to embrace its Black practitioners. The American Bar Association refused to accept African Americans until 1943. Local Northern California bar associations would admit Blacks, but the role they would be permitted to play was perceived as restricted. In some Bay Area courts, these Black lawyers faced intense hostility from the bench. Outside of the courtroom, they contended with a few competitive white attorneys who bad-mouthed them to potential clients, circulating false rumors and scaring away business. Even without the spread of these rumors, people generally seemed to prejudge Black lawyers as less competent than their white counterparts. These attitudes towards the Black lawyer made the task of developing a successful practice difficult.

It was founder Richard Bancroft, a graduate of Howard Law School, who proposed that the Law Club take the name of Charles Hamilton Houston, the celebrated American civil rights lawyer, teacher, and activist who strategized the legal plan that would one day topple America's "separate but equal" doctrine of legalized discrimination. The membership agreed. Charles Houston exemplified the type of lawyers they aspired to be.

Over the next twenty years, between 1955 and 1975, the Charles Houston Law Club continued to grow. Annual events like the Christmas party and summer barbecue ripened into tradition. From this solid foundation, professional careers flourished.

Despite these obstacles, the number of Black attorneys in Northern California grew. Unwelcomed by many of the communities they sought to serve, they turned to each other for support. During these times, when a recent Black law school graduate passed the bar exam, he would often be extended the opportunity to start his legal career in the office of a more experienced Black practitioner. For decades, Black lawyers used this intimate system of employment and training to cultivate new talent in the profession.

In 1955, the African-American lawyers in Northern California were summoned together to formalize their bond as Black practitioners. A law club, the likes of which had never been seen before in Northern California, was formed. At first, these founding members met monthly at each other's offices after work. There, they discussed ways to promote their practices and counter the racial bias that affected them personally and professionally. They also used this time to share knowledge and experience with one another. They exchanged ideas and strategies for handling individual cases, served as each other's mentors, and strengthened friendships.

The original Law Club members, our founders, consisted of thirty-two lawyers. They were: John D. Drake, Lawrence Sledge, George R. Vaughns, George D. Carroll, Carl B. Metoyer, Terry A. Francois, Clinton W. White, Lionel Wilson, Claude O. Allen, Thomas L. Berkley, Charles E. Wilson, Sherman W. Smith, Richard Bancroft, Franklin Williams, Wiley W. Manuel, Raymond J. Reynolds, Francis S. Heffron, Murvill C. Abels, Edward D. Mabson, H. Leroy Cannon, Joseph G. Kennedy, John Adams Jr., John W. Bussey, Hiawatha T. Roberts, William C. Dixon, Cecil Poole, Maurcie Hardeman, Armeka T. Jackson, Solomon Johnson, Garfield Steward, Wilmont Sweeney, and Charles Blagburn. John C. Henderson, one of the pioneer Black lawyers of the Bay Area who had practiced in Oakland since 1934, passed away in May of 1952 but was included on the original Law Club roster in memoriam.

These ambitious men would go on in their professional careers to become judges, mayors, ambassadors, city supervisors, and successful businessmen. Almost all of them were active in the NAACP and helped support its litigation efforts. At least eight of them led NAACP branches as officers, including six presidents of Bay Area NAACP offices. Franklin Williams worked directly with Thurgood Marshall and the Legal Defense Fund on important equal protection cases and would later be appointed United States Ambassador to Ghana. Ten of these founders would become judges, one of whom — Wiley W. Manuel — broke ground as the first African American Justice to sit on the California Supreme Court. Two others, John W. Bussey and Lionel Wilson, became the first African American judges on the San Francisco and Alameda County benches, respectively. Judge Bussey was also personally responsible for training a large bevy of lawyers, White and Black, to pass the tough California bar exam.

Growth into a Bar Association

Benjamin Travis graduated as the only African American in his law school class in 1960 and promptly began working with Hiawatha T. Roberts, a member of the Charles Houston Law Club. At Robert's invitation, Travis joined the club in 1961 and profited from the social and professional support. In 1973, he became the group's president and embarked on a mission to transform the local law club into a nationally recognized bar association. Travis, aided by another prolific young attorney named Robert L. Harris, coordinated a reorganization of the group into a community-conscious political force that extended its collective voice to advocate against racial injustice wherever it arose — locally, statewide, and nationally. Under their leadership, the lawyers' group gained official recognition as a specialty bar association under the State Bar of California in 1975 and became an affiliate of the National Bar Association. The Charles Houston Bar Association, or "CHBA" as it has come to be known, was incorporated in 1976.

Joined by colleagues from the association including George Holland, Alfred Reginald Brown, Henry Ramsey, Horace Wheatley, Gordon Baranco, Ruth Herch, Thomas Broome, Annette Green, Ruth Blackwell, Geoffrey Carter, Dale Rubin, Donald P. McCullum, and too many others to list here, Travis and Harris created the blueprint for the organization as it stands today. CHBA would soon become instrumental in breaking down barriers and opening doors of professional opportunity. Leading by example, Benjamin Travis accepted judicial appointment to the Alameda County bench. Robert L. Harris, after serving as CHBA President, went on to become the first National Bar Association President from west of the Mississippi River and the youngest president in that organization's history.

Since 1976, CHBA has remained proactive in its efforts to increase diversity in the legal profession, to advance African American access to the courts, to bring services to under-served Bay Area communities, and to counsel youth. To that end, each year, CHBA's Legal Affairs and Community Action Committees conduct neighborhood outreach and administer programs to benefit the community. The Young Lawyers Committee reaches out to support law school students and the many Black Law Students Association chapters of Northern Californian law schools. CHBA's annual College Awareness Advisory Program focuses on high school students to discuss preparing for college.

CHBA members have been innovative in organizing groups and programs that benefit many people. In April of 1977, members co-founded, along with jurists from Southern California, the California Association of Black Lawyers (CABL), the first and only statewide alliance of predominantly African American bar associations. In 1982, our members helped create the Wiley W. Manual Law Foundation, a charitable organization providing scholarships to Bay Area students and administering an annual mock trial competition for students.

CHBA has also been involved in litigation aimed at protecting the legal rights of the African American community. In 1976, CHBA successfully sued the County of Alameda over perceived unfairness in the assignment of criminal defense cases involving indigent defendants.

In 1978, CHBA members defended, pro bono, the NAACP after police officers sued the association for libel and slander. In that case, CHBA's motion for summary judgment was granted on the ground that the NAACP's criticism of the police department was protected by the First Amendment. Lead counsel, Robert L. Harris, received the NAACP's prestigious William Robert Ming Award for his successful advocacy.

In the early 1980s, CHBA and CABL sponsored anti-ku klux klan legislation, now codified at California Penal Code of Civil Procedure section 527.7 [allowing an injunction to be obtained against a group which is meeting and taking substantial action in furtherance of the commission of acts of violence if it can be shown that the group will probably engage in those acts].

In 1983, the association joined with other community groups to submit an amicus curiae brief to the United States Supreme Court on behalf of African-American firefighters in Memphis, Tennessee, who had been threatened by impending layoffs under an unfair seniority system. That same year, CHBA successfully petitioned the California State Supreme Court to review a Court of Appeals decision that held that the Unruh Civil Rights Act did not apply to charitable and volunteer organizations.

Throughout the 1970s and 1980s, CHBA supported affirmative action in state and federal cases. This fight continues today. In 1995, CHBA joined forces with numerous community groups to oppose Proposition 209. In February 2003, CHBA again spoke out to advocate for diversity in education when it joined an amicus brief, authored in part by member Eva Paterson, supporting the University of Michigan in the United States Supreme Court cases of Grutter v. Bollinger and Gratz v. Bollinger, lawsuits attacking the school's student admission policies.

The success of the Charles Houston Bar is due to the leadership of the association's past presidents and the hundreds of board members and committee chairpersons who, over the years, have volunteered much of their precious time and energy to realize the organization's benevolent goals. The association is equally indebted to the many Bay Area law firms and corporations who support CHBA's endeavors. It is this wealth of talent and dedication of spirit that enables CHBA to continue its mission. Our work has not gone unnoticed. The organization's efforts have earned recognition from the National Bar Association as one of its Most Outstanding Affiliates in 1977, 1986, 2002 and in 2004.

In 2005, CHBA celebrated its 50th Anniversary. April 22nd of that year, the anniversary of Charles Hamilton Houston's death, was declared "Charles Houston Bar Association Day" by the Alameda County Board of Supervisors in honor of the association's significance to the community.

"The most hopeful sign about our legal defense is the ever-increasing number of young Negro lawyers, competent, conscientious, and courageous, who are anxious to pit themselves (without fee) against the forces of reaction and injustice. . . The time is soon coming when the Negro will be able to rely on his own lawyers to give him every legal protection in every court." – Charles Hamilton Houston History researched and written by Chad Smiley

History Of The California Association Of Black Lawyers

The California Association of Black Lawyers (CABL) has an illustrious history and lineage of courage, activism and participation in the political process. During the 1976 National Bar Association Convention in Houston, Texas, several California attorneys and judges met and discussed the need for a statewide bar organization to address issues facing Black lawyers and judges in California. After that NBA Conference, a series of informal meetings were held in Northern and Southern California. After several meetings, held both in Oakland and in Los Angeles, it was decided that a statewide association should be formed and that the initial meeting should be held in Los Angeles in April. This meeting was sponsored and planned primarily by the leadership of the Charles Houston Bar Association and the John M. Langston Bar Association. They were assisted by the Black Lawyers of San Diego County (now the Earl B. Gilliam Bar Association) and the Black Women Lawyers of California.

On April 23, 1977, at the Airport Marriott in Los Angeles, Robert L. Harris, President of the Charles Houston Bar Association, called the first session of this historic meeting to order. The initial bylaws of the association were adopted and thereafter several panel discussions were held on current issues. The key panel of the morning dealt with reverse discrimination. The case discussed was Bakke v. U.C. Regents, which was working its way through the judicial process at the time. Moderated by Judge Ben Travis and Judge Stanely Malone, the panel consisted of several noted legal scholars, including Elihu M. Harris, Billy Hunter, Professor Emma Jones, Professor Charles Lawrence, and Judge Robert M. Takasugi.

After the luncheon address, which was delivered by Justice Wiley W. Manuel, who a month earlier had become the first Black Supreme Court Justice in California's history, the afternoon session opened with Robert L. Robertson, President of the John M. Langston Bar Association, presiding. To ensure the viability of the Association, elections were held to guide the Association into its first year of operations. Upon the nomination of Assemblyman Willie L. Brown, Jr., Donald McCullum of Oakland, California, a noted civil rights and longtime NAACP attorney, was elected CABL's first president. Other officers elected were Naomi Young as Vice President – North, Ivey Dailey as Vice President – South, Irma Brown as Secretary, and John L. Burris as treasurer. Judge Ben Travis was elected Chair of the Judicial Section of CABL.

The primary motivating factor for the organization's formation was to change the face of the judiciary in California and to influence the course of events pertinent to Black people. The objectives and purposes included "the stimulation of Black lawyers in organized bar activities, to seek out and eradicate the roots and causes of racism, and to prepare the high standards of integrity, honor, and courtesy in the legal profession." Other objectives included to vigorously defend Black people from those who would consciously or otherwise deny them basic human and legal rights.

This historic gathering of the first statewide conference of Black lawyers and judges attracted over 200 prominent attorneys, judges, and other interested dignitaries and legal giants including the President (Carl Character of Cleveland) and the President-Elect (Mark T. McDonald of Houston) of the National Bar Association ('NBA"). Others attending included Tom Daugherty, David Cunningham, Lawrence Jones, Clinton W. White, Vince Monroe Townsend, Maxine Thomas, George Holland, Thomas Broome, Horace Wheatley, and Dan Weber, to name a few. Governor Jerry Brown and the State Attorney General also spoke at the conference.

From its inception, the organization has challenged inequities in the legal system and has grown both in membership and influence. CABL continues to be instrumental in increasing the number of African-American judges throughout California. Meeting regularly with members of the State Legislature and the Governor's Judicial Appointments Secretary, CABL has been effective in its advocacy of issues facing African Americans and others of similar experience and situation. Moreover, CABL is proud to have produced six distinguished presidents of the NBA. They include Robert L. Harris (the first Californian ever to be elected an officer of the NBA), Thomas J. Broome, James O. Cole, the Honorable Allen J. Webster, Randy K. Jones and Demetrius Shelton. Today, the California Association of Black Lawyers represents 6,000 African-American attorneys, judges, law professors and students.

The History of the John M. Langston Bar Association

The John M. Langston Bar Association has a long and impressive history. Founded in the 1920's in Los Angeles, when attorney Crispus Attucks Wright and other pioneering lawyers began what was then a "law club." The Association was originally known as the Blackstone Club and was founded in response to other bar associations' policy of excluding African Americans as members. The Blackstone Club became the Langston Law Club in 1943, but it was not until the mid-1960s that the Los Angeles County Bar Association recognized the Langston Law Club (and other minority bar groups) as dues-paying bar associations.

Langston Law Club officially became the John M. Langston Bar Association in 1968. In 1990, the organization incorporated as a California nonprofit corporation named The John M. Langston Bar Association of Los Angeles, Inc. The John M. Langston Bar Association of Los Angeles, Inc. is a 501(c)(3) publicly supported charity.

Under the leadership of distinguished Presidents and active board members, the John M. Langston Bar Association has provided its members and the community with exceptional programs and events. Some of its activities include awarding scholarships to deserving law students at the installation and awards gala; providing free bar exam tutorials to assist law students in passing the bar examination; inducting accomplished legal practitioners and pioneers of our Bar into the Langston Hall of Fame; mentoring activities for law students and young lawyers; facilitating community law clinics; sponsoring continuing legal education programs for members; and hosting the Langston Law Institute where bar members and the community discuss solutions to legal issues affecting our community.

History of John Mercer Langston

One of the most prominent African Americans in the United States before and during the Civil War, John Mercer Langston was one of the first African Americans to hold elective office in the United States (he became Brownhelm, Ohio, township clerk in 1855), he helped establish Howard University's school of law, and he topped off his long illustrious political career by becoming the first Black ma*n to represent Virginia in the U.S. House of Representatives. He was a Republican.

Born the youngest of four children as a free Black in Louisa County, Virginia on December 14, 1829, Langston gained distinction as an abolitionist, politician, and attorney. Despite the prominence of his slave owner father, Ralph Quarles, Langston took his surname from his mother, Lucy Langston, an emancipated slave of Indian and Black ancestry.

At fourteen, Langston began his studies at the Preparatory Department at Oberlin College. Known for its radicalism and abolitionist politics, Oberlin was the first college in the United States to admit Black and White students. Langston completed his studies in 1849, becoming the fifth African American male to graduate from Oberlin's Collegiate Department. Langston received a B.A. in 1849 and an M.A. in theology in 1852 from Oberlin. Langston wanted to become a lawyer because it was a profession only three Black men in the nation had officially achieved nationwide in the early 1850s.

In 1854, Langston married Caroline Matilda Wall, who also attended Oberlin College. From North Carolina, she was the daughter of an enslaved mother and Colonel Stephen Wall, a wealthy white planter who freed his mixed-race daughters Sara and Caroline, and sent them to Ohio to be raised in an affluent Quaker household and educated. An intellectual partner of Langston, Caroline had five children with him, one of whom died in childhood.

In 1855, Langston was elected town clerk of Brownhelm Township in Ohio, becoming the first Black elected official in the state. In addition to his law practice and activities as town clerk, Langston and his brothers, Gideon and Charles, participated in the Underground Railroad. John Mercer Langston caught the attention of Frederick Douglass, who encouraged him to deliver antislavery speeches.

During the Civil War, Langston recruited Black volunteers for the Massachusetts 54th Infantry Regiment, officially the country's first African American military unit. In 1867, Langston served as Inspector General of the Freedmen's Bureau, touring the postwar South and encouraging freedmen to seek educational opportunities. He regularly spoke out against segregated facilities, including churches. For the first two decades of the postwar era, Langston held prominent political and educational appointments.

In 1868, Langston moved to Washington, D.C. to help establish the nation's first Black law school at Howard University. He became its first dean and served briefly as acting president of Howard in 1872. President Ulysses S. Grant appointed Langston as a member of the Board of Health of the District of Columbia, and he was elected its Secretary in 1875. In 1877, President Rutherford B. Hayes appointed Langston U.S. Minister to Haiti. He returned to the U.S. in 1885 and became president of Virginia Normal and Collegiate Institute (now Virginia State University).

In 1888, Langston ran for a seat in Congress as an Independent against a white Democratic opponent. The election results were contested for 18 months. Langston was finally declared the winner and served the six remaining months of his term. Langston lost his reelection bid in 1890. Partly because of his prominence, the Oklahoma Territory town of Langston, and the college created in the town, Langston University, were named after him. After a lifetime of "firsts" and numerous accomplishments, Langston died in Washington, D.C. on November 15, 1897 at the age of 67.

The History of the Wiley W. Manuel Bar Association

Brown Picks Woman, Black for High Court

First Such Choices in State; Rose Bird to Be Chief Justice

Rose Bird

Wiley W. Manuel

Justice Wiley William Manuel

The Wiley Manuel Bar Association of Sacramento County, formerly known as the Sacramento Association of Black Attorneys, (SABA), was founded in the fall of 1977, through the initial efforts of four attorneys in the Sacramento area, David Seals, Milton Armistead, Nathaniel Colley and Joseph Russell. These four attorneys saw a need for a bar association which would address the concerns of the Black community as well as the Black lawyers in the Sacramento area and along with thirteen others, held the first meeting of SABA. The seventeen individuals in attendance were: David Seals (President), Milton Armistead (Vice President), Harold Machen (Parliamentarian), Otis Benning, Clarence Brown, Timothy Chandler, Nathaniel Colley, Randolph Cooke, Joseph Cooper, Amos Freeman, L'Archie Harris, James Long, Gary Ransom, Vance Raye, Joseph Russell, Renard Shepard, and Herman Smith.

The stated purpose of the organization was "to provide an organized bar affiliation to represent the professional interests of the legal community in Sacramento, with special emphasis on Black attorneys; to promote the administration of justice; and to make use of legal tools and Legal discipline for the advancement of the economic, political, educational, and social interest of Sacramento, especially the Black community.

In 1981, after the untimely death that year of Justice Wiley William Manuel, the first African American appointed to the California Supreme Court, the SABA changed its name to the Wiley Manuel Law Society. Justice Manuel was a distinguished leader in the legal field in the never-ending battle for equality and justice for all people, regardless of race, creed or national origin. It was this leadership that prompted the association to change its name in his honor. The next year, the Society affiliated with the State Bar of California and became the Wiley W. Manuel Bar Association of Sacramento County. In 1984, Wiley Manual Bar Association (WMBA) became affiliated with the Sacramento County Bar Association. It also maintains affiliate status with the National Bar Association and was founding affiliate association to the California Association of Black Lawyers (CABL), which was also established in 1977, WMBA and its members continue to be a vital part of the Sacramento legal community.

Wiley William Manuel was the first African-American to be appointed as a justice to the California Supreme Court.

Governor Edmund G. Brown, Jr. appointed Wiley Manuel to the California Supreme Court on February 12, 1977. On November 7, 1978, Justice Manuel was elected to a twelve-year term on the California Supreme Court. 42 Justice Manuel received his Bachelor of Law degree from Hastings College of Law in 1953. Prior to his appointment to the California Supreme Court, he enjoyed a 23-year career with the California Department of Justice as a Deputy Assistant Attorney General and Chief Assistant Attorney General in the San Francisco office. In 1963, Wiley Manuel served as President of the Charles Houston Bar Association.

Justice Manuel's twelve-year term would have expired in 1990. However, on January 5, 1981, he succumbed to a strenuous battle with cancer.

Justice Manuel's legal career and his personal life were marked by dedication to hard work, public service and concept of equal justice for all segments of society.

In addition to the Wiley W. Manuel Bar Association of Sacramento County, there is also a non-profit scholarship foundation in Northern California, and an Oakland courthouse named in his honor.

The History of the Black Women Lawyers Association of Northern California

Honorable Patricia Ann McKinley (deceased)

Honorable Judith Ford (Retired)

Following in the footsteps of Annie Coker, California's first African-American woman lawyer, many of California's early Black women attorneys settled in the San Francisco Bay Area. Concentrated primarily in the East Bay, these women often felt isolated amongst their male peers, frustrated with the discrimination they faced, and unwelcomed within the greater legal community. But they did not despair. Instead, they turned to each other for support, inspiration, and encouragement. Early pioneer Estella Dooley, one of the first African-American women admitted to the California Bar and the first Black woman deputy public defender in the state, held gatherings of Black women lawyers at her home in San Francisco in the 1960s. In the mid-1970s, another group of Black women lawyers began to gather under the leadership of attorneys like Julia Blackwell, Dianne Millner, Barbara Parker, and Naomi Young. These women inspired those who followed them to create an enduring organization that would be a both catalyst for change for Black women in the legal profession and, in the words of Inaugural President Cloey Hewlett, "a safe space for Black women to thrive."

In the summer of 1979, a group of women that included Geraldine Chavis, Cloey Hewlett and future judges Maria-Elena James, Patricia McKinley, Judy Johnson, and Brenda Harbin-Forte gathered at the home of the Honorable Judith Ford (Ret.) over wine, great food, and amazing company to support and encourage one another as Black women navigating the legal profession. It was from that meeting that the organization we know today as Black Women Lawyers Association of Northern California was formed. Since 1979, Black Women Lawyers Association of Northern California has been a safe haven, voice, and sisterhood for Bay Area Black women in the law. Our events range from in-depth roundtable discussions on business development and career advancement to networking and social events to dinner discussions with frank and open dialogues unique to the needs and experiences of Black women attorneys.

Today, Black Women Lawyers Association of Northern California ("BWLNC") is 501(c)(6). BWLNC is an affiliate member of the National Bar Association (NBA) and a member of the California Association of Black Lawyers (CABL) and the Minority Bar Coalition (MBC). Our membership is comprised of senior level executives and in-house attorneys, law firm partners and associates, solo practitioners, government attorneys, judges, law professors, and law students from some of the best institutions in the country. 49

Honorable Patricia Ann McKinley

The Honorable Patricia Ann McKinley was born in San Francisco on April 11, 1949 and raised in the City of Richmond. A demonstrated leader at an early age, Judge McKinley entered the University of California at Berkeley in 1967. Embracing her love of travel, Judge McKinley spent a year studying at the University of Bordeaux in France where she became fluent in French. After graduating with a degree in French, Judge McKinley attended Boalt Hall School of Law.

Following her graduation from Boalt in 1971 and her extended travels to North and West Africa, Judge McKinley entered private practice in Oakland, California where she made a name for herself as a civil and criminal attorney. It was in these early years of her career that Judge McKinley became involved in various alumni, civic, and legal organizations. In 1979, Judge McKinley, along with Judge Judith Ford, invited several Black women lawyers to a meeting at Judge Ford's home to discuss forming an organization to not only combat the discrimination and isolation that many of them faced but also to support one another and to be a catalyst for change for Black women within the legal profession. It was from this historic meeting that Black Women Lawyers Association of Northern California ("BWLNC") was born.

In 1980, Judge McKinley accepted an offer to join the Richmond City Attorney's office where she balanced her desire to be an exceptional advisor to the City with her need to be an advocate for the poor, minority, and disenfranchised residents of her hometown. She also continued to travel the globe and added Turkey, Japan, and the South Pacific to her already extensive repertoire of international experiences.

By 1982, Judge McKinley's legal talents had come to the attention to Governor Jerry Brown who appointed her to the Bay District Municipal Court District. At 33, Judge McKinley was the youngest and first African American woman to be appointed to that court where she presided over civil and criminal cases in Contra Costa County. Judge McKinley admittedly welcomed this challenge because her hometown was within her jurisdiction. After three short years on the bench, Judge McKinley's colleagues on the bench named her Presiding Judge.

In 1986, after running unopposed and winning her judicial seat in 1984, Judge McKinley tragically lost her battle with cancer at the age of 37, but her legacy lives on. BWLNC celebrates the trailblazing accomplishments of Judge McKinley.

Honorable Judith Ford

The Honorable Judith D. Ford (Ret.) is a pioneer in the legal field and in the history of Black Women Lawyers Association of Northern California ("BWLNC"). In 1979, Judge Ford hosted a gathering of Black women who worked in the legal field, and it was there that BWLNC was formed.

A California native and a graduate of the University of California at Berkeley, Judge Ford graduated from Boalt Hall School of Law in 1974. After graduation, Judge Ford joined the law firm of Petty, Andrews, Tuffs & Jackson as an associate. In 1978, she became an Assistant District Attorney for the City and County of San Francisco. Judge Ford left the District Attorney's Office in 1980 to join the Federal Trade Commission where she served as Regional Director. In 1982, Governor Jerry Brown appointed Judge Ford to the Municipal Court for the Oakland-Piedmont-Emeryville Judicial District where she became Presiding Judge in 1987. Judge Ford became an Alameda Superior Court Judge in 1998 upon the unification of the courts, and she served in that capacity until her retirement in 2002.

During her distinguished career, Judge Ford was repeatedly recognized for her work in improving the administration of justice, particularly in the area of courtroom technology. She chaired the state's Court Technology Advisory Committee in 1998. While leading the panel, Judge Ford helped develop standards for privacy and access to electronic court information and pushed for improved case management systems. She also spearheaded a Tactical Plan for Court Technology to ensure effective management of technology resources in the state's court system. After leaving the state panel, Judge Ford served as a member of the national Joint Technology Committee and helped develop a Business Process Enhancements Guide and Manual for Courts. In 2002, Judge Ford received he first-ever LexisNexis CourtLink Excellence in Legal Technology award which recognized her for her "leadership, innovation and championing of technology to deliver breakthrough advances in the efficient practice of litigation in the courts."

The very next year, Judge Ford received the National Center for State Courts' Distinguished Service Award as a result of her career commitment to improving the justice system.

Despite her many career heights and achievements, Judge Ford has never lost her commitment to BWLNC. Our resident historian and storyteller, Judge Ford has been committed to the members of this organization since its inception, and for her pioneering spirit, mentorship, and support, BWLNC is truly thankful.

The History of the Black Women Lawyers Association of Los Angeles, Inc.

Black Women Lawyers Association of Los Angeles, Inc. is a non-profit corporation whose mission is dedicated to charitable, educational and community-based services. BWL was founded in 1975 after a small group of Los Angeles based African-American women judges and attorneys held a luncheon meeting to discuss the marked absence of an organization which addressed the needs and concerns of African-American women in the legal profession. The dialogue and events that followed became the genesis of BWL. Over the years, BWL branched out and grew through its various community projects and committee activities.

The first BWL scholarship luncheon was held in 1975 at the Medallion Restaurant. Since then, BWL has raised scholarship funds annually for second and third year law students through its annual fundraising efforts by the Black Women Lawyers Association of Los Angeles Foundation.

In 1982, BWL and Women Lawyers Association of Los Angeles ("WLALA") co-founded the Harriet Buhai Center for Family Law ("Center"). The Center has evolved into one of the primary providers of pro bono family law services in Los Angeles County. In recognition of BWL's significant community contributions as a founder and co-sponsor of the Center, the National Conference of Women Bar Associations presented its first annual Public Service Award to BWL and WLALA in July 1985. In 1991, BWL was among the various ethnic minority bar associations that formed the Multicultural Bar Alliance.

Through its continued involvement and support of this alliance, BWL offers a needed channel for communication for attorneys of color, both outside and within the African-American community. In 1992, the BWL Foundation was established to support and fund BWL's numerous charitable, educational and community-based services. BWL also gives holiday food baskets to needy families, donations to shelters for the homeless and battered women, and strives to expand its outreach programs to schools .The viability of BWL's programs is dependent upon your support and commitment. Thank you for your interest in our organization.

The Black Women Lawyers Association of
LOS ANGELES, INC. 2025 – 2026 BOARD OF DIRECTORS

Justice Richard T. Fields

The History of the Richard T. Fields Bar Association

The bar association is named after the Honorable Richard T. Fields, who was the first African-American jurist in Riverside County. He was appointed as a Commissioner in 1991, and in April 2000, he became the first African-American judge in Riverside County. Judge Fields has presided in the courts of Riverside County 26 years. In 2007 and 2008, Judge Fields served as the Presiding Judge of the entire Riverside County court system. In 2017 he was appointed to the California 4th District Court of Appeal.

Prior to his appointment to the bench, Judge Fields served as a Reginald Heber Smith National Poverty Law Fellow with the Legal Aid Foundation of Los Angeles. He was associated with the Law Offices of Susan R. Wasserman, and he also served for several years as a Riverside County deputy public defender.

Justice Fields has received many awards. In 2007, he received the Southwest Bar Association's Judge of the Year award. In 2008, he was named as Judge of the Year by the Riverside-San Bernardino Chapter of the American Board of Trial Advocates. In June 2009, he received the Outstanding Jurist Award from the Leo A. Deegan Inn of Court. In 2013, he received the Alba Witkin Humanitarian Award from the California Judges Association. He also been honored for judicial excellence by the California Association of Black Lawyers and the 100 Black Men of the Inland Empire. In 2016, he was named the Leo A. Deegan Inn of Court Douglass E. Weathers Distinguished Honoree and received the Champions of Justice Award from Fair Housing Council of Riverside County Inc. In 2017, he received the California Association of Black Lawyers Judicial Section South's prestigious Black Gavel Award.

The History of the Las Vegas Chapter of the National Bar Association

The Las Vegas Chapter of the National Bar Association (LVNBA) was originally incorporated in 1981 and reincorporated in 2005. Over the years, the LVNBA has grown from a small group of fourteen trailblazing attorneys and judges to a large and vibrant organization.

The National Bar Association (National Bar) was founded in 1925 when there were fewer than 1,000 African-American lawyers in the nation, and less than 120 belonged to the (National Bar). By 1945, there were nearly 250 members representing 25% of the African-American members of the bar. Over the past 75 years, the National Bar has grown enormously in size and influence.

When the LVNBA was founded in 1981, there were fewer than 20 African-American attorneys in state of Nevada. Currently in Nevada, circa 125-150 African-American attorneys comprise approximately 1% of the membership of the State Bar of Nevada. Since its founding, the LVNBA has grown in size and influence and LVNBA members own their own law firms, are partners and associates at small, medium, and large size firms throughout Clark County, are students and law professors at community colleges and the University of Nevada, pursue justice for clients as prosecutors and public defenders, serve in the Nevada Legislature, are members of the Nevada judiciary, and represent cities, counties, the Attorney General's Office, and the Department of Justice.

Founders of the Las Vegas Chapter of the National Bar Association

The LVNBA was originally incorporated in 1981 by a small group of fourteen trailblazing African-American legal pioneers. The original fourteen founding members are: Robert Archie (1941-1996), Andras F. Barbero, B. Jeanie Banks, Marcus Cooper, James Davidson, Michael Allen Davis (1951-2012), David Dean (1934-1986), Booker T. Evans, Judge Addeliar D. Guy, III (1923-1997), James O. Porter, Judge Johnnie B. Rawlinson, Dan Winder, Arthur L. Williams, Jr., and Justice of the Peace Earle W. White, Jr. (1933-2005).

Presidents of the Las Vegas Chapter of the National Bar Association

LVNBA presidents are leaders in the Las Vegas legal community and beyond. In addition to serving as LVNBA officers, LVNBA presidents have held offices in numerous other legal and community organizations in Nevada.

- 2023- - Caleb Green
- 2021-2023 - Angela Cook
- 2019-2021 - Augusta Massey
- 2017-2019 - Kali Fox Miller
- 2015-2017 - Karl Riley
- 2013-2015 - Professor Rachel Anderson
- 2011-2013 - Doreen Spears Hartwell
- 2009-2011 - Judge Richard Boulware
- 2007-2009 - F. Travis Buchanan
- 2004-2007 - U.S. Attorney for the District of Nevada Jason Frierson
- 2002-2004 - Arthur L. Williams, Jr.
- 2001-2002 - Uri L. Clinton
- 1999-2001 - Geraldine Kirk-Hughes
- 1996-1999 - Bryan K. Scott
- 1995-1996 - Cutbert E.A. Mack
- 1993-1994 - John R. Bailey
- 1991-1992 - Lizzie R. Hatcher
- 1989-1990 - Timothy C. Williams
- 1987-1989 - Justice Michael L. Douglas (Ret.)
- 1985-1987 - Lizzie R. Hatcher
- 1983-1985 - Arthur L. Williams, Jr.
- 1981-1982 - Robert Archie (1934-1986)

Judge Hayzel Burton Daniels

The History of the Arizona Black Bar

The Arizona Black Bar is the successor organization to the Hayzel B. Daniels Bar Association, which was formerly known as the Arizona Black Lawyers Association. The Arizona Black Lawyers Association was originally founded in 1971 and underwent a name change in 1993 to honor its founder, the Honorable Hayzel B. Daniels. To date, the Arizona Black Bar boasts a statewide membership of law students and legal professionals from both the private and public sectors, including municipal, state, tribal, and federal judges.

Hayzel B. Daniels (1913-1992), or 'Haze' as he was known, was an upstart, outspoken and courageous man who dedicated his life to education and his country

Haze attended law school on the G.I. Bill and later graduated from the University of Arizona Law School in 1948. After becoming the first African-American to pass the Arizona State Bar examination, Haze opened a law office in Phoenix and became involved in politics and was a major supporter of the NAACP.

In 1950, Haze became one of the first two black elected state representatives in the Arizona legislature. As a legislator, he fought for the integration of Phoenix public schools-then still segregated by law.

With the support of the NAACP, Haze initiated lawsuits on behalf of black children attacking the constitutionality of the statute. With no funding available, Haze along with attorney Herbert B. Finn, volunteered his services on Phillips, et. al. v. Phoenix Union High School District. Haze even paid the filing fee out of his own pocket. This turned out to be a wise investment because Arizona Superior Court Judge Fred C. Struckmeyer, Jr., soon ruled that there was no lawful authority for the segregation of black children in Carver High School.

Recognizing the limitations of this decision on November 12, 1953, Haze and Herb Finn filed suit against the Wilson Elementary School District in Heard et al v. Davis, et. al.. This time, in a bold and direct decision, Arizona Superior Court Judge Charles C. Bernstein ruled specifically that segregation in public schools was an unconstitutional deprivation of the equal protection of the laws guaranteed by the Fourteenth Amendment.

While the States appeal from that decision was pending, the United States Supreme Court requested a copy of Judge Bernstein's order. Although we will probably never know how much the Court was influenced by the Heard decision, when the landmark decision of Brown v. Board of Education was issued on May 17, 1954, striking down the concept of separate, but equal the Supreme Court had concluded just as directly as Judge Bernstein that racial segregation in public schools was unconstitutional.

In the spotlight once again, Haze made national news when he was appointed as a Phoenix City Court judge in 1965, thus becoming the first African-American judge in the history of the State of Arizona. Well respected, he served with distinction for 13 years receiving numerous awards and accolades including the alumni distinguished citizen award from the University of Arizona.

The History of the Loren Miller Bar Association (Washington State)

From its founding in August 1968 to the present, the Loren Miller Bar Association ("LMBA") has grown from its 13 founders to its current membership of over 250 attorneys statewide. LMBA's membership growth and organizational development has coincided with its successful creation and implementation of numerous community programs. On October 14, 1978 the Loren Miller Bar Club members officially changed the Club's name to the Loren Miller Bar Association and incorporated LMBA as a nonprofit 501(c)(4) corporation. In 1997, LMBA created the Philip L. Burton Memorial Foundation as a nonprofit 501(c)(3) corporation to administer LMBA's scholarship fund for the University of Washington, Seattle University and Gonzaga University law students.

At its core, the LMBA is first and foremost a civil rights organization. From its infancy, LMBA adopted a vigorous platform of confronting institutionalized racism and the myriad social and economic disparities affecting the African-American community. In the 1960's and 70's, LMBA's members confronted discrimination in employment, housing, education, public contracting and disparate treatment of African-American athletes at the University of Washington. In the 1980's and 90's, LMBA maintained its civil rights agenda, but expanded its sphere of influence within Washington's majority bar and among other African-American attorneys nationwide. Examples of this can be seen in LMBA's screening of judicial candidates for the bench, its co-founding of the Northwest Minority Job Fair, its member representation on Washington State Bar Association and King County Bar Association standing committees, and its hosting of the National Bar Associations annual conventions in 1984 and 1994. Over the past 30 years, LMBA has spearheaded or been intimately involved with a number of significant historical events.

Ensuring American Athletes at the University Equal Treatment of African-American Athletes at the University

In the late 1960's and early 1970's, African-American athletes on the University's football team alleged that they were being discriminated against because their ability to compete for and play positions on the team was limited by the coaching staffs designation of certain positions for white players only. LMBA members represented the athletes who challenged the University's discriminatory practices. As a result, the University changed its coaching regime, hired African-American administrators in the Athletic Department, and hired African-American football coaches to ensure that the African-American athletes were able to compete for positions that were previously closed.

Providing Instruction to African-American Law Students Studying for the Washington State Bar Examination

In the mid-1970's, LMBA started a program designed to raise the bar passage rate for African-American students taking the Washington bar examination. The program involved writing exercises and coaching on prior examination questions similar to modern-day bar review courses. The program is credited with the bar admission of numerous LMBA members.

Creating Employment Opportunities for African-American Law Students Through the Northwest Minority Job Fair

In the 1980's, LMBA sought to change the face of Seattle's large corporate law firms where there was a dearth of African-American attorneys and persistent claims of unavailable qualified applicants. LMBA co-founded the Job Fair to allow minority students the opportunity to showcase their talents for firms that were genuinely in search of qualified applicants.

In the 1980's, LMBA sought to change the face of Seattle's large corporate law firms where there was a dearth of African-American attorneys and persistent claims of unavailable qualified applicants. LMBA co-founded the Job Fair to allow minority students the opportunity to showcase their talents for firms that were genuinely in search of qualified applicants.

Reaching Across the State to Spokane's African-American Community and Gonzaga University's Law Students

In 1997, LMBA held its first general meeting in Spokane, Washington, at Gonzaga University's law school. The original purpose of the meeting was to show LMBA support for Gonzaga's African-American law students who were the victims of race-hate mail and threats by white supremacist or white Gonzaga law students who were sympathetic to the white supremacist cause. The meeting developed into a community forum where African-American citizens from Spokane shared their concerns about the racial environment in the city and, for the first time, had an African-American attorney audience to address those issues.

Historically, the LMBA has provided leadership by example to the African-American community and, as the focal point of Washington's African-American attorneys, is poised to continue the promotion of civil rights and the professional development, social and economic well-being, and professional interests of its current and potential members into the 21st Century.

Tipping the Balance of the 1972 Washington Supreme Court Race Between Wright and Shorett

King County Superior Court Judge Lloyd Shorett struck down the University's Law School affirmative action program in De Funis v. Odegaard, 82 Wn.2d 111973), and in the wake of his decision ran for election to the Washington Supreme Court. Fearing the long-term detrimental effects of a racially insensitive Court, LMBA members successfully mobilized a grassroots campaign throughout the Washington African-American community in favor of Judge Shorett's opponent, Charles Wright, who narrowly won the election by 5,000 votes. LMBA's efforts significantly raised the organization's credibility within the majority bar and lead to future judicial candidates actively seeking LMBA's endorsement.

Preserving the City of Seattle's Selective Certification/ Affirmative Action Program for Underrepresented Women and Minorities in the Seattle Fire Department

In 1976, Claude Harris (who later became Seattle's first African-American Fire Chief) was chosen to be a Battalion Chief for the Seattle Fire Department through the City's selective certification/affirmative action program for underrepresented women and minorities ("Program"). His selection and the Program were challenged by white firefighters in a reverse discrimination lawsuit filed against the City. LMBA members intervened on behalf of Battalion Chief Harris and, in concert with the City's attorneys, successfully tried the case, then won the appeal preserving the Program in Maehren v. City of Seattle, 92 Wn.2d 480 (1979), cert. denied, 452 U.S. 938 (1981).

Obtaining Financial Assistance from the Bar for African-American Law Students

In the mid-1970's, the King County Bar Foundation and the then King County Bar President, Bill Gates, Jr., were encouraged by LMBA to increase the number of minority lawyers in the Washington Bar by creating minority scholarships, initially for students at the University of Washington and later for students at the other law schools.

REGION TEN

Region 10 of the National Bar Association encompasses the legal communities in the states of Oklahoma, Colorado, Kansas, Utah, Wyoming and New Mexico and it plays a crucial role in the overall success of the organization and the advocacy for civil rights in the United States. Region 10 includes three active affiliate chapters – The New Mexico Black Lawyes Association, The Oklahoma City Association of Black Lawyers, and the Utah Black Lawyers Association.

Region 10's history is intertwined with the broader history of the National Bar Association itself, which emerged during the era of segregation and racial discrimination in America. The NBA was founded in response to the exclusion of Black attorneys from the American Bar Association (ABA) and to create a space where African American legal professionals could network, advocate, and support each other.

The population of Black attorneys in Region 10 is about 3% of the legal community. While the population is small, Region 10 has been home to several influential leaders who have shaped the legal landscape in their states and nationwide. Region 10 has also had continuous representation on the National Bar Association Board of Governors. Region 10 Directors have included – Eleanor Thompson, a member of the National Bar Association Hall of Fame and served as Regional Director for over forty years, the Honorable Shammara Henderson, the first Black Judge on New Mexico's Court of Appeals, Tiece I. Dempsey, former law clerk to the first Black United States District Judge in the Tenth Circuit, and the Honorable Shauna Graves-Robertson, who has served on Salt Lake County Justice Court for over twenty-five years.

Today, NBA Region 10 remains a vital part of the National Bar Association, continuing its tradition of advocating for social justice, equality, and the advancement of African American attorneys and judges. The region provides critical support to its members through its affiliates, ensuring that African American legal professionals in Oklahoma, Colorado, Kansas, Utah, Wyoming and New Mexico have the resources, connections, and opportunities needed to excel in their careers and make an impact in their communities.

The region is also dedicated to building bridges with other legal organizations and community groups in an effort to address the intersection of race, law, and social justice. Region 10 is active in providing scholarships, organizing annual conferences, and supporting legislative efforts aimed at protecting the rights of African Americans.

Region X of the National Bar Association
would like to congratulate
the National Bar Association on

its Centennial Anniversary!

NATIONAL BAR ASSOCIATION

EST. 1925

Region X Board

Regional Director: Judge Shauna Graves-Robertson

Secretary: Aja Brooks

Treasurer: Tiece Dempsey

NATIONAL BAR ASSOCIATION REGION X

New Mexico Black Lawyers Association

ABL

Region X Town Hall

The Fight for Justice for Greenwood

Public Nuisance Litigation Repairing the Continued Harm of the Tulsa Race Massacre

April 28, 2021
7PM EST

Tricia "CK" Hoffler
NBA President

Damario Solomon-Simmons
Managing Partner, Solomon-Simmons

Tiece Dempsey
Region X Director

NATIONAL BAR ASSOCIATION
EST. 1925

Co-sponsored by:
Charles Hamilton HOUSTON INSTITUTE For Race & Justice

Honoring Living Legends

Justice Tom Colbert (Retired)
Oklahoma Supreme Court

Judge Shammara Henderson
New Mexico Court of Appeals

Judge Shauna Graves-Robertson
Salt Lake County Justice Court

Alfred Dennis Mathewson
Emeritus Professor of Law & Former Co-Dean of the University of New Mexico School of Law

HOW DO I GET INVOLVED?

NATIONAL BAR ASSOCIATION 100 YEARS
IGNITING JUSTICE FOR 100 YEARS

SEE OLD FRIENDS. MAKE NEW ONES.

THE LISTENING & ENGAGEMENT TOUR

MEET UP. SHORE UP.

SALT LAKE CITY
UTAH

Join the largest nationwide grassroots movement of lawyers and judges in history.

APRIL 4 2025

6-9PM | **HOLLAND & HART**
222 South Main St
Suite 2200
Salt Lake City, UT 84101

RSVP TODAY SCAN QR CODE

SHARE YOUR STORY. GET INVOLVED. MAKE AN IMPACT.

POWERED BY

Holland & Hart

Utah Black Lawyers Association

EMAIL US AT RECRUITMENT100@NATIONALBAR.ORG | FOLLOW US AT @NATIONALBAR

REGION TWELVE

History of the Washington Bar Association (1925-2025)

While the Washington Bar Association (WBA) is celebrating its 100th anniversary in 2025, the deep roots and history of the black lawyers in Washington, D.C., date back to the admission of the first black lawyers during the Reconstruction Period. In 1869, George Boyer Vashon was the first black person admitted to the bar of the District of Columbia. Later, in 1872, Charlotte E. Ray was admitted as the first black woman lawyer in both the District of Columbia and the country. In 1902, during the post-reconstruction period, Robert H. Terrell would become the first black lawyer appointed a municipal court judge in the District of Columbia. Unfortunately, during this same period, and afterward, black lawyers and judges were excluded from membership in both the local white District of Columbia Bar Association (DCBA), and the American Bar Association (ABA).

Notwithstanding the exclusion of black lawyers from white local and national bar associations, the emergence of qualified and ambitious Black lawyers in the nation's capital would continue to achieve admissions to the bar of the District of Columbia. Eventually, seasoned black lawyers recognized the need to organize and formally associate in order to survive, to thrive, and for "their mutual benefit and protection" in an unwelcoming legal profession that was dominated by hostile white lawyers and a white judicial system that did not accord equal justice under law to all. Thus, around 1916, William L. Houston and other older black lawyers in the nation's capital formed the District of Columbia Colored Bar Association (DCCBA). Members of this organization, and their progeny, would later join and lead the Washington Bar Association and the National Bar Association. Black lawyers in the District of Columbia, and from around the country, some of whom would fight in "the War to end all wars" were themselves engaged in the moral equivalence of war in the District of Columbia, confronting unjust and racially exclusionary laws and practices known as "Jim Crow" and other vestiges of racial slavery and overt racism.

Out of the rising racial consciousness of the "roaring twenties" and the "New Negro Movement," in 1925, the Washington Bar Association (the "WBA") was founded by a new generation of young, gifted and black lawyers who looked away from the pace and approach of the "Colored Bar Association" in the District of Columbia, and decided to totally commit themselves to the formation of a new kind of bar association with a dedicated mission of making the concept of "equal justice under law" a reality for all.

The seven founders of the Washington Bar Association included the precocious son of William L. Houston - - Charles Hamilton Houston - - and six other black lawyers who became uncompromising, equal justice pioneers dedicated to using the law for the advancement of human rights and civil rights, equally, for all. The seven WBA founders, who incorporated the Washington Bar Association on May 26, 1925, were: Charles Hamilton Houston, George E.C. Hayes, J. Franklin Wilson, Isaiah Lisemby, Louis R. Mehlinger, Charles E. Robinson and Ulysses S. Garnes. George E. C. Hayes served as the first president of the WBA, Charles Hamilton Houston was the third WBA President and Charles E. Robinson served as fourth WBA President. Joshuah R. Turner is the current and 55th WBA President. To date, 13 members of the WBA have also served as presidents of the NBA, starting with William Lepre Houston, the NBA's 9th President (1937- 1939) and ending with the NBA's 77th President, Alfreda Robinson (2019-2020). In 1930, the WBA hosted the NBA 6th Annual Meeting in D.C., and in 2020, the WBA hosted the NBA first Virtual Annual Meeting, due to the COVID-19 pandemic. With the NBA National Headquarters strategically located in the nation's capital, the WBA has served as host to numerous National Bar Association's Annual Meetings and countless Wiley Branton Symposiums, Mid-Year Meetings and other meetings.

Over the years, the WBA and its members have continued to be a force in the general welfare of the District of Columbia, pleading that the local and federal courts, the administrative staffs of the courts in that Circuit, the Office of the Corporation Counsel and the U.S. Attorney's Office for the District of Columbia were competently staffed and occupied by people of color, women, and fair minded personnel who were in touch with all the citizens of the District. Members of the WBA have contributed significantly to the development of effective equal justice theories, practices and precedents and pursued them all the way to the U.S. Supreme Court. It was the equal justice advocacy and practice of many WBA members and other Black lawyers that formed the jurisprudence that underpinned the Supreme Court's 1954 decisions of Brown vs. Board of Education (1954) and Bolling vs. Sharpe (1954)

Further, the WBA has consistently provided leadership from its membership, founders and leadership regarding the significant roles played by the black lawyers in the development and improvement of the legal profession and democracy in America. For example, the two highest awards bestowed by the WBA are named in Charles Hamilton Houston and Ollie May Cooper, two WBA members who were also active NBA members and supporters.

In addition, the 28th WBA Past President Dr. J. Clay Smith wrote the authoritative book entitled *Emancipation: The Making of the Black Lawyer-1844-1944* (1993). Moreover, WBA Co-Founder and 3rd WBA President, Charles Hamilton Houston, while a member of the law faculty and later Dean of Howard University Law School, investigated, researched and prepared a preliminary report on a survey of activities by Negro lawyers throughout the country which he sent to, among others, Dean Roscoe Pound of the Harvard Law School. In his historic report, Charles H. Houston characterized the strengths and weaknesses in the black bar associations located around the country. In fact, while making specific references to the equal justice work of the WBA, he concluded as follows: "*The Washington, D.C. Bar Association is now taking an increasingly active part in matters affecting the conduct of the profession.*" *Tentative Findings re Negro Lawyers, p.14 (1928)*.

For the past century, the equal justice record of the WBA demonstrates that the same challenges that faced Black people and Black lawyers at its founding in 1925, have remained in various guises throughout the years. True to its founding mission, the WBA has continued its leadership and development into all aspects of the legal community in our country and in the nation's capital. With continued dedication to its core equal justice mission, and legacy, the WBA will continue to ensure that constitutional guarantees are not further diluted, civil rights laws are properly enforced and that the rights, dignity and humanity of the citizens of the District of Columbia, and the nation, are protected. In keeping with this perpetual equal justice thrust, mission and legacy, on January 18, 2025, in Washington, D.C., Charles Hamilton Houston III was the Keynote Speaker at the WBA Centennial Year Kickoff Reception in the George E.C. Hayes Fellowship Hall where a "Call to Commemoration–1925-2025" was issued with the theme: Centennial Salute to the Washington Bar Association Founders, Leadership and its Legacy of Pursuing Equal Justice Under Law.

GWAC History 2025 Journal

The Greater Washington Area Chapter (GWAC) of the Women Lawyers Division, National Bar Association, stands as a beacon of empowerment and advocacy for African American women attorneys in the D.C. metropolitan area. Established in 1974 by the visionary Barbara Whiting-Wright, GWAC has grown from a modest assembly of approximately 20 members to a robust network of over 400 legal professionals, including students, practitioners, and judges.

The Greater Washington Area Chapter, Women Lawyers Division, National Bar Association (GWAC) is a network of African American women attorneys dedicated to the professional development of its members. GWAC is committed to improving the quality of life in the Greater Washington D.C. through a variety of activities, including educational programs and community service projects. GWAC's mission is to address the concerns of the D.C. metropolitan community, with a particular emphasis on African American women in the legal profession.

Founding Vision and Early Leadership

In 1974, Barbara E. Whiting-Wright, a trailblazing attorney and advocate, co-founded the Greater Washington Area Chapter (GWAC) of the Women Lawyers Division, National Bar Association. Recognizing the unique challenges faced by African American women in the legal profession, Whiting-Wright established GWAC to create a supportive network that would empower these women through mentorship, professional development, and community engagement.

Whiting-Wright's own career was marked by significant milestones. She was the first Black woman to serve as a customs law specialist at the U.S. Customs Service, beginning her tenure in 1964.

Her commitment to service extended beyond her professional achievements; she was deeply involved in mentoring young attorneys and advocating for greater inclusion within the legal community. Her leadership set the tone for GWAC's enduring mission to uplift African American women lawyers and address the broader concerns of the D.C. metropolitan community.

Growth and Community Impact

Since its inception, GWAC has grown from a modest group of approximately 20 members to a robust organization of over 400 legal professionals, including students, practitioners, and judges. The chapter has been instrumental in providing educational programs, community service projects, and advocacy initiatives aimed at improving the quality of life in the Greater Washington D.C. area.

In 1993, GWAC expanded its reach by establishing the GWAC Foundation, Inc., a 501(c)(3) charitable arm dedicated to empowering the African-American community. The Foundation focuses on fostering the education and training of African-American law students, enriching the lives of African-American children, and improving the quality of life for the elderly, particularly within the African-American community. gwacdc.org

Continuing the Mission

As GWAC celebrates its 50th anniversary, the organization remains steadfast in its commitment to empowering African American women in the legal profession. Under the leadership of President Tracey G. Jackson, Ph.D., Esq., GWAC has launched the "50 for 50" campaign, aiming to recruit 50 new members, welcome back 50 former members, and engage 50 law students.

GWAC's enduring legacy is a testament to the vision of its founder, Barbara Whiting-Wright, and the countless members who have contributed to its mission. Through unwavering commitment to service, mentorship, and advocacy, GWAC continues to be a pillar of support and a catalyst for change within the legal community.

GWAC Foundation

In 1993, GWAC expanded its reach by establishing the GWAC Foundation, Inc., a 501(c)(3) charitable arm dedicated to empowering the African-American community. The Foundation focuses on fostering African-American law students' education and training, enriching African-American children's lives, and improving the quality of life for the elderly, particularly within the African-American community.

GWAC's 5oth Anniversary

As GWAC celebrates its 50th anniversary, the organization continues to honor its legacy while looking forward to a future filled with promise and possibility. Under the leadership of President Tracey G. Jackson, Ph.D., Esq. (2024–2025), GWAC remains steadfast in its commitment to professional development, community service, and advancing African American women in the legal field. During the 50th jubilee year, GWAC recognized several Women of Wonder and launched the "50 for 50" campaign to recruit 50 new members, welcome back 50 former members, and engage 50 law students. This initiative reflects GWAC's dedication to growth, inclusivity, and the nurturing of future leaders.

Leadership Legacy

GWAC's strength lies in its dynamic leadership. Each president has contributed to the organization's growth and adaptability, ensuring its relevance in an ever-evolving legal landscape. Notable president-elect, president, and past presidents include:

Patricia-Joy Walker (2025-2026) (President-Elect)	**Tracey G. Jackson, PhD, Esq. (2024-2025)**	**Keela Seales (2023-2024)**
Bayliss Fiddiman (2022-2023)	Renee Mims (2021-2022)	Erinn D. Martin (2020-2021)
Maryam Hatcher (2019-2020)	Carla Jordan-Detamore (2018-2019)	Janea Hawkins (2017-2018)
Alicia M. McNeal (2016-2017)	Brandes S. G. Ash (2015-2016)	Melanie E. Bates (2014-2015)
Shara Chang (2013-2014)	Meredith P. Graves (2012-2013)	Josephine Nelson Harriott (2011-2012)
Valencia Rainey (2010-2011)	Nakeasha L. Sanders (2009-2010)	Lani P. Shaw (2008-2009)
Michelle Thomas (2007-2008)	Ayoka Campbell (2006-2007)	Kirra L. Jarratt (2005-2006)
Rita Sampson (2002-2005)	Tara J. Fentress (2001-2002)	Norma Brown Hutcheson (1999-2001)
Elicia Pegues Spearman (1997-1999)	Kim Kendrick (1995-1997)	Cheryl L. Ziegler (1993-1995)
Grace E. Speights (1991-1993)	Gloria R. Sulton (1989-1991)	Kathryn A. Ellis (1988-1989)
Belva D. Newsome (1986-1988)	N. Denise Wilson-Taylor (1984-1986)	Cecilie A. Vaughters-Johnson (1982-1984)
Ruth R. Banks (1980-1982)	Lenore H. Cameron (1978-1980)	
Barbara Whiting-Wright: (1976-1978) President Pro Temp 1974-1976		

SECTIONS AND DIVISIONS

NATIONAL BAR ASSOCIATION
EST. 1925

SECTIONS

Administrative Law TBD	**Alternative Dispute Resolution Law** Carl Turpin www.nba-adr.org	**Appellate Law** Tilman Breckenridge
Bankruptcy Law Donald Bell	**Civil Rights Law** Tanya Clay House	**Civil Rights Law** Tanya Clay House
Civil Trial Advocacy Law Vanita M. Banks	**Commercial Law** Rashida MacMurray Abdullah www.nbacls.com	**Communications Law** N/A
Corporate Law Otto Meyers	**Criminal and Juvenile Justice Law** Kevin Jones	**Entertainment, Sports, & Arts Law** Ricky Anderson
Environmental, Energy, & Public Utilities Law Benjamin F. Wilson	**Family Law** Princess Woodward	**Government Procurement Law** N/A
Health Law Stephanie D. Barnes	**Immigration Law** Allen Orr	**Insurance Law** Karen Dodson
Intellectual Property Law Jennifer Fisher-Golden	**International Law** Barbara A. Simmons	**Labor & Employment Law** Kevin D. Reese
Law & Religion Section J. Machelle Sweeting	**Privacy, Cybersecurity & Technology Law Section** Leah Perry	**Real Property, Trusts, and Estates Law** Terrance Quinn www.nba-rpte.org
Small Business Law Goodwille Pierre, M.Ed., JD	**Tax Law** Michelle Hallman	**Veteran Affairs & Military Law** Louis "Jamie" Boston

***Note: This summary reflects available information; not all NBA sections submitted updates or historical information.**

ALTERNATIVE DISPUTE RESOLUTION

National Bar Association – Alternative Dispute Resolution Section

Carl Turpin, Chair

Rebekah RatliU, 1 st Vice Chair

Yvette Gibbons, 2nd Vice Chair

Dean Burrell Treas

Yonelle Moore, Secretary

Steven Hunter Board

Joanna Bracy Board

Verlyn Francis, Board

Paul Garrison, Board

freida Kenny, Board

Robie Beatty, Parliamentari

President Wiley Adams, NBA ADR Section and ILS Traveled to Accra, Ghana. By Rebekah Ratliff, NBA ADR Section 1st Vice Chair

President Wiley Adams traveled to Accra, Ghana with a delegation representing the NBA ADR and ILS Sections to celebrate the April 5th historic signing (ceremony) of the MOU with the African Continental Free Trade Area (AfCFTA).

The MOU proposes capacity building and upskills training in ADR (and other areas) to better prepare diplomats, entrepreneurs, women and youth for investment and trade on the continent. This trip was used as an exploratory mission to ascertain the processes, protocols and potential for a mutually beneficial partnership between the NBA and the AfCFTA to provide needed consulting expertise and other resources for investment and trade to design mechanisms for economic transformation on the continent. AfCFTA Initiative Co-chairs Barbara A.

Simmons (Chair of the ILS Section) and ADR/ILS section member, Attorney Johanna LeBlanc planned a full itinerary of meetings and activities in Ghana with our partners, to solidify relationships and discuss strategy with the various stakeholders. As one of the architects of the MOU, 1st Vice Chair, Rebekah Ratliff was part of the delegation and will be leading the ADR capacity building piece of the project, which will include training.

Rebekah also met with the Insurance Commissioner of Ghana, the President of the Africa Insurance Organization (AIO) and the President of the Chartered Insurance Ladies Association of Ghana (CILAG), of which she is a member. The insurance and financial services industry will be a key partner in supporting all trade and commerce activities.

The celebration continued on Monday, April 7th with a private reception, hosted by the Adomi Advisory Group PLLC at the scenic Bridge View Resort in Akosombo, Ghana, with the delegation arriving by police escort. April 8 was a day of connection with visits to the Court of Appeals, the Ghana School of Law, American Chamber of Commerce, Office of the Attorney General and Ministry of Justice, ending at the Office of Diaspora Affairs (Office of the President). ADR is a priority, as the laws surrounding free trade on the continent of Africa will need to be restructured to accommodate the opportunities that exist through the AfCFTA and (streamlined) protocols will need to be put in place to ensure access. It is anticipated that dispute management will be of the utmost importance.

After a comprehensive debrief of the delegation members, information will soon follow, regarding opportunities for members of the ADR Section with particular skills sets to participate in defined working groups in accordance with project needs. The opportunities are endless, stay tuned.

NBA ADR Section 2024-2025 Programs

During the 2024-2025 bar year the NBA ADR Section had several important programs to advance our knowledge of ADR

National Bar Association Commercial Law Section
Centennial Celebration

Established in 1987, the National Bar Association Commercial Law Section (NBA-CLS) has been a driving force for diversity, education, and professional excellence within the legal community. Its foundation lies in the vision of connecting NBA members in the commercial law practice with institutional corporate clients, creating pathways for Black attorneys to serve as outside counsel. This vision materialized in the groundbreaking 1988 Corporate Counsel Conference (CCC) in Chicago, led by Chair Cora T. Walker. The participation of over 25 major corporations, including IBM, Ford, and Shell, marked the beginning of transformative attorney-client relationships.

Today, the annual CCC remains the NBA-CLS's signature event, having grown significantly in scope and influence. Serving as a model for diversity, equity, and inclusion initiatives, it's estimated that over 1,000 NBA-CLS members have connected with over 100 corporations through this vital platform over the past three decades.

By creating a dynamic interface between outside counsel and in-house legal teams actively seeking to diversify their external partnerships, NBA CLS directly addresses the critical need for greater representation within the legal landscape. The networking and CLE programming that NBA CLS provides are invaluable, offering practitioners a space to exchange expertise, stay abreast of evolving commercial law trends, and cultivate professional relationships that can lead to collaborative opportunities and career advancement. Furthermore, NBA-CLS' commitment to community service and expanding the pipeline of Black law students entering the legal profession contributes to a more inclusive and equitable legal field, enriching the profession with diverse perspectives and talent. Ultimately, NBA-CLS not only empowers its members but also actively works to shape a more representative, knowledgeable, and interconnected legal community.

Mission and Initiatives

The mission of the NBA-CLS is to:

- Bring together outside counsel members with in-house counsel who seek to increase the diversity of their outside counsel ranks;
- Provide networking and education forums to address the interests of members practicing in the area of Commercial Law; and
- Expand the pipeline of African Americans entering the legal profession.

Our mission is exemplified in impactful programs such as:

Annual Corporate Counsel Conference:

- NBA-CLS' annual Commercial Counsel Conference, held each February, stands as its marquee event for the Section. This significant event serves as a central gathering point for commercial law practitioners, in-house counsel, and other legal professionals. This three-day conference offers a robust platform for in-depth discussions on cutting-edge legal developments, critical industry trends, and best practices within commercial law. Through engaging panel discussions, insightful presentations, and valuable networking opportunities, attendees gain substantive knowledge, forge meaningful connections, and contribute to the ongoing dialogue shaping the field. As the CLS's flagship event, CCC is essential for expertise enhancement, network expansion, and staying at the forefront of commercial law.

Peek Behind the Corporate Veil:

- PBTCV is an exclusive program available to NBA-CLS top tier sponsors. It provides a unique opportunity for sponsoring law firms partners and NBA-CLS' Executive Committee to network while gaining exposure to the interworking of a corporate legal department. This initiative invites participants into the inner workings of reputable corporations, offering invaluable insights into their culture, operational processes, and the diverse range of legal matters they handle. By offering a firsthand look behind the scenes, the program aims to equip outside counsel with a deeper understanding of potential clients' needs and priorities, fostering stronger partnerships and enabling them to better serve these organizations.

Scholarships and Community Contributions:

- NBA-CLS demonstrates its commitment to empowerment and service through scholarships for deserving law students and contributions to initiatives such as the Dr. Martin Luther King Jr. Drum Major for Justice Oral Advocacy Program.

Black Lawyers Matter Internship Program:

- Launched in 2020, this program was launched to match law students with internship opportunities with various corporate and non-profit organizations. Through fellowship and grants, law students interviewed and were paired with organizations to gain greater exposure to the different career paths of lawyers.

Section of the Year Award:

- NBA CLS has been recognized several times at the NBA Annual Convention as the Outstanding Section of the Year for its contributions to advancing the NBA mission.

As the National Bar Association celebrates its centennial, the NBA CLS stands proud of its legacy and looks forward to continuing its impactful work in partnership with the NBA. With unwavering commitment to diversity and inclusion, the section will undoubtedly continue to shape the future of the legal profession and empower generations to come.

NBA Corporate Law Section

It is with great enthusiasm and honor that the Corporate Law Section of the National Bar Association (NBA) celebrates and participates in the various activities commemorating this NBA 100th Annual Conference.

The Corporate Law Section (initially known as the Institutional/Corporate Law Section) has been an integral component of the success of the NBA and the delivery of its mission for almost half a century. As with the original founding of the section, the Corporate Law Section (may be referenced as "Section" hereafter) continues to champion its purpose, namely (a) to provide, improve and promote the participation of lawyers who practice in one or more areas of corporate law; (b) to improve and promote the presence of attorneys of African descent in the practice of corporate law; (c) to promote adherence to the highest ethical standards in the practice of corporate law and to the legal competency in the members of the Section through continuing legal education; (d) to promote a communications network and create a sense of community among lawyers practicing corporate law; (e) to promote, speak for and advance the cause of civil and human rights in corporate environments as well as other national and global environments; (f) to promote concern and action among corporate law practitioners, their respective organizations and other organizations, with the legal welfare of the poor, minorities and underrepresented communities, and; (g) to provide a vehicle for effective and sustainable change that leads to more professional opportunities for Section members and equity across corporate ecosystems.

We are proud and yet humbled to share, that the Section has delivered and continues to deliver, on all elements of its purpose and mission. From the Section's annual Gateway to Success Conference and its highly acclaimed quarterly newsletter to its much appreciated collaborations with other NBA sections and divisions to host the annual Corporate Counsel Leadership Summit (Summit), the Annual Networking Reception and substantive continuing legal educations sessions and webinars. At this upcoming, NBA 100th Annual Convention, we will also celebrate the 17th Annual Summit which was founded by a member of our Section, NBA Past President John Page.

A prime directive for our Section is to enhance and nurture a pipeline of future lawyers and corporate law practitioners. To this end, in the most recent three (3) years, the Section has given out over $130,000 in scholarships to both undergraduate and law school students and over $20, 000 grants to Morris Brown College. We seek to provide similar grants and/or endowments with other Historically Black Colleges and Universities (HBCUs).

Our scholarship and legal professional development deliverables was significantly enhanced with the founding of the Gateway to Success Conference by Past Section Chair Catherine Costict and Section member Sharon Bridges, which held its inaugural conference at Jackson State University, a nationally recognized HBCU.

Years later, the Gateway to Success Conference (Gateway) continues to be impactful by providing the opportunity for both law students and lawyers to enhance their legal acumen, providing national scholarships and building substantive relationships with HBCUs by striving to host most of our Gateway conferences at HBCU law schools and/or undergraduate programs across the nation.

In our Section's 2025 1st Quarter Newsletter (Link: https://cls-q1-2025.tiiny.site/), our NBA Law Student Fellow, August Bennett, authored a fantastic article entitled "A Legacy of Great Leadership of the Corporate Law Section." The article highlighted many of the past section chairs, such as Freida Wheaton, Debra Matlock, Past NBA President Vanita Banks, Catherine Costict, Lamonika Hurst, Twanda Turner Westbrook, Kevin Armstrong and Otto O. Meyers III, who is also a past and now current chair of the Section. A common denominator through these decades of leadership has been the passion and commitment to enhance opportunities for minorities in the practice of corporate law, building and nurturing the pipeline of future practitioners and providing opportunities for our members to sharpen their legal skills while building authentic personal and professional networks.

While the Section has been blessed with great leadership through each of its past chairs and current chair, one of the Section's greatest strengths and value-advantages, is its members, especially those members who volunteer on the Section's various committees. We take this opportunity to, once again, thank our members for their membership, commitment and action in support of the Corporate Law Section and the National Bar Association. Another blessing and integral to the success of our Section activities are our phenomenal sponsors - Thank you!!

We close with an exuberant salute to the NBA and its 100th Annual Convention. We pledge our commitment and service to delivering and celebrating another future 100 years of service to the NBA, its members, and the communities its serves.

Criminal Law and Juvenile Justice Section

The National Bar Association (NBA) is one of the oldest and largest national organizations of predominantly African American lawyers and judges in the United States. Founded in 1925, the NBA has played a significant role in advocating for civil rights and social justice, with various sections dedicated to specific areas of law. Among these is the Criminal Law Section, which focuses on criminal law and justice issues, providing a platform for legal professionals to address critical challenges within the criminal justice system.

Formation and Early Years

Establishing the Criminal Law and Juvenile Justice Section is part of the NBA's commitment to address the unique challenges African Americans face in the criminal justice system. In the early years, the section focused on promoting fair legal representation and combating racial discrimination in criminal prosecutions. The NBA's efforts were and continue to be crucial during times of rampant racial injustices and the legal rights of African Americans are overlooked. Later, the section added the Juvenile Justice component to address the disparities of juveniles in the criminal justice system. Arguably, the Criminal Law and Juvenile Justice Section is the cornerstone of NBA and continues to be an intricate and vital part of the organization because of the continued systemic efforts to criminalize black and brown existence.

Key Milestones

1. Advocacy for Legal Reforms:

- Over the decades, the Criminal Law Section has been at the forefront of advocating for reforms aimed at reducing racial disparities in sentencing, wrongful convictions, and police misconduct. The section has organized numerous conferences and seminars to educate its members and the public about these issues.

2. Training and Resources:

- The section has also provided training programs and resources for attorneys practicing criminal law, emphasizing the importance of professional development and ethical standards in legal practice. We have conducted countless CLE Sessions at each conference and Annual Convention, showcasing some of the nation's prominent Black Attorneys.

3. Community Engagement:

- Recognizing the importance of community involvement, the Criminal Law and Juvenile Justice Section has initiated outreach programs to inform and empower communities about their rights within the criminal justice system. This includes workshops, legal clinics, and partnerships with local organizations. Most notable for the Know Your Rights Campaign, Challenges to the Death Penalty, and Unconstitutionality of Life Sentencing of Juveniles.

In recent years, the Criminal Law and Juvenile Justice Section has expanded its focus to include contemporary issues such as mass incarceration, the impact of drug laws on minority communities, and the need for comprehensive criminal justice reform. The section has actively participated in national discussions, collaborating with other organizations and stakeholders to advocate for policy changes and challenge the attach on legal professionals to include lawyers and judges.

Some Notable Initiatives and Contributors

- **Criminal Justice Reform Agenda:** The section has developed a comprehensive agenda addressing systemic issues within the criminal justice system, advocating for legislative changes at both state and federal levels.

- **Mentorship Programs:** To inspire the next generation of legal professionals, the Criminal Law and Juvenile Justice Section has implemented mentorship programs connecting experienced attorneys with law students and young lawyers, fostering a new wave of advocates for justice.

- **Notable Members:** The list of section members is extensive, including Charles Hamilton Houston, Justice Thurgood Marshall, Johnny Cochran, and Darryl Parks to name a few.

- **Chairs of the Section:** Between 2005 and 2020, Lei-Chala Wilson served as Chair for approximately 16 years, with Terry Wiley serving a few years in between. Leslie Thomas Jones became Chair in 2021- 2022. After serving as Vice-Chair under Leslie Thomas Jones, Kevin L. Jones was elected Chair in 2022 and continued serving through the Centennial Celebration.

The Criminal Law and Juvenile Justice Section of the National Bar Association continues to be a vital force in shaping the discourse around criminal law and justice in the United States. Its historical contributions and ongoing initiatives reflect a commitment to ensuring equitable treatment within the legal system for all individuals, particularly those from marginalized communities.

As the section looks to the future, it remains dedicated to addressing the evolving challenges within criminal law, striving for a justice system that upholds the principles of fairness and equality even in the lawless era of the Trump Administration.

Submitted by:

Chair Kevin L. Jones, Esq
2022-Present

National Bar Association
Entertainment, Sports & Arts Law Section

Attn:Attorney Ricky Anderson
4265 San Felipe Street, Suite 1100
Houston, Texas 77027
(713) 929-6463
Ricky@AttorneyRickyAnderson.com

Entertainment Law is a specialized area of legal practice that focuses on the legal services related to the entertainment industry, including film, television, music, theater, publishing, and digital media. Entertainment law encompasses a wide range of legal disciplines that affect the creation, production, and distribution of artistic and commercial entertainment. It combines elements of:

- **Contract Law** – drafting and negotiating agreements such as talent contracts, production deals, and licensing agreements.
- **Intellectual Property Law** – protecting copyrights, trademarks, and rights of publicity.
- **Labor and Employment Law** – dealing with union agreements, employment disputes, and talent representation.
- **Litigation** – resolving disputes over ownership, royalties, defamation, or breaches of contract.
- **Corporate and Finance Law** – structuring entertainment companies, financing projects, and mergers/acquisitions.

Entertainment lawyers represent a wide range of clients including artists, writers, producers, studios, record labels, agents, and digital content creators. They help navigate the legal landscape to ensure creative work is protected, properly monetized, and lawfully distributed.

Entertainment Law
(Music | Film | Digital Media)

Music Law

Focus: Protects the rights of artists, songwriters, and producers.

- Copyrights – Covers songs (composition) and recordings (masters)
- Publishing & Royalties – Collecting income from various uses
- Recording Contracts – Terms between artists & labels
- Performance Rights – Managed by ASCAP, BMI, SESAC
- Sampling & Licensing – Legal clearance for using music

Film Law

Focus: Manages legal aspects of film development, production & distribution.

- Option & Purchase Agreements – Buying rights to scripts/books
- Talent & Crew Contracts – Covering actors, directors, staff
- Production Legal – Insurance, releases, union compliance
- Distribution Deals – Agreements with studios, streamers, etc.
- Clearances – For music, logos, or footage in films

Digital Media Law

Focus: Protects and monetizes online content and creator rights.

- Content Licensing – Streaming agreements, platform rights
- DMCA & Copyright Takedowns – For online infringement
- Influencer Agreements – Sponsorship & brand deals
- Privacy & Data Law – Especially for apps and platforms
- Platform Terms & Monetization – Navigating YouTube, TikTok, etc.
- Web3/NFT Law – Blockchain-based content ownership

Sports Law

Sports Law is a specialized field that encompasses a variety of legal issues affecting the world of professional and amateur athletics. It involves the intersection of contract law, labor law, antitrust, intellectual property, and tort law, tailored to the unique dynamics of sports organizations, athletes, agents, and governing bodies.

Areas of Sports Law:

- Contracts & Negotiations Covers player contracts, endorsement deals, coaching agreements, and sponsorships.
- Labor & Collective Bargaining Involves player unions, collective bargaining agreements (CBAs), salary caps, free agency, and dispute resolution through arbitration.
- Agent Representation Legal rules for athlete agents, including compliance with regulations like the Uniform Athlete Agents Act (UAAA).
- Intellectual Property Protecting the rights to team logos, trademarks, broadcast rights, and an athlete's right of publicity.
- Regulatory & Compliance Includes NCAA rules, league governance, anti-doping regulations, and Title IX compliance for gender equity in sports.
- Personal Injury & Risk Management Managing liability for injuries, insurance issues, and safety protocols.
- Dispute Resolution Litigation, arbitration, and mediation for contract disputes, discipline, or eligibility issues.

Sports Law includes athletes, teams, leagues, coaches, agents, governing bodies, and sponsors.

Football (NFL & College)

Legal Issues:

- Collective Bargaining Agreement (CBA): NFL CBA governs salaries, benefits, drug policies, and conduct rules.
- Franchise Tag & Salary Cap: Regulates player movement and team payroll.
- Concussions & Player Safety: Major area of litigation and settlement (e.g., NFL concussion settlement).
- Name, Image & Likeness (NIL): College athletes can now monetize their NIL under NCAA rules.
- Agent Regulation: Agents must be NFLPA-certified; strict NCAA agent rules for college players.
- Broadcast & Licensing Rights: Massive television deals and merchandising regulations.

Basketball (NBA & NCAA)

Legal Issues:

- Player Mobility: Trades, free agency, and max contract structures are tightly regulated.
- NBA Draft & Eligibility Rules: Age limits, early entry, and "one-anddone" NCAA concerns.
- Collective Bargaining: NBA CBA includes luxury tax provisions and detailed revenue sharing.
- Endorsement Deals: Major focus for high-profile players; often more lucrative than salaries.
- NIL in College: Explosive growth of sponsorships and personal branding opportunities.
- Player Discipline & Conduct: Managed through league office and arbitration processes.

Baseball (MLB)

Legal Issues:

- Antitrust Exemption: MLB is exempt from federal antitrust laws—unique among sports leagues.
- Arbitration System: Players can pursue salary arbitration after a set number of years.
- Guaranteed Contracts: Most MLB contracts are fully guaranteed, unlike in the NFL.
- Drug Policy: Strict policies under the Joint Drug Prevention and Treatment Program.
- Minor League Structure: Recently scrutinized for labor conditions and player compensation.
- Collective Bargaining: Covers revenue sharing, service time manipulation, and playoff structure.

Soccer (MLS & International)

Legal Issues:

- Transfer System: Players often move between clubs for a fee, governed by FIFA transfer rules.
- Collective Bargaining: MLS has a CBA with its players union; includes free agency and salary minimums.
- Designated Player Rule: Allows clubs to pay marquee players beyond the salary cap.
- International Contracts: Players may face cross-border contract disputes and visa/work issues.
- Governing Bodies: FIFA, UEFA, and national federations impose rules impacting contracts, discipline, and competition.
- Gender Equity & Pay Disputes: Legal battles (e.g., U.S. Women's National Team lawsuit) spotlight equal pay and treatment.

Insurance Law Section

Formation, Leadership and Members

- The National Bar Association passed a motion to launch the Insurance Law Section ("NBA-IS") at its Mid-Year Conference in Louisville, KY on April 27, 2023. The Section's mission focuses on trial, corporate law, and regulatory issues relating to the business of insurance and the content of insurance policies, with emphasis on consumer policies and the regulation of claim handling. The Section serves as a guidepost for critical issues involving the insurance industry and all insurance attorneys are encouraged to become members. This Section also provides a platform and pipeline for those in the industry to access the NBA's full membership and network of 65,000 lawyers, judges, law professors and law students.

- Karen Dodson is the NBA-IS Chair. Karen is also Managing Counsel for Travelers Insurance, where she supervises a staff of attorneys and support staff in the areas of auto, construction liability, workers' compensation, public sector, subrogation, general liability, and trucking cases. Karen joined Travelers in 1999 as an attorney in the Staff Counsel organization, rising up through the ranks in New York, New Jersey, and now Georgia. She has held various leadership roles in the National Bar Association, and most recently helped to launch the NBA-IS.

- The Section's officers and committee leaders include: Vice-Chair, Maria John, Secretary, Erika Oates, Treasurer, Tangela Thomas, CLE Programming Chair, Roger Johnson and Marketing Committee Chairs, Tahirah Smith and Janeen Thomas. The Section's Advisory Board includes: Catherine Costict (Chair), Terrance Evans, Arlene Knighten, Kenyon Moore, and Rodney Barganier.

- To date, the Section has grown to **approximately 40 paid** members and continues to attract insurance attorneys to the NBA, some of whom had not previously been active NBA members. Our members include in-house counsel, defense and plaintiff litigators, coverage attorneys, regulatory attorneys, arbitrators, and other insurance professionals.

- In addition to attracting new members to the NBA, the NBA-IS also collaborates with other sections and divisions (including Corporate, WLD, ADR, Health Law and YLD) to present CLEs, webinars, networking events, and other activities.

The Commitment to Continuing Education

The NBA-IS has presented the following dynamic CLEs at the 99th Annual Convention:

- Diversity, Equity, & Inclusion and its relation to Insurance Law
- Preserving Trust: Legal Responses to Fraudulent Activities in Insurance and Health Law (partnering with the Health Law Section); and
- Preparing for Trial – A Perspective from Both Sides - Litigation Skills (partnering with the Young Lawyers Division).
- Defending Experts in Evidentiary Depositions & Jury Impact

Engagement through Sponsorship

- The NBA-IS hosted a Brunch Reception where the keynote speaker was Darryl Lewis, Chief Legal Officer of Universal Property & Casualty Insurance Company ("Universal"). The Brunch was co-sponsored by the National Association of Insurance Commissioners (NAIC), the title sponsor and by Travelers Insurance Company.
- Insurance Innovators Panel featuring speakers from NAIC and Universal
- Meet & Greet Event in the Region IX Suite Sponsored by Duane Morris

Partnership with Sections and Divisions to provide Webinars

The NBA-IS has hosted the following webinars since its inception:

- "Careers in Insurance: My Life as an Insurance Lawyer," in collaboration with the NBA's Women's Lawyers Division(2024)
- "Ladies First: Women Trailblazers in the Insurance Law Industry"
- "Artificial Intelligence & Insurance Law – Where Do We Go from Here?"
- "Mediator Matters: Selecting the Right Panel for Complex Insurance Cases" co-hosted by JAMS
- "HERSTORY: African American Women in Workers' Compensation"
- "Insurance Matters: Risky Business and the Future of ADR" co-hosted by the NBA ADR Division
- "Careers In Insurance" 2025

NBA-IS' Support of Events

In addition to its ongoing participation in the NBA's Annual Convention, the Section has also supported:

- The NBA Corporate Law's Gateway to Success Conference: *Turning Adversity into an Energy Source for Success; and*
- The National Black Law Student Association Career Conference

Global Advocate: National Bar Association's International Law Section

As the National Bar Association (NBA) celebrates its 100th anniversary, its legacy of advocacy extends beyond American courtrooms. Its International Law Section (ILS) has forged global partnerships and served as a force for justice abroad. From anti-apartheid efforts to election monitoring and legal training, the ILS has built powerful international partnerships and advanced the rule of law worldwide.

The NBA's international work began in the 1980s with solidarity missions to apartheid-era South Africa. A pivotal 1982–83 delegation led by Judge A. Leon Higginbotham Jr. encouraged local Black lawyers to establish the Black Lawyers Association (BLA) of South Africa. This collaboration planted the seeds for a lasting transatlantic partnership. With Judge Higginbotham's encouragement, the BLA established a Continuing Legal Education Center, supported by American legal experts and major U.S. foundations. These programs trained Black South African attorneys for leadership in a democratic future. Simultaneously, the NBA passed resolutions demanding Nelson Mandela's release and co-authored a pivotal report titled "Namibia: The Crisis in United States Policy Toward Southern Africa," which urged an end to South Africa's intransigence in then-occupied Namibia and condemned the U.S. "constructive engagement" policy with the apartheid regime. The report received unanimous endorsement from the Organization of African Unity. NBA's global engagement formally expanded its reach through the ILS and International Affiliates Meetings in the early 1990s.

In 1991, the NBA expanded its global reach with its first overseas affiliate chapter meeting in Senegal and Côte d'Ivoire. In the years that followed, the NBA convened affiliate chapter meetings across the globe: London, England (1992); Johannesburg, South Africa (1993 and 1995); Toronto, Canada (1994) (and 2017); Accra, Ghana (1996); Bahia, Brazil (1997); Tanzania and Kenya (1998); Israel and Jordan (1999); London and Paris (2000); Madrid, Spain (2001); Johannesburg, South Africa, Gaborone, Botswana (2004); and Barcelona, Spain (2005).

The 1992 legal tour of South Africa fostered crucial knowledge exchange as apartheid laws were dismantled. In April 1994, the NBA was the only bar association authorized to monitor South Africa's first democratic election. Nine ILS members, including Executive Director John Crumpa, and Deputy Director Maurice Foster, observed s millions of Black South Africans voted for the first time. This moment validated the NBA's years of advocacy. Post-apartheid, the NBA shifted to institution-building and expanded its footprint across Africa. In 1995, it hosted legal leaders from Ghana, Kenya, Tanzania, and Uganda for a U.S. study tour. Reciprocal visits soon followed, with discussions focused on governance and legal education.

In the early 2000s, the NBA signed a Memorandum of Understanding with South Africa's Ministry of Justice. Delegations visited Botswana, Zimbabwe, and South Africa, providing legal education seminars and engaging top officials, including heads of state and Constitutional Court Justices. A high point came in 2004 when a 40-member NBA delegation co-hosted an international meeting with the BLA in Johannesburg. Attendees included South Africa's Justice Ministers and Justice Albie Sachs. The event deepened mutual respect and inspired BLA members to attend future NBA meetings. Since that time, there has been a consistent delegation of Black South African lawyers who attend the NBA National Convention. Such exchanges have enabled Black lawyers from Africa, America, Canada, and the Caribbean to share strategies on issues ranging from judicial diversity, civil rights enforcement as well as addressing human rights violations. The result is to strengthen all communities in the process. Activities of the NBA's International Law Section have transformed the NBA from a domestically focused bar association into a truly international advocate for justice.

As it enters the next century, the International Law Section stands prepared to expand its focus to play a critical role in the international trade arena. In 2025, the National Bar Association signed a landmark Memorandum of Understanding (MOU) with the African Continental Free Trade Area (AfCFTA) Secretariat. This agreement reflects the NBA's growing role in shaping the intersection of law, trade, and economic integration across the African continent. The African Continental Free Trade Area is a comprehensive trade agreement aimed at transforming African into a more integrated and prosperous continent by promoting trade, investment, and the free movement of people and capital. The NBA has the good fortune of having the opportunity of becoming a partner with the AfCFTA Secretariat in assisting in the implementation of the AfCFTA Agreement. This marks a bold step into shaping law and trade in Africa's next chapter.

The partnership with the AfCFTA Secretariat complements the 2023 Cooperation and Collaboration Agreement signed with the Pan African Lawyers Union (PALU) and positions the NBA as a strategic legal partner in Africa's transformation agenda. PALU is the largest organization of African lawyers and associations on the Continent. Both Agreements were initiated by the International Law Section.

As the NBA moves into its second century, the International Law Section remains a testament to the power of legal solidarity. By building bridges across continents, the ILS reaffirms that justice truly knows no borders and neither should economic empowerment.
The International Law Section welcomes all who have a desire to make a difference in the international arena. The Section is open to expanding to include additional international areas of interest. Join the Section as it takes its rightful place as international advocates. Also, stay tuned as the Section will publish an extended version of its history.

Submitted by:
Barbara A. Simmons, Chair ILS, and
Leroy Wilson, Jr. NBA Life Member and former NBA Vice President

Law and Religion Section

The Vital Role of the Law and Religion Section of the National Bar Association

As the National Bar Association (NBA) celebrates its historic 100th Annual Convention in Chicago, Illinois, it is fitting to reflect on the indispensable contributions of one of its most meaningful arms —the Law and Religion Section. As the oldest and largest association of African American lawyers and judges, the NBA has long stood at the forefront of legal excellence, social justice, and community empowerment. Within this legacy, the Law and Religion Section occupies a unique and sacred space where the practice of law meets the moral compass of faith.

The Law and Religion section was established at the Board of Governors meeting at the 81st annual NBA convention in Detroit Michigan in 2006 by the visionary and spiritual leadership of a proposal submitted by NBA members and scholars Kwame O. Reed, Esq. and Rev. Dr. Larry Delano Coleman, Esq. Kwame O. Reed was elected as the Section's first Chair.

At the heart of this section is a commitment to exploring and strengthening the intersection between law and religion—two powerful forces that have shaped the arc of justice and liberation in the African American experience. Our houses of worship have long been more than places of prayer; they have been sanctuaries of advocacy, education, and activism. Understanding the legal rights and responsibilities of faith-based institutions is not only prudent—it is essential to their survival and their power to serve.

In addition to its active participation in organizing Continuing Legal Education (CLE) programs at the annual NBA convention, the Law and Religion Section also hosted its own groundbreaking conferences designed to empower religious institutions with legal knowledge, fortify their administrative operations, and affirm their role as community anchors. Whether addressing zoning and tax issues, safeguarding First Amendment protections, or responding to civil liability concerns, the section equips faith leaders with the tools to navigate an increasingly complex legal landscape.

The section's inaugural conference was held April 30, 2010 - May 1, 2010 at the Sheraton Columbia Town Center Hotel in Columbia, Maryland under the theme: "The Church and the Law: Practical Considerations for Church Leaders and Church Lawyers." Led by Section Chair Rev. William "Bill" Bennett, Esq. and conference Co-Chairs Arlene D. Knighten, Esq. and Jo Glasco, Esq. the conference's goal was to assist attendees better understand the religious and legal environment in which religious institutions operate and to provide tools and insights which can help attorneys and church leaders operate more effectively." The keynote speaker was Congressman Elijah Cummings, United States House of Representatives, 7th Congressional District Maryland.

The following year, under the theme "Empowering and Protecting the Church" the now annual conference was held April 29, 2011 - April 30, 2011, and was Co-Chaired by Arlene Knighten, Esq. and Ian Clarke Esq., at the Georgia Tech Hotel and Conference Center in Atlanta, Georgia. Integral to the conference's success, was the support of various sponsors and section guardians: Charles Byrd Jr Esq., Pamela Means, Esq., Robin Perry, Esq., and Alfreda Robinson, Esq. Divinely, the third annual conference was held on April 27, 2012 - April 29, 2012 in Chicago, Illinois - the place of our centennial convention - under the theme: "Faith, Law and Politics."

A cherished hallmark of the section's work is its support of the annual NBA Prayer Breakfast, a spiritually enriching tradition that invites legal professionals to pause, reflect, and reconnect with their faith and purpose. It is a sacred moment of unity—where robes, titles, and courtroom agendas give way to shared prayers, testimonies, and the enduring belief that justice and mercy must walk hand in hand.

As the Law and Religion Section looks to the future, it seeks to expand its membership, deepen its outreach, and continue playing an integral role in the life of the NBA. Just as our houses of worship have historically nurtured our aspirations and shaped our calling to law, this section remains committed to honoring that foundation. Through collaboration, education, and spiritual reflection, it will continue to serve as a beacon—guiding the legal profession not just in the pursuit of justice, but in the pursuit of righteousness.

Congratulations to the NBA on this milestone 100-year anniversary. It is with fervent prayer that we have come this far by faith, leaning on the Lord. May the prayers and support of the law and religion section continue to inspire us all to act justly, love mercy, remain united in spirit and persevere as we continue to walk faithfully in truth and with purpose in the years ahead.

Yours in the power of prayer, faith, and justice,

Hon. J. Machelle Sweeting

Hon. J. Machelle Sweeting
Chair, NBA Law and Religion Section

PAST SECTION CHAIRS

Kwame O. Reed and Larry Delano Coleman, *Section Founders*
Kwame O. Reed, Esq. (Minneapolis, MN)
Rev. Dr. Larry Delano Coleman, Esq. (Raytown, MO)
Rev. William Bennett, Esq. (Washington, DC)
Juan Thomas, Esq. (Aurora, IL)
Arlene Knighten, Esq. (Baton Rouge, LA)
Rev. Dr. Rickey Nelson Jones, Esq. (Laurel, MD)
Hon. J. Machelle Sweeting (New York, NY)

DIVISIONS

Government Lawyers Arlene Knighten	**Judicial Council** Hon. Brendette Brown Green Visit website
Law Professors Dean Tamara Lawson	**Law Students** Omarosa Manigault Newman
Legislative Law Dartesia Pitts	**LGBTQ Division** Antonio Lee
Partners in Majority Firms Grasford Smith www.minoritypartners.org	**Small Firms & Solo Practitioners** Marwan Porter
Women Lawyers Division Doreen Rachal	**Young Lawyers Division** Alex Smith www.nbayld.org

***Note: This summary reflects available information; not all NBA divisions submitted updates or historical information.**

Government Lawyers Division

The Government Lawyers Division's mission is to serve the distinctive needs of government and public lawyers. Our Division believes that by championing causes that benefit society as a whole, government and public interest lawyers uphold the principles of democracy and equality, striving to create meaningful change and ensure the legal system works for everyone. Their work is not just a profession but a mission to serve the greater good.

The Division provides informational and continuing legal education programs that benefit public attorneys, fosters ethics and professionalism, and provides a unique insight into the role of the Government and Public Lawyer. The Division includes not only those attorneys working for local, state, and national governments and their various agencies, it also includes attorneys working in the public sector such as state bar associations, legal services and other public service agencies. The Government Lawyers Division is one of the oldest divisions of the National Bar Association and has throughout its tenure had a strong commitment to integrity and excellence. The Government Lawyers Division fosters unity among Government and Public Interest lawyers and guarantees their voice is represented at the National Bar Association Board meetings and events.

Chairs of the Division have served in all aspects of the Government from the Us Attorneys officer, the National Labor Relations Board, and other state and government agencies. The present chair of the Government Lawyers Division is Arlene Knighten, former Executive Counsel for the Louisiana Department of insurance.

NATIONAL BAR ASSOCIATION JUDICIAL COUNCIL

Congratulates

THE NATIONAL BAR ASSOCIATION EST. 1925 100 YEARS

on its Centennial Anniversary.

HONORABLE
BRENDETTE BROWN GREEN
Circuit Judge - Birmingham, Alabama
NBA Judicial Council, 2024-2025 Chair

Our Mission

The Council shall exist for the education, the encouragement and the support of its members in their individual and collective efforts to achieve the following objectives:

- *the eradication of racial and class bias from every aspect of the judicial and the law enforcement process;*
- *the improvement of the public's confidence in courts and in the determination of the judiciary to listen, to understand and to fashion effective remedies for the legitimate grievances of the deprived, the depressed and the dehumanized in our society;*
- *to develop, analyze, and improve the judicial, managerial and administrative systems for the purposes of eradicating the civil and criminal case backlogs and for the marked improvements of the entire criminal justice system–particularly as it relates to the interrelationships between police, courts and corrections;*
- *to provide seminars, conferences, and forums for the exchange of judicial experiences for the training of new Council members and for the continuing education of veteran council members, and*
- *to bring about a better balance in the Federal and State judiciaries of ethnic judges.*

WWW.NBAJUDICIALCOUNCIL.ORG

Our History

The rapid increase in the number of black judges in the United States prompted the National Bar Association's National President, Edward F. Bell, to suggest the coordination of a separate judicial body within the parent organization. With the cooperation of the National Bar Foundation, the financial assistance from the Ford Foundation and the considerable interest expressed by the National Bar Association and judges around the country, a panel of judges was convened in Miami, Florida early in January 1971 to discuss organizing plans. As a result, a Planning Committee was chosen to begin formal organization of the new Council.

The committee subsequently proposed a resolution for the organization of the Judicial Council, which was adopted by the Executive Board of the National Bar Association on January 9, 1971.

The resolution stated that the Judicial Council shall be an independent, autonomous section of the National Bar Association with its own officers, bylaws, program, and treasury. Foremost among its objectives was the eradication of racial and class bias from every aspect of the judicial and law enforcement process.

Later that year, from August 3-6, 1971, black judges across the country assembled in Atlanta, Georgia for the founding convention. Judge George Crockett Jr. was elected Chairperson, and U.S. Circuit Court of Appeals Judge William H. Hastie was the keynote speaker. Over fifty-four chairs have led the organization since.

WWW.NBAJUDICIALCOUNCIL.ORG

Honorable Brendette Brown Green
Circuit Judge
NBA Judicial Council, 2024-2025 Chair
Birmingham, Alabama

Over the Years

It is with **deep honor** and **immense privilege** that I assume the role of the 54th Chair of the National Bar Association Judicial Council (NBAJC). I am committed to *Continuing the Legacy of Leadership and Service* established by the distinguished jurists who have preceded me.

In these challenging times, it is crucial that we unite to support one another and amplify our collective impact across the nation. I invite each of you to actively participate in the vital work of the NBAJC. Our membership is comprised of federal and state judges, justices, magistrates, and hearing officers from all jurisdictions. Together, we can learn from each other, promote access to justice for underserved communities, advocate for increased diversity within the judiciary, and support judicial wellness and professional development. 2025 marks a momentous occasion as we celebrate the 100th anniversary of the National Bar Association.

In 1971, the National Bar Association (NBA), with the assistance of the Ford Foundation, established the NBA's Judicial Council. Judge George Crockett, Jr. served as the Judicial Council's first chair. Black power meant producing more black judges. At its founding meeting, the Judicial Council pledged to increase black representation in federal and state judiciaries.

"The Judicial Council's logo reflected the cultural nationalism of this period. Founders redrew LADY Justice as an urban black woman with an Afro. The newly reconstituted figure held the scales of justice in her left hand and was lifting her blinders with her right hand. The Judicial Council's log read, "Let us remove the blindfold from the eyes of American justice. Too long has it obscured the unequal treatment accorded to poor people and black people under our law.

In 1975, Justice Sara J. Harper became the first female Chair of the National Bar Association Judicial Council. She served as the fifth Chair. She opened the door for many female Chairs. To date, twenty-two female Chairs have followed.

After graduating from Cleveland College in 1948, Sara J. Harper went on to become the first African-American woman to graduate from Case Western Reserve University's School of Law when she earned her degree in 1952. Harper became a prosecutor in the 1960s. In 1990, she and another woman became the first to win seats on the Ohio Court of Appeals. Then, in 1992, she sat on the Ohio Supreme Court as the first African-American woman to do so. Harper also was the first woman to serve on the judiciary of U.S. Marine Corps Reserve and she co-founded the country's first victim's rights program. She also was the Cleveland NAACP president in the early 1980s.

The members of the Judicial Council of the National Bar Association believe that our system of justice will only survive and keep the confidence and support of all segments of society, when those responsible for its trust continue to be the main catalysts for constructive change.

Therefore, the Judicial Council will continue to review itself in terms of past performance, and future potential. Our Bench will always be prepared to define its values and accept its responsibilities, to make meaningful progress toward making "Equal Justice Under Law" a reality for all. Judge Joseph C. Howard, Sr., from Baltimore, Maryland, served as the second National Bar Association Judicial Council Chair. He served from 1972-1973.

— Excerpt from "Why We Organize" 1971

WWW.NBAJUDICIALCOUNCIL.ORG

Honorable Brendette Brown Green
Circuit Judge
NBA Judicial Council, 2024-2025 Chair
Birmingham, Alabama

Past Chairs

NATIONAL BAR ASSOCIATION JUDICIAL COUNCIL

1971-1972	Judge George W. Crockett	Detroit, Michigan
1972-1973	Judge Joseph C. Howard	Baltimore, Maryland
1973-1974	Judge Lloyd O. Brown	Cleveland, Ohio
1974-1975	Judge Robert N.C. Nix, Jr.	Chicago, Illinois
1975-1976	Judge Sara J. Harper	Cleveland, Ohio
1976-1977	Judge Glenn T. Johnson	Chicago, Illinois
1977-1978	Judge Theodore R. Newman, Jr.	Washington D.C.
1978-1979	Judge Horace T. Ward	Atlanta, Georgia
1979-1980	Judge Russell R. DeBow	Chicago, Illinois
1980-1981	Judge Eugene W. Sharpe	New York, New York
1981-1982	Judge Alice A. Bonner	Houston, Texas
1982-1983	Judge H.T. Lockhard	Memphis, Tennessee
1983-1984	Judge Revius O. Ortique, Jr.	New Orleans, Louisiana
1984-1985	Judge Jack Tanner	Tacoma, Washington
1985-1986	Judge Charles W. Fleming	Cleveland, Ohio
1986-1987	Judge Thelma Wyatt Moore	Atlanta, Georgia
1987-1988	Judge Joyce London Alexander	Boston, Massachusetts
1988-1989	Judge Howard E. Bell	New York, New York
1989-1990	Judge Williams Thompson	Washington, D.C.
1990-1991	Judge Veronica Simmons-McBeth	Los Angeles, California
1991-1992	Judge Webster L. Brewer	Indianapolis, Indiana
1992-1993	Judge John L. Braxton	Philadelphia, Pennsylvania
1993-1994	Judge Richard Scott	Austin, Texas
1994-1995	Judge Benjamin H. Logan	Grand Rapids, Michigan
1995-1996	Judge William Cousins, Jr.	Chicago, Illinois
1996-1997	Judge Renee Jones Weeks	Newark, New Jersey
1997-1998	Judge Bernette Johnson	New Orleans, Louisiana
1998-1999	Judge Shelvin Louise Marie Hall	Chicago, Illinois
1999-2000	Judge Morris L. Overstreet	Austin, Texas
2000-2001	Judge Sylvia A. James	Inkster, Michigan
2001-2002	Judge Cecil Patterson	Phoenix, Arizona
2002-2003	Judge Patricia Banks	Chicago, Illinois
2003-2004	Judge Earnestine Hunt Dorse	Memphis, Tennessee
2004-2005	Judge Craig S. Strong	Detroit, Michigan
2005-2006	Judge M. Lynn Sherrod	Huntsville, Alabama
2006-2007	Judge Michael G. Bagneris	New Orleans, Louisiana
2007-2008	Judge Jon R. Gray	Kansas City, Missouri
2008-2009	Judge Peggy A. Quince	Tallahassee, Florida
2009-2010	Judge Robert D. Rucker	Indianapolis, Indiana
2010-2011	Judge Marcella Holland	Baltimore, Maryland
2011-2012	Judge Yvette Alexander	Baton Rouge, Louisiana
2012-2013	Judge Patrice Hinnant	Greensboro, North Carolina
2013-2014	Judge Denise Langford Morris	Pontiac, Michigan
2014-2015	Judge Randa Trapp	San Diego, California
2015-2016	Judge Leonard Murray	Chicago, Illinois
2016-2017	Judge Johnny Hardwick	Montgomery, Alabama
2017-2018	Judge Anne-Marie Clarke	St. Louis, Missouri
2018-2019	Judge Luke LaVergne	Baton Rouge, Louisiana
2019-2020	Judge Shauna Graves-Robertson	Salt Lake City, Utah
2020-2021	Judge Cenceria Edwards	Brooklyn, New York
2021-2022	Judge Monte Watkins	Nashville, Tennessee
2022-2023	Judge Kimberly Esmond Adams	Atlanta, Georgia
2023-2024	Judge Harry Cantrell Jr.	New Orleans, Louisiana

Continuing the Legacy of Leadership and Service

WWW.NBAJUDICIALCOUNCIL.ORG

Congratulations

THE NATIONAL BAR ASSOCIATION EST. 1925 | 100 YEARS

HONORABLE BRENDETTE BROWN GREEN
BIRMINGHAM, ALABAMA
Circuit Judge Jefferson County
NBA Judicial Council, Chair

HONORABLE FREDDRENNA M. LYLE
CHICAGO, ILLINOIS
Illinois Appellate Court
NBA Judicial Council, Chair- Elect

HONORABLE ALISHA RUFFIN MAY
BIRMINGHAM, ALABAMA
Circuit Court Judge
NBA Judicial Council,
Recording Secretary

HONORABLE HARRISON GREGG, JR. (RET.)
MISSOURI CITY, TEXAS
2nd Administrative Region
State of Texas
NBA Judicial Council, Financial Secretary

HONORABLE NICOLE SHEPPARD
NEW ORLEANS, LOUISIANA
Orleans Parish Civil District Court
NBA Judicial Council, Treasurer

HONORABLE DAVID J. HOBDY
BESSEMER, ALABAMA
Presiding Circuit Judge
(Bessemer Division)
NBA Judicial Council, Historian

HONORABLE CASSANDRA COLLIER-WILLIAMS
CLEVELAND, OHIO
Common Pleas Court
General Division
NBA Judicial Council, Parliamentarian

HONORABLE ALARIC MAY
BIRMINGHAM, ALABAMA
Circuit Court Judge
NBA Judicial Council, Chaplain

HONORABLE YVETTE MANSFIELD ALEXANDER
BATON ROUGE, LOUISIANA
Baton Rouge City Court
NBA Judicial Council, Chief of Protocol

HONORABLE LUKE A. LAVERGNE (RET.)
BATON ROUGE, LOUISIANA
The Family Court of
East Baton Rouge
NBA Judicial Council, Executive Director

HONORABLE HARRY CANTRELL (RET.)
NEW ORLEANS, LOUISIANA
Criminal District Court for the
Parish of Orleans
NBA Judicial Council, Immediate Past Chair

NATIONAL BAR ASSOCIATION JUDICIAL COUNCIL *Officers*

Congratulations

THE NATIONAL BAR ASSOCIATION EST. 1925 100 YEARS

JUSTICE
SARA J. HARPER (RET.)
CLEVELAND, OHIO
Eight District Court of Appeals
5th NBA Judicial Council Chair
1975 - 1976

JUDGE
ALICE A.BONNER (RET.)
HOUSTON, TEXAS
80th Civil Division Court
11th NBA Judicial Council Chair
1981 - 1982

JUDGE
JOHN L. BRAXTON (RET.)
PHILADELPHIA, PENNSYLVANIA
Philadelphia Court of Common Pleas
22nd NBA Judicial Council Chair
1992 - 1993

CHIEF JUSTICE
BERNETTE JOHNSON (RET.)
NEW ORLEANS, LOUISIANA
Louisiana Supreme Court
27th NBA Judicial Council Chair
1997 - 1998

JUSTICE
SHELVIN LOUISE MARIE HALL (RET.)
CHICAGO, ILLINOIS
Illinois Appellate Court
Cook County Circuit Court
28th NBA Judicial Council Chair
1998 - 1999

JUDGE
PATRICIA BANKS (RET.)
CHICAGO, ILLINOIS
Circuit Court of Cook County
32nd NBA Judicial Council Chair
2002 - 2003

JUDGE
EARNESTINE HUNT DORSE (RET.)
MEMPHIS, TENNESSEE
Memphis Municipal Court
33rd NBA Judicial Council Chair
2003 - 2004

JUDGE
MARTHA LYNN SHERROD (RET.)
HUNTSVILLE, ALABAMA
District Judge
35th NBA Judicial Council Chair
2005 - 2006

JUDGE
JON R. GRAY (RET.)
KANSAS CITY, MISSOURI
Circuit Court of Jackson County
37th NBA Judicial Council Chair
2007 - 2008

JUSTICE
ROBERT D. RUCKER (RET.)
INDIANAPOLIS, INDIANA
Indiana Supreme Court
39th NBA Judicial Council Chair
2009 - 2010

JUDGE
MARCELLA HOLLAND SENIOR JUDGE (RET.)
BALTIMORE, MARYLAND
Circuit Court of Baltimore City.
47th NBA Judicial Council Chair
2010 - 2011

CHIEF JUDGE
YVETTE MANSFIELD ALEXANDER
BATON ROUGE, LOUISIANNA
Baton Rouge City Court
41st NBA Judicial Council Chair
2011 - 2012

NATIONAL BAR ASSOCIATION JUDICIAL COUNCIL *Past Chairs*

Congratulations

THE NATIONAL BAR ASSOCIATION EST. 1925 100 YEARS

JUDGE
PATRICE A. HINNANT
GREENSBORO, NORTH CAROLINA
Superior Court
42nd NBA Judicial Council Chair
2012 - 2013

JUDGE
DENISE LANGFORD MORRIS
PONTIAC, MICHIGAN
Oakland County Circuit Court
43rd NBA Judicial Council Chair
2013 - 2014

JUDGE
RANDA TRAPP (RET.)
SAN DIEGO, CALIFORNIA
San Diego Superior Court
44th NBA Judicial Council Chair
2014 - 2015

JUDGE
LEONARD MURRAY (RET.)
CHICAGO, ILLINOIS
Circuit Court of Cook County
45th NBA Judicial Council Chair
2015-2016

JUDGE
JOHNNY HARDWICK (RET.)
MONTGOMERY, ALABAMA
15th Judicial Circuit
46th NBA Judicial Council Chair
2016 - 2017

JUDGE
ANNE -MARIE CLARKE (RET.)
ST. LOUIS, MISSOURI
47th NBA Judicial Council Chair
2017 - 2018

JUDGE
LUKE A. LAVERGNE (RET.)
BATON ROUGE, LOUISIANA
48th NBA Judicial Council Chair
2018 - 2019

JUDGE
SHAUNA GRAVES-ROBERTSON
SALT LAKE CITY, UTAH
Salt Lake County Justice Court
49th Chair NBA Judicial Council
2019 - 2020

JUSTICE
CENCERIA P. EDWARDS, CPA
BROOKLYN, NEW YORK
New York State Supreme Court
Appellate Division, Second Judicial Department
50th NBA Judicial Council Chair
2020 - 2021

JUDGE
MONTE D. WATKINS (RET.)
NASHVILLE, TENNESSEE
51st NBA Judicial Council Chair
2021 - 2022

JUDGE
KIMBERLY M. ESMOND ADAMS
ATLANTA, GEORGIA
Superior Courts of Georgia
Atlanta Judicial Circuit
52nd NBA Judicial Council Chair
2022 - 2023

JUDGE
HARRY CANTRELL JR. (RET.)
NEW ORLEANS, LOUISIANA
Criminal District Court for the Parish of Orleans
53rd NBA Judicial Council Chair
2023 - 2024

NATIONAL BAR ASSOCIATION JUDICIAL COUNCIL *Past Chairs*

Congratulations

THE NATIONAL BAR ASSOCIATION EST. 1925 100 YEARS

JUDGE SHARON V. BURRELL
ROCKVILLE, MARYLAND
Circuit Court of Montgomery County, Maryland
NBA Judicial Council Board Member

HONORABLE BONITA COLEMAN
CHICAGO, ILLINOIS
Circuit Court of Cook County
NBA Judicial Council Board Member

HONORABLE LONNIE THOMPSON
MEMPHIS, TENNESSEE
General Sessions Court Judge
NBA Judicial Council Board Member

JUDGE MIESHA DARROUGH
MIAMI, FLORIDA
Eleventh Judicial Circuit of Florida
NBA Judicial Council Board Member

HONORABLE ANDREW DIXON, III
TALLAHASSE, FLORIDA
Administrative Law Judge
NBA Judicial Council Board Member

JUDGE J. IMANI DREW
KANKAKEE COUNTY, ILLINOIS
Associate Judge
NBA Judicial Council Board Member

JUDGE ALICE SPRINKLE GRAY (RET.)
LITTLE ROCK, ARKANSAS
Pulaski County Circuit Court
Civil Division
NBA Judicial Council Board Member

JUDGE DEBORAH M. TURNER
CLEVELAND, OHIO
Cuyahoga County Court of Common Pleas
NBA Judicial Council Board Member

HONORABLE KARELIA R. STEWART
SHREVEPORT, LOUISIANA
First Judicial District Court
Caddo Parish
NBA Judicial Council Board Member

NATIONAL BAR ASSOCIATION JUDICIAL COUNCIL *Executive* BOARD MEMBERS

Congratulations

THE NATIONAL BAR ASSOCIATION EST. 1925 100 YEARS

JUDGE AMANDA N. HEATH
AUGUSTA, GEORGIA
Superior Court
Augusta Judicial Circuit
NBA Judicial Council Board Member

JUDGE JANET JAMES MAHON
ORLANDO, FLORIDA
Administrative Law Judge
Federal Social Security Administration
NBA Judicial Council Board Member

JUDGE HERMAN MARABLE, JR.
FLINT, MICHIGAN
67th District Court
NBA Judicial Council Board Member

JUDGE AUDREY MOOREHEAD
DALLAS COUNTY, TEXAS
Dallas County Criminal Court #3
NBA Judicial Council Board Member

HONORABLE RODNEY SMITH
FT. LAUDERDALE, FLORIDA
United States District Judge
Southern District of Florida
NBA Judicial Council Board Member

JUDGE ROBIN D. PITTMAN
NEW ORLEANS, LOUISIANA
District Court Judge
Criminal District Court, Section F
NBA Judicial Council Board Member

HONORABLE J. MACHELLE SWEETING
NEW YORK, NEW YORK
Supreme Court of the State of New York
NBA Judicial Council Board Member

JUDGE ALFREDA TALTON-HARRIS (RET.)
SUFFOLK, VIRGINIA
Juvenile and Domestic Relations District Court
Fifth Judicial District of Virginia
NBA Judicial Council Board Member

HONORABLE LATRICE WESTBROOKS
JACKSON, MISSISSIPPI
Court of Appeals of the State of Mississippi
NBA Judicial Council Board Member

NATIONAL BAR ASSOCIATION JUDICIAL COUNCIL *Executive* BOARD MEMBERS

Congratulations

THE NATIONAL BAR ASSOCIATION EST. 1925 100 YEARS

HONORABLE
NOELL F. ALLEN
INDIANAPOLIS, INDIANA
Administrative Law Judge
U.S. Social Security
Administration

HONORABLE
TANGELA BARRIE
STONE MOUNTAIN, GEORGIA
Superior Court of
Dekalb County

HONORABLE
SHAHEENA BENNETT
MONCKS CORNER, SOUTH CAROLINA
Chief Municipal Court Judge
Town of Moncks Corner

HONORABLE
RAHKEL BOUCHET
WASHINGTON, D.C.
Magistrate Judge
District of Columbia
Superior Court

HONORABLE
TANYA BRINKLEY
MIAMI, FLORIDA
Circuit Court Judge
Eleventh Judicial
Circuit of Florida

HONORABLE
PAMILA J. BROWN
ELLICOTT CITY, MARYLAND
Howard County
District Court

JUDGE
BERNETTA D. BUSH (RET.)
CHICAGO, ILLINOIS
Circuit Court of Cook County

HONORABLE
JAYNE CHANDLER
MEMPHIS, TENNESSEE
Municipal
Court Judge

HONORABLE
JOHN M. T. CHAVIS, II
INDIANAPOLIS, INDIANA
Presiding Judge
Marion Superior Court

HONORABLE
AKUA D. COPPOCK
WASHINGTON, D.C.
Administrative Law Judge
Office of Administrative Hearings
For the District of Columbia

HONORABLE
DEDRA DAVIS
HOUSTON, TEXAS
270th District
Court

HONORABLE
BERNICE BOUIE DONALD
MEMPHIS, TENNESSEE
U.S. Court of Appeals,
6th Circuit

HONORABLE
VERETTA L. FRAZIER
DALLAS, TEXAS
Presiding Judge of the
44th Civil District Court

NATIONAL BAR ASSOCIATION JUDICIAL COUNCIL *Members*

Congratulations

NATIONAL BAR ASSOCIATION 100 YEARS

HONORABLE
TERRINEE L. GUNDY
ATLANTA, GEORGIA
Atlanta Municipal Court

HONORABLE
SHERRI HALE
JOLIET, ILLINOIS
12th Circuit Court

HONORABLE
URSULA A. HALL
HOUSTON, TEXAS
Presiding Judge (Former)
165th District Court, Harris County, TX
Associate Judge (Former) City of Houston
Texas, Municipal Court

HONORABLE
TERESA HAMMONS (RET.)
VIRGINIA BEACH, VIRGINIA
Virginia Beach
General District Court

HONORABLE
DEBORAH HENDERSON
MEMPHIS, TENNESSEE
General Sessions
Civil Court Judge
Division IV

HONORABLE
CHARLENE EDWARDS HONEYWELL
TAMPA, FLORIDA
United States
District Judge
Middle District of Florida

HONORABLE
GARY M. JACKSON
DENVER, COLORADO
Denver County
Senior Judge

HONORABLE
DEBRA A. JAMES
NEW YORK, NEW YORK
New York State Supreme Court
Civil Bench

HONORABLE
KENYA M. JOHNSON
ATLANTA, GEORGIA
Chief Judge
Fulton County
Probate Court

HONORABLE
CASSANDRA LEWIS (RET.)
CHICAGO, ILLINOIS
Circuit Court Judge
Cook County

HONORABLE
JULIA R. MALVEAUX
DALLAS, TEXAS
Presiding Judge
The Probate Court

HONORABLE
H. ALEXANDER MANUEL (RET.)
WASHINGTON, DC
U.S. Administrative
Judge

NATIONAL BAR ASSOCIATION JUDICIAL COUNCIL *Members*

Congratulations

THE NATIONAL BAR ASSOCIATION EST. 1925 100 YEARS

HONORABLE
EARNEST E. MORRIS, JR.
ST. CROIX, VIRGIN ISLANDS
Superior Court of
Virgin Islands

HONORABLE
JULIE HARRIS NELSON
MIAMI, FLORIDA
Miami – Dade
11th Judicial Circuit
Criminal Division

HONORABLE
LISA S. OTTLEY
KINGS COUNTY, NEW YORK
Associate Justice, Appellate Term
2nd, 11th & 13th Judicial District
New York State Supreme Court

HONORABLE
MONICA MCCOY PURDY
DALLAS, TEXAS
Presiding Judge
95th State Civil District Court

HONORABLE
SYLVIA HINDS-RADIX (RET.)
NEW YORK STATE
Associate Justice, Appellate Division
New York State Supreme Court
Second Judicial Department

HONORABLE
EDWINA G. RICHARDSON
NEW YORK CITY, NY
Deputy Chief
Administrative Judge

HONORABLE
SANDRA ELENA ROPER
NEW YORK, NY
Civil Court of the
City of New York

HONORABLE
LOYCE L. RYAN (RET.)
MEMPHIS, TENNESSEE
Memphis, Shelby County
Tennessee

HONORABLE
SONYA L. SACKS
ALEXANDRIA, VIRGINIA
18th Judicial District
Court of Virginia

HONORABLE
JULIE SIMONE SNEED
TAMPA, FLORIDA
United States
District Judge

HONORABLE
MARY MAXWELL THOMAS (RET.)
CHICAGO, ILLINOIS

HONORABLE
PATRICIA J. TITUS (RET.)
LOS ANGELES, CALIFORNIA
Superior Court of California
County of Los Angles

HONORABLE
WAVNY TOUSSAINT
NEW YORK STATE
Presiding Justice
Appellate Term
Supreme Court of the
State of New York
2nd, 11 & 13th Judicial Districts

NATIONAL BAR ASSOCIATION JUDICIAL COUNCIL *Members*

The Louisiana Judicial Council

celebrates

THE NATIONAL BAR ASSOCIATION EST. 1925 100 YEARS

Judge Carl E. Stewart
U.S. Fifth Circuit Court of Appeals

Justice John Michael Guidry
Louisiana Supreme Court

Judge Karelia R. Stewart
First Judicial District Court

Judge Kern A. Reese
Orleans Parish Civil District Court

Judge Kimya M. Holmes
Orleans Criminal District Court

Magistrate, Judge Juana M. Lombard
Orleans Criminal District Court

Judge Ranord J. Darensburg
New Orleans Juvenile Court

Judge Aisha S. Clark
Monroe City Court

Chief Judge Lisa Woodruff-White, Retired
East Baton Rouge Parish Family Court

Judge Kirk A. Williams
Baker City Court

The Louisiana Judicial Council

celebrates

THE NATIONAL BAR ASSOCIATION EST. 1925 100 YEARS

Justice Piper D. Griffin
Louisiana Supreme Court

Judge Paula A. Brown
4th Circuit Court of Appeal

Judge Rachael D. Johnson
4th Circuit Court of Appeal

Judge E. Adrian Adams
24th Judicial District Court

Judge June B. Darensburg
24th Judicial District Court

Chief Judge Lee V. Faulkner, Jr.
24th Judicial District Court

Judge Robin D. Pittman
Orleans Parish Criminal District Court

Chief Judge D. Nicole Sheppard
Orleans Parish Civil District Court

Fiat Justitia Ruat Coelum
Louisiana Judicial Council - NBA

Judge Tammy D. Lee
Monroe City Court

Chief Judge Sheva M. Sims
Shreveport City Court

IN RECOGNITION OF THE

THE NATIONAL BAR ASSOCIATION EST. 1925 CENTENNIAL *Celebration*

The Louisiana Judicial Council Foundation

SALUTES LOUISIANA PAST CHAIRS OF THE NBA JUDICIAL COUNCIL

Justice Revius Oliver Ortique, Jr.
Supreme Court of Louisiana

Chief Justice Bernette J. Johnson
Supreme Court of Louisiana

Chief Judge Luke A. LaVergne, Retired
19th Judicial District Family Court

Judge Michael G. Bagneris, Retired
Orleans Parish Civil District Court

Judge Harry E. Cantrell Jr., Retired
Orleans Parish Magistrate Court

Chief Judge Yvette M. Alexander
Baton Rouge City Court

Fiat Justitia Ruat Coelum
Louisiana Judicial Council - NBA

OFFICERS

Chief Judge Yvette M. Alexander, Chairwoman
Justice Piper D. Griffin, Vice Chairwoman
Judge June B. Darensburg, Treasurer
Chief Judge Luke A. LaVergne, Retired, Secretary
Judge James E. Stewart, Sr., Retired, Parliamentarian

BOARD OF DIRECTORS

Attorney Keith A. Doley
Attorney Dwayne M. Murray
Attorney James M. Williams
Judge Kern A. Reese

NATIONAL BAR ASSOCIATION®
EST. 1925

EST. 1925
MCBA 100
MARION COUNTY BAR ASSOCIATION
FAIRNESS JUSTICE EQUALITY

The Judicial Council of the Marion County Bar Association (Indianapolis) congratulates the National Bar Association on its Centennial Anniversary, as we also celebrate our 100th year.

Judicial Council Members from the U.S. Court of Appeals for the Seventh Circuit, U.S. District Court Southern District of Indiana, Indiana Court of Appeals, Marion Circuit Court, Marion Superior Court, and Marion County Small Claims Courts:

Front Row: Magistrate Roxana Bell, Judge Tara Melton, Judge Charnette Garner, Senior Judge Barbara Crawford, Judge Clayton Graham, Judge Rudolph Pyle III (Indiana Court of Appeals), Chief Judge Tanya Walton Pratt (U.S. District Court Southern District of Indiana), Judge Doris Pryor (U.S. Court of Appeals for the Seventh Circuit), Retried Judge Carr Darden (Indiana Court of Appeals), Judge Geoffrey Gaither, Judge Linda Brown, Magistrate Regina Tidwell, Magistrate Eleanor Finnell, and Magistrate Duane Merchant.
Back Row: Magistrate Terrance Tharpe, Magistrate Leon Keith, Magistrate Stefanie Crawford, Judge Amber Collins, Retired Magistrate Susan Boatright, Judge Kimberly Bacon, Magistrate Yoni Moise, Judge Ryan Gardner, Judge Melanie Kendrick, Judge Marshelle Broadwell, Judge Garland Graves, and Judge John Chavis II.

Congratulations

to the National Bar Association

on 100 Years of Championing the Rule of Law for A

Honorable J. Michelle Childs
Circuit Judge
U.S. Court of Appeals for the D.C. Circuit
(2022 – present)

We honor a century of leadership, advocacy, and unwavering commitment to justice.

JUDICIAL POSTS

U.S. District Court for the District of South Carolina (2010 – 2022)

South Carolina Circuit Court (2006 – 2010)

Federal Judges Association
President (2023 – 2025)

NATIONAL BAR ASSOCIATION

Judicial Council (2012 – present)

Member (2010 – present)

Wiley Branton Symposium Award (2018)

Junius W. Williams Young Lawyers Division Award (2002)

NOTABLE ACCOMPLISHMENTS

American Inns of Court
Board of Trustees (2025 – present)

Rodel Institute
Judicial Fellow (2022 – present)

American Law Institute (2010 – present)

University of South Carolina Honorary Doctorate Degree in Public Service (2021)

The Judicial Section of the Gate City Bar Association
GATE CITY BAR ASSOCIATION
Judicial Section
Congratulates the
NATIONAL BAR ASSOCIATION
100
YEARS OF
Service
AT THEIR
Centennial Convention
Celebrating 20 Years of Transformative
Legal Programming in Atlanta, Georgia
OVER $300,000 IN LAW SCHOOL SCHOLARSHIPS WITH THE SUPPORT OF
Rodney Bullard, Esq. • Chick-Fil-A • C.K. Hoffler, Esq.
Legacy Programs
Judicial Fellowship Institute
Law Student Mentorship
Legal Field Trips
Community In The Courthouse Programs
Wellness for Judges
Community Law Clinics
Youth Reading Programs
Pathway To The Bench Bootcamp
GATECITYJUDICIAL.ORG

Chief Judge Yvette Alexander
Judiciary Excellence Award Honoree

Chief Judge Alexander began her legal career as counsel for the Louisiana State House of Representatives and Louisiana State Senate. And later began working at the East Baton Rouge Parish Public Defender's Office and the law firm of Moore and Moore in Baton Rouge, Louisiana. From 1988-1995, she served as Chief Legal Counsel for the Louisiana Department of State under Secretary of State Fox McKeithen and as an Ex-Officio Member of both the Louisiana State Bond Commission and the Louisiana School Employees Retirement System. Chief Judge Alexander also served as an Assistant Attorney General for the Louisiana Attorney General's Office. She practiced law for over 17 years before being elected as the first African-American woman to the Baton Rouge City Court in 1995, to Division D, where she sits currently. Judge Alexander is the first African-American woman to serve as Chief Judge of that court.

Chief Judge Yvette Mansfield Alexander became interested in community and public service at a young age, after working on her father's mayoral election campaign. She believes that public service is the rent we pay for the space we occupy. Early in her legal career she realized that she wanted to become a judge because she despised the inferior treatment of defendants by many judges. Judge Alexander vowed to work towards changing this inhumane practice. However, she believes that in order to change a system, one must be in a decision-making role within that system. Having been elected as a Judge for multiple terms, she has worked diligently towards her goal of administering justice with fairness and compassion. Her campaign slogan was "Your Voice for Justice". She believes that all Judges should strive to administer justice with fairness and compassion.

As a Judge she continues to stand as the community's voice for justice conveying her role in advocating for fairness, equality and the rights of individuals, especially those who may not have the means or ability to speak out for themselves. She is dedicated to ensuring that justice is served and that the legal system is used to protect and uphold the rights of ALL people.

Chief Judge Yvette Mansfield Alexander's mantra is: "Let go of what you think life should be and enjoy the life you have. That doesn't mean you shouldn't strive for a better life, it only means that you should not be consumed by what you don't have and miss out on enjoying the amazing life you have."

THE AFRICAN-AMERICAN JUDGES OF FLINT, (GENESEE COUNTY) MICHIGAN

On the north lawn of the Genesee County Courthouse—APRIL 2025

(From left to right): 67th District Court Judges Herman Marable, Jr.; G. David Guinn; & Tabitha Marsh and 7th Circuit Court Judges Mary Hood; & Khary Hanible

*Not pictured: 67th District Court Judge William Crawford II.

*The **Association of Black Judges of Michigan** is Honored to Recognize and Congratulate the **National Bar Association** on this Historic Milestone.*

2025-2026 Officers

Hon. Tenisha R. Yancey, President
36th District Court

Hon. Nicole N. Goodson, President-Elect
Third Circuit Court

Hon. Cynthia M. Ward, Secretary
54-A District Court

Hon. Jeremy Bowie, Treasurer
50th District Court

Board of Directors

Hon. E. Lynise Bryant
36th District Court

Hon. Bradley Cobb
Third Circuit Court

Hon. Rebekah Coleman
32A District Court

Hon. Kenyetta Stanford Jones
36th District Court

Hon. Lisa Martin
34th District Court

Hon. Cylenthia LaToye Miller
Third Circuit Court

Hon. Alisa L. Parker-LaGrone
8th District Court

Hon. Kristen Simmons
54-A District Court

Hon. Adrienne Scruggs
Third Circuit Court

NATIONAL BAR ASSOCIATION®

EST 1925

100 YEARS

Congratulations To The

NATIONAL BAR ASSOCIATION

ON 100 YEARS

From the Outstanding Women Jurists

of Birmingham, Alabama

Left to Right

Front Row: Judge Marshell Jackson Hatcher, Judge Tamara Harris Johnson, Judge Janine Hunt-Hilliard, Presiding Judge Elisabeth French, Judge Debra Weston-Pickens, Judge Shera Grant, Judge Shanta Owens.

Back Row: Judge Brendette Brown Green (54th NBAJC Chair), Judge Alisha Ruffin May, Judge Kechia Davis, Judge Monica Agee, Judge Tiara Hudson, Judge Maria Fortune, Judge Martha Cook, Judge Chuantae Brown, Judge Tanita Cain, Judge Adrienne Powell, Judge Jacquelyn Grant Jones, Judge Kandice Pickett

CONGRATULATIONS TO THE NATIONAL BAR ASSOCIATION ON ITS CENTENNIAL ANNIVERSARY

CALIFORNIA JUDICIAL OFFICERS (RETIRED AND SITTING): FEDERAL, STATE SUPREME COURT, APPELLATE COURT, TRIAL COURT, COMMISSIONERS, STATE BAR COURT AND ADMINISTRATIVE LAW JUDGES

ASSOCIATION OF AFRICAN AMERICAN CALIFORNIA JUDICIAL OFFICERS (AAACJO)
CALIFORNIA ASSOCIATION OF BLACK LAWYERS JUDICIAL COUNCIL (CABL JC)

NATIONAL BAR ASSOCIATION
EST. 1925

Congratulations

NATIONAL BAR ASSOCIATION ON 100 YEARS!

"THE HOUSTON 19"

LEFT TO RIGHT: JUDGE LUCIA BATES - JUDGE ERICA HUGHES - JUDGE SANDRA PEAKE JUDGE CASSANDRA HOLLEMAN (DECEASED) - JUDGE GERMAINE TANNER - JUDGE RONNISHA K. BOWMAN - JUDGE LINDA MARIE DUNSON - JUDGE ANGELA GRAVES-HARRINGTON - JUDGE MARIA JACKSON - JUDGE DEDRA DAVIS - JUDGE SHANNON B. BALDWIN - JUDGE LATOSHA LEWIS PAYNE - JUDE TONYA JONES - JUDGE RAMONA FRANKLIN - JUDGE SHARON M. BURNEY - JUDGE MICHELLE MOORE - JUDGE LORI CHAMBERS GRAY - JUDGE TORIA J. FINCH - JUDGE LASHAWN A. WILLIAMS

Congratulations

100 Years

NATIONAL BAR ASSOCIATION®

EST. 1925

LATIMER-HAWKINS FLORIDA JUDICIAL COUNCIL

Judge Bradley Harper (Co-Chair) | Judge Michael Robinson (Co-Chair)

Judge Faye Allen, Judge Michael Andrews, Judge Panayotta Augustin-Birch, Judge Jeramy Beasley, Judge Christopher Benjamin, Judge Samuel Bookhardt III, Judge Tanya Brinkley, Judge Sandra Champ, Judge Sheree Cunningham, Judge Miesha Darrough, Judge Michelle Delancy, Judge Stephen Everett, Judge Fabienne Fahnestock, Judge Keathan Frink, Judge Donna Goerner, Judge Hubert Grimes, Judge Charlene Honeywell, Judge Chiaka Ihekwaba, Judge Alicia Latimore, Magistrate Yves Laventure, Judge LeAnn Mackey-Barnes, Judge June McKinney, Judge Julie Nelson, Judge George Odom, Judge Rhonda Peoples-Waters, Judge Alicia Peyton Robinson, Judge Jackie Powell, Judge Peggy Quince, Judge Meshon Rawls, Judge Michael Robinson, Judge Mary Robinson, Judge Gabrielle Sanders-Morency, Judge Rodney Smith, Judge Julie Sneed, Judge Emerson Thompson, Judge Gloria Walker, Judge Shands Walker, Judge Reginald Whitehead, Judge Tanya Wilson

LATIMER - HAWKINS FLORIDA JUDICIAL COUNCIL
NATIONAL BAR ASSOCIATION

www.hawkinsjudicial.com

HOWARD UNIVERSITY SCHOOL OF LAW-CLASS OF 1982: *JUDGES & MAGISTRATES*

Judge Steven Brister, JMC
(Municipal Court NJ)

Magistrate Flora Jackson
(Family Court FL)

Judge Kathie Davidson
(Dean NY State Judicial Institute)

Administrative Judge Sheryl C. Sears
(Employee Appeals Court D.C. Federal)

Judge George B. Pearson
(General District/Juvenile VA)

Chief Judge Joi Jeter Taylor
(Circuit Court VA retired)

Chief/Administrative Judge Sheila R. Tillerson Adams
(Circuit Court MD retired)

Judge Keith C. Harvest, JMC
(Municipal Court NJ)

Judge Donald R. Havis
(Circuit Court IL)

Presiding Justice Wavny Toussaint
(Appellate Term NY)

Judge Evelyn M. Gunn
(Social Security Administration CA Federal)

Judge Sam D. Walker
(NY Supreme Court retired)

Judge David Eugene Cheek, Sr.
(Circuit Court VA retired)

Judge Mirlande Tadal
(Immigration Court NJ Federal retired)

It is our esteemed honor to support the historic milestone and celebration of the National Bar Association's Centennial Year (1925 – 2025)!

~CONGRATULATIONS~

The Illinois Judicial Council *salutes the* National Bar Association *on its Centennial.*

On behalf of our membership, we celebrate the progress of African American Jurists in Illinois.

NATIONAL BAR ASSOCIATION
EST 1925

Supreme Court of Illinois

Justice
P. Scott Neville

Justice
Lisa Holder White

Justice
Joy V. Cunningham

Congratulations to our Past President,

Illinois Appellate Court Justice

Freddrenna M. Lyle

on her election as the incoming

Chair of the Judicial Council of the National Bar Association

THE JUDICIAL COUNCIL
NATIONAL BAR ASSOCIATION

2024-2025 OFFICERS & EXECUTIVE BOARD

Hon. Allen P. Walker, *President*

Hon. Tiana Blakely, *President Elect*
Hon. Lionel Jean-Baptiste, *Asst. Secretary*
Hon. Tyria B. Walton, *Asst. Treasurer*
Hon. Vincent Cornelius, *Board At Large*
Hon. Sheree D. Henry, *Board At Large*
Hon. Steven G. Watkins, *Board At Large*

Hon. Toya T. Harvey, *Secretary*
Hon. Kevin T. Lee, *Treasurer*
Hon. Bonita Coleman, *Board At Large*
Hon. J. Imani Drew, *Board At Large*
Hon. Freddrenna M. Lyle, *Board At Large*
Hon. Kimberly D. Lewis, *Ex Officio*

Congratulations

TO THE NATIONAL BAR ASSOCIATION ON 100 YEARS OF EXCELLENCE

Judge

BERNICE B. DONALD *Retired*

First African American Female Judge for the Sixth Circuit Court of Appeals

First African American Female U.S. District Court Judge in the history of the state of Tennessee

First African American Female Bankruptcy Judge in the United States

First African American Female Judge in the history of the state of Tennessee

Partner - Burch, Porter & Johnson, PLLC

Secretary - American Bar Association

President - American Bar Foundation

President - National Association of Women Judges

Recipient - Inaugural Sandra Day O'Connor Award

Recipient - Gabelli Distinguished Jurist in Residence for Rule of Law National Judicial College

Founder - Spirit of Excellence Award (ABA)

Chair - Human Rights Center, ABA

Board Member - Federal Judicial Center

Education Chair - National Bar Association Judicial Council

ARBITRATOR MEDIATOR SPECIAL MASTER

JAMS Local Solutions. Global Reach.

Congratulations

to the National Bar Association on 100 Years of Commitment to the Rule of Law for all Citizens.

Honorable Carl E. Stewart

Circuit Judge
United States Fifth Circuit Court of Appeals
1994 - present
(Chief Judge 2012 - 2019)

First Judicial District Court
1985 - 1991
Louisiana Second Circuit Court of Appeal
1991 - 1994
Recipient of the National Bar Association Judicial Council William H. Hastie Award
July 30, 2008
President of the American Inns of Court Foundation
2014 - 2018
2018 National Bar Association Hall of Fame Inductee

Recipient of the 35th Annual Edward J. Devitt Distinguished Service to Justice Award in 2019.
Our nation's highest honor bestowed upon an Article III federal judge.

Congratulations

JUDGE LORRAINE W. PRINGLE (RET.)

SALUTES

National Bar Association On its 100th Anniversary

Standing for Justice and Equality

Congratulations

TO THE NATIONAL BAR ASSOCIATION (NBA)
The Oldest and Largest Network of Black Lawyers,
Judges and Legal Professionals in the United States on this

HISTORIC

100-YEAR ANNIVERSARY

Through Bold Leadership, Dedicated Service and Transformative Advocacy, The NBA Remains a Powerful Force for Justice, Equality and the Advancement of Civil Rights and Continues to Inspire Future Generations of Leaders to Shape the Legal Landscape and to Pursue Careers in Law.

HONORABLE J. MACHELLE SWEETING
ACTING JUSTICE, NEW YORK STATE
SUPREME COURT – CIVIL TERM

HARLEM, NEW YORK
Certified Chaplain, National Registered Parliamentarian (RP)
Chair, NBA Law and Religion Section 2024-2025
Executive Committee Member and Resolutions Committee Chair, NBA Judicial Council

May the Legacy of the NBA that is entrenched in the courageous pursuit of justice persist in perpetuity.
- Congratulations on the Centennial Anniversary of Service in the Law (1925-2025) -

JUDGE SANDRA ELENA ROPER

NEW YORK JCC, RPH, JD, LLM
NBA LIFETIME MEMBER

My legacy in the Law is each memorandum, amicus curiae brief, legislative bill proposal, legislative bill support, pleading and ultimately decision and order.

New York City Criminal Court Judge Sandra Roper in her chambers at 100 Centre Street in NYC....(Photo by David Handschuh/NYLJ)

Decision of the Day: Upholding $3M Personal Injury Verdict, Judge Says Insinuating Her Past Medical Experience With Jurist Role Is 'Unethical'

This ruling was selected and summarized by the New York Law Journal's decision editors. October 30, 2023 at 09:30 AM 2 minute read

Cases and Courts | By ALM Staff | October 30, 2023 at 09:30 AM

THE GENERATIONAL LEGACY

Parents: Ralph & Norma Roper
Grandparents: Lionel & Cecilia Scott

My Children: Donald (Shalonda) & Norma, Esq. (Brian, Esq).

My Grandchildren: Dyan, Donald, Jeremiah, Treasure, Lyric, Miracle, Isabella Yesenia, Sofia SandraElena & Sandra LaReina

KINGS | CIVIL PROCEDURE

Case Dismissed; Plaintiff Ignored Judicial Orders

Plaintiff brought an action against defendant. Defendant moved to dismiss. The motion was granted. The court held plaintiff's six-year continued failure to obey judicial orders, even where considered a calculated litigation tactic, was an affront to the judiciary, abuse of the administration of justice, abuse of judicial efficiency and abuse of judicial economy. Plaintiff continued to violate the courts' orders as mere suggestions and not consequential enforceable judicial orders. Plaintiff disobeyed judicial orders resulting in the striking of plaintiff's Notice of Trial and another judicial order explicitly warned plaintiff that disobedience may escalate the punitive penalty to dismissal of the complaint.

Judge Sandra Elena Roper
Civil Court

Chiropractic Testing Service of New York, P.C. v. State Farm Mutual Auto Ins. Co., 725164/17 (March 10)

To Whom Much is Given, Much is Required
(Luke 12:48)

Judicial Friends Association
Congratulates
NATIONAL BAR ASSOCIATION®
EST. 1925
on its centennial anniversary
JudicialFriends.org
345 Fifth Avenue
New York, NY 10016
Hon. Cheryl J. Gonzales, President
Hon. Paul Wooten, 1st Vice President
Hon. Alvin Yearwood, 2nd Vice President
Hon. Christel Garland, Treasurer
Hon. Lisa Headley, Secretary

Congratulations & WELL DONE

JUSTICE SHELVIN LOUISE MARIE HALL

ILLINOIS APPELLATE COURT JUSTICE (RET.)
28TH NBA JUDICIAL COUNCIL CHAIR

For your exemplary service as **Chair of the 2025 National Bar Association Judicial Council's Thurgood Marshall Luncheon** held during the **National Bar Association's Centennial Celebration** on July 30, 2025, in Chicago, Illinois.

From **JUSTICE L. PRISCILLA HALL (RET.)**
Second Department
Appellate Division of the
State of New York
NBA Judicial Council Member

"The first elected BLACK SISTER trial judges and the first BLACK SISTER appellate court justices in the United States."

Congratulations to the
NATIONAL BAR ASSOCIATION

on celebrating 100 years in the fight for justice!

"Where you see wrong or inequality or injustice, speak out, because this is your country. This is your democracy. Make it. Protect it. Pass it on."
—Justice Thurgood Marshall

Hon. Tricia Ferrell
Supervising Judge Nassau County District Judge

Hon. Darlene Harris
Nassau County
Family Court

Hon. Victoria Gumbs-Moore
Suffolk Family Court

Hon. Valerie M. Cartright
NYS Supreme Court

Hon. Eckor Joseph
Administrative Law Judge

Hon. Geoffrey N. Prime
Nassau County District Court

Hon. Alonzo G. Jacobs
Suffolk County
District Court

FROM THE CHAMBERS OF
THE HONORABLE JUDGE AMANDA N. HEATH
SUPERIOR COURT JUDGE, AUGUSTA JUDICIAL CIRCUIT
AUGUSTA, GEORGIA

Congratulations to the
National Bar Association for
100 Years of Advocacy and Service to the Community

NBA Law Professors' Division

The Law Professors' Division has long contributed to the expertise, service, and leadership of the National Bar Association. This summary is only a glimpse of the rich history and robust contributions of this Division to the National Bar Association and the legal profession at large. The Law Professors Division's active engagement goes well beyond the names able to be listed here but instead represents an ethos of impact for advancement of the legal profession from its origins at the 200 American law schools.

Several of our members serve in leadership roles throughout higher education, including as University Presidents (Danielle Holley-Mount Holyoke), Provosts (Chris Bracey – GWU), and Law Deans & Associate Deans, Roger Fairfax (Howard), Blake Morant (GWU), Leonard Baynes (U Houston), Cassandra Hill (Northern Illinois), Angela Onwuachi-Willig (Boston U), Nikki Boothe (U Illinois), Felicia Epps (U North Texas), Everett Bellamy (Georgetown), Michael Thompson (Yale), as well as in Distinguished and Chaired Professors roles, Professors Paul Butler (Georgetown), Mario Barnes (UC Irvine), Spencer Overton (GWU), Wendy Greene (Drexel), Kristin Johnson (Emory), Deleso Alford (U New Mexico), Mitch Crusto (Loyola, New Orleans), Gregory Parks (Wake Forest), Carlton Waterhouse (Howard), David Green (North Carolina Central), George Edwards (IU, McKinney), and Loren Mulraine (Belmont).

Significantly, in additional to the academic expertise that our members provide, the Law Professors' Division has a strong legacy of service in elected roles and presidential appointments on the Board of Governors including President, Vice President, Treasurer, and Board Member at Large: Past President Dean Alfreda Robinson (GWU), Past President Professor Beverley McCleary Smith (Touro), former Treasurer Professor Rachel Anderson (U Nevada, Las Vegas), and former Board Member at Large Dean Tamara Lawson (U Washington).

The Law Professors' Division has been extremely active in Continuing Legal Education presentations both at the annual meetings, Wiley Branton conferences, judicial council symposia, and NBA Presidents' international trips, including Morocco, Brazil, Cuba, Dubai, India, Bermuda, Amsterdam/The Hauge, and Paris.

LGBTQ Division

Established in 2018 by Jonathan Patterson, the Lesbian, Gay, Bisexual, Transgender, Queer (LBGTQ+) Division of the National Bar Association (NBA) was created to explore the intersectionality between Black and LGBTQ+ communities, including the ways in which laws affect LGBTQ+ people of color and the evolution of legal precedent developed around minorities. This Division represents LGBTQ+ lawyers within the NBA, and works to cultivate diverse membership with allies.

Due to historical challenges stemming from the intersectionality of race and sexual orientation in the Black community, Black LGBTQ+ legal professionals are not organized nationally, nor unified in their standpoints on various issues inside and outside the legal community. The LGBTQ+ Division works to create a space for members and allies, educate communities on pivotal issues, and develop NBA's advocacy on LGBTQ+ issues.

In 2022, Antonio C. Lee from Chicago, Illinois was the first LGBTQ+ Division member to serve as Board Member-at-Large on the NBA Board of Governors. He subsequently served as Chair of the LGBTQ+ Division in 2023. During NBA's 2023-2024 year under Chair Lee's leadership, the Division launched its inaugural Luminary Awards Ceremony, which was created to celebrate the unparalleled brave and courageous lawyers, judges, community stakeholders, and allies across the nation, whose work significantly contributed to improving the lives of LGBTQ+ people of color. The Division convened its first Luminary Awards Ceremony during NBA's 99th Annual Convention in Las Vegas, which garnered over 70 attendees to honor awardees of the Division's Judge Deborah A. Batts Vanguard Award, Exemplary Service Luminary Award, Leadership Luminary Award, and Ally Luminary Award. That same bar year, the Division awarded $7,500 in scholarships to three LGBTQ+ law students, who detailed their interests in advancing protections for the LGBTQ+ community. Notably, Chair Lee represented the Division as a panelist at Yale Law School for their inaugural Pauli Murray Symposium entitled "Pauli's Legacy and Intersectional Journeys: Black LGBTQIA+ Voices in the Legal Field." The symposium served as a platform to discuss pressing issues faced by LGBTQ+ community within the framework of intersectionality. During the 2023-2024 bar year, NBA Past President Dominique D. Calhoun awarded the LGBTQ+ Division with NBA's Outstanding Division of the Year Award.

The LGBTQ+ Division and its Board of Directors frequently collaborate with various community stakeholders, including the National LGBTQ+ Bar Association and the American Bar Association's (ABA) Commission on Sexual Orientation and Gender Identity (SOGI).

For example, the Division created a CLE in 2024 entitled State of the Law: Addressing Systemic Racial Barriers Impacting Black LGBTQ Communities, and Its Perpetuation Through Emerging Policies and Legal Doctrines, which was presented during the NBA 99th Convention then subsequently at the National LGBTQ+ Bar Association's Lavender Law Conference. During the 2024-2025, Chair Lee served as Chair of the LGBTQ Division and Commissioner to the ABA's SOGI Commission. The Division was also invited to present the National Minority AIDS Council's Coalition for Justice and Equality Across Movements conference in Puerto Rico.

Lastly, the LGBTQ+ Division works tirelessly to increase the pipeline of LGBTQ+ law students to lawyers by partnering with the National Black Law Student Association on various webinars and conferences. The Division also posts educational videos on social media to raise awareness about issues in our community.

NATIONAL BAR ASSOCIATION

SMALL FIRMS & SOLO PRACTITIONERS

DIVISION

Patricia Rosier, Esq.
National Bar Association
Small Firms Solo
Practitioners' Division
Founder

Michael Rosier, Esq.
National Bar Association
Small Firms Solo
Practitioners' Division
Founder

John Moore, Esq.
National Bar Association
Small Firms Solo
Practitioners' Division
Past Chair

Tonya Primus, Esq.
National Bar Association
Small Firms Solo
Practitioners' Division
Past Chair

Marwan Porter, Esq.
National Bar Association
Small Firms Solo
Practitioners' Division
Current Chair

Summary:

As the National Bar Association celebrates 100 years of advancing justice and empowering Black legal professionals, the Small Firms and Solo Practitioners Division (SFSPD) proudly reflects on its own impactful legacy. Founded in **1998** by visionary attorneys **Michael Rosier** and **Patricia Rosier**, SFSPD was created to meet the distinct needs of solo and small firm attorneys—legal entrepreneurs who serve as trusted advocates, community leaders, and business owners. Recognizing that this growing sector of the NBA required targeted support and representation, the Rosiers and subsequent leaders built a division grounded in inclusion, empowerment, and excellence.

Highlights:

Leadership within SFSPD has always been a core value, beginning with its founders, **Michael and Patricia Rosier**, who paved the way for generations of NBA leadership. Their early guidance set a tone of purpose and professionalism that continues today. The Division has since been led by dedicated chairs including **Tonya Primus, John Moore,** and most recently, **Marwan Porter**. Under Mr. Porter's stewardship, SFSPD has continued to build on its strong foundation—offering CLEs, mentorship opportunities, and programs like the NBA International Leadership Conference that bring members together for professional growth and shared vision. As the NBA marks its centennial, SFSPD stands as a testament to the enduring leadership, service, and strength that small firm and solo attorneys bring to our communities and to the profession at large.

National Bar Association Women Lawyers Division: A Celebration Of Our History

The Women Lawyers Division (WLD) is the oldest and largest division within the National Bar Association (NBA). Our Division was founded in 1972 as a mechanism for women lawyers to address challenges impacting Black women in law by the following phenomenal women: Joan A. Burt; Hon. Theresa Doss; Hon. Golden Johnson; Hon. Lucile A. Watts; Hon. Joyce L. Alexander; Ruth Banks; Hon. Alice Bonner; Ruth Harvey Charity; Florence Jackson; Arthenia Joyner; Allie Weeden Latimer; Hon. Gabrielle McDonald; Ethel Ollivierre; Hon. Eileen Peterson; Savannah Potter; Hon. Clara Rich; Alice Rucker; and Dorothy Sampson founded the WLD.

Since 1972, WLD's mission and vision has expanded, in part, because of the elevation of programming which was inspired by the leadership of the Division during the last 53 years: Hon. Lucile A. Watts (1972-1974); Hon. Golden Johnson (1974-1975); Hon. Theresa Doss (1975); Joan A. Burt (1975-1977); Edith Corlette (1979-1980); Hon. Renee Jones Weeks (1977-1979); Jacqueline Rucker (1982-1983); Dolores Pegram Wilson (1980-1982); Carolyn Y. Howard (1983-1985); Pinkie Carolyn Wilkerson (1985-1987); Emma H. Pendergrass (1987-1989); Brenda A. Girton (1989-1991); Jacqueline A. Walker (1991-1993); Gloria A. Brimberry (1993-1995); Debra D. Matlock (1995-1997); Camille Stearns Miller (1997-1999); Hon. Sharon E. Strickland (2001-2003); Iris McCollum Green (1999-2001); Margo Bouchet (2003-2005); E. Jean Johnson (2005-2007); Hon. Cylenthia LaToye Miller (2007-2009); Gloria Johnson (2009-2010); DeMonica Gladney (2010-2012); Antoinette Barksdale (2012-2014); Monica Dula (2014-2016); Rosalyn Henderson Myers (2016-2018); Valencia Rainey (2018-2020); Sharon Bridges (2020-2022); Desiree Boykin (2022-2024); Doreen Rachal (2024 – present).

Through the WLD, women have made significant contributions to the NBA providing a strong, reflective voice on issues that disproportionately affect women, such as wage disparities and barriers to career advancement. The WLD has also lead four main initiatives: developing a pipeline of future women lawyer leaders, mentoring young ladies (as young as 5), creating pathways for advocacy at the highest level, the United States Supreme Court, and providing professional and personal development programming. We give back and elevate those within the NBA, the broader community and partner with other organizations nationally to drive change.

Annual Breakfast
Each year, we host our annual breakfast, renamed during this centennial year to the Gertrude E. Rush Annual Breakfast, to renew our commitment to the Division and honor and celebrate legal trailblazers, organizations, and individuals who make meaningful and impactful contributions to communities of color, aligned with our mission. This is our sole fundraiser each year. The proceeds support our initiatives, including our WE Empower program, our scholarships, and our Respect Yourself program. These programs foster meaningful connections, propel women of all ages to pursue legal careers, and offer opportunities for leadership development, financial literacy, and civic engagement—tools essential for success in today's world.

Respect Yourself Program
Our Respect Yourself program incorporates teamwork, leadership building skills, and oratorical skills. Together, we are building our future attorneys, judges, law school professors, prosecutors, non-profit leaders, and entrepreneurs. During the Centennial Convention, we will host over 100 young ladies as part of our Respect Yourself program, geared to embrace, educate, and empower our future leaders.

WE Empower Program
Celebrating its 5th year anniversary, the WE Empower program was created to provide mentoring support and leadership development to current Black women law school students. The program pairs law school students with seasoned lawyers, who serve as a resource for the students during the program.

Annual Supreme Court Swearing-In
Each year, the Division hosts an annual swearing-in ceremony at the United States Supreme Court, to provide all NBA members an opportunity to advocate at the highest level.

Impactful and Intentional Programming (2024-2025 Bar Year)

This bar year, our Division's theme is: Empower, Elevate, and Escalate.

- Empower: We must EMPOWER each other to achieve our individual and collective personal and professional goals.
- Elevate: As we climb and achieve success, we must ELEVATE our members and ensure the success of all.
- Escalate: We will ESCALATE, soar, and transcend beyond glass ceilings– and OUR time is NOW.

Aligned with this theme, we have developed, executed, and participated in the following programming and look forward to our Centennial Conference programming to include CLEs, our annual breakfast, our Respect Yourself program, and our Annual Retreat.

Wiley Branton Symposium Discussion
WLD hosted a powerful discussion focused on: The Power of Her Voice: The Intersection of Voting Rights and Black Women's Empowerment, where dynamic panelists, Tanya Clay House, Rebekah Caruthers, and Antoinette Barksdale, explored the pivotal roles of Black women, like Fannie Lou Hamer and Shirley Chisholm, in the voting rights movement. The conversation addressed the ongoing relevance of their legacy, the power of Black women in voting, and the intersections between voting rights and economic empowerment.

WLD Voting Rights Advocacy Campaign
We disseminated throughout the United States our call to action for all members to assist with the protection of voting rights before and during the November 2024 election. We showed up, and we showed out throughout the US! We had boots on the ground throughout the country – supporting each other and the underserved communities that we serve. We also hosted a powerful a post-Election sister-to-sister conversation, that provided a safe space to express our emotions and thoughts as we move forward together.

Membership Drive Throughout The United States
Aligned with the Division's mission to increase membership in WLD by at least 100 this bar year, the Membership Committee and the Personal and Professional Development Committee have hosted networking events with local affiliate chapters throughout the United States, with the sole purpose of helping to increase NBA membership, WLD membership, and encourage sisterhood throughout the country. Entitled: Centennial Celebration of Excellence, our focused cities for this year include: Washington, DC, Boston, Atlanta, Miami, Dallas, New York, New Orleans, Michigan, Chicago, and Los Angeles. We are also a co-host of the NBA's listening national tour.

Honoring Gertrude E. Rush

During this year's Gertrude Rush Mid-Year Conference, WLD hosted two events: Zumba and a CLE. Focused on mental health and physical wellness, WLD curated a Zumba-focused session, providing all NBA members an opportunity to connect with WLD members, to receive a fun full-body workout through dance accompanied by rhythmic music and movements, and to release endorphins, promoting relaxation while decreasing stress. We showed up – and we showed out for our CLE focused on: Impact of the 92%: Black Women Embracing Our Resilience and Redefining Our Purpose, focused on our resilience, our collective goals, and critical areas of continued advocacy. We filled the room to hear the impactful words of our sisters: Dean Adrien Wing, Marcia Sells, and Barbara Arnwine. We rounded out this momentous occasion of recognizing the only Black woman founder of the National Bar Association by paying tribute to Gertrude Rush at her grave site.

WLD 100 for 100 Centennial Scholarship

In celebration of 100 years of Black women attorneys' engagement through the National Bar Association, the Division created the WLD 100 for 100 Centennial Scholarship Giving Society to support and empower current women law school students through scholarship awards. This essay contest encourages current law school to provide a statement on the impact of 100 years of Black women attorneys.

NATIONAL BAR ASSOCIATION WOMEN LAWYERS DIVISION

NATIONAL BAR ASSOCIATION 100 YEARS

EMPOWER • ELEVATE • ESCALATE

1972-2025

EMPOWER, ELEVATE, AND ESCALATE

INTO THE NEXT 100 YEARS!

History of the National Bar Association Young Lawyers Division

"The Lifeblood of the National Bar Association"

The Young Lawyers Division (YLD) of the National Bar Association has long been recognized as the heartbeat of the organization—providing energy, leadership, and a vision for the future. Its powerful story begins during the civil rights era, a time when young Black attorneys were not only entering the profession in larger numbers but were also demanding a seat at the table and a voice in shaping justice in America.

In Chapter 12 of Unfinished Agenda, attorney and civil rights leader Junius Williams recounts the formative years of the YLD. Motivated by the social and political challenges of the 1960s and '70s, Williams and a coalition of young, bold attorneys sought to create a division within the NBA that reflected the needs and values of their generation.
Their efforts led to the creation of the Young Lawyers Division—a group that has since become known as "the lifeblood of the National Bar" for its unwavering commitment to justice, leadership, and community empowerment.

Timeline of Key Events in YLD History

Early 1970s
Junius Williams and others advocate for a youth-focused division within the NBA.

1971
Official formation of the Young Lawyers Division within the NBA.

1974
First official YLD programming appears at NBA Annual Convention.

1980s
YLD expands national footprint through legal clinics and civil rights initiatives.

1990s
Launch of YLD Leadership Training Program for early-career attorneys.

2000s
YLD alumni begin to take key leadership roles within the NBA and judiciary.

2010s
Focus intensifies on mentorship, diversity in law, and criminal justice reform.

2020s
YLD leads digital advocacy and social justice campaigns post-George Floyd.

Present Day
YLD continues to produce trailblazing leaders, staying at the forefront of change.

Sidebar: Notable YLD Alumni

Meet just a few of the distinguished legal professionals who began their leadership journey through the NBA Young Lawyers Division:

- Hon. Ketanji Brown Jackson – Associate Justice, U.S. Supreme Court (YLD alum who has inspired a generation)
- Junius Williams – Civil Rights Attorney, Author of Unfinished Agenda, and founding voice of the YLD
- Angela Rye – Political Strategist, Attorney, and Media Commentator
- Hon. Carlton Reeves – U.S. District Court Judge, Southern District of Mississippi
- Kristen Clarke – Assistant Attorney General, U.S. Department of Justice, Civil Rights Division
- Benjamin Crump – Civil Rights Attorney, known for national advocacy on racial justice cases

Young Lawyers Division Board for the Centennial Convention: Chair Alex Mitchell; Vice Chair Caleb Green; Chair-Elect Bria Kemp; Treasurer Ashley Weathers; Secretary/Historian Arielle Comer; Parliamentarian Patric Koseni; Immediate Past Chair Amy Depuy

AFFILIATE CHAPTERS

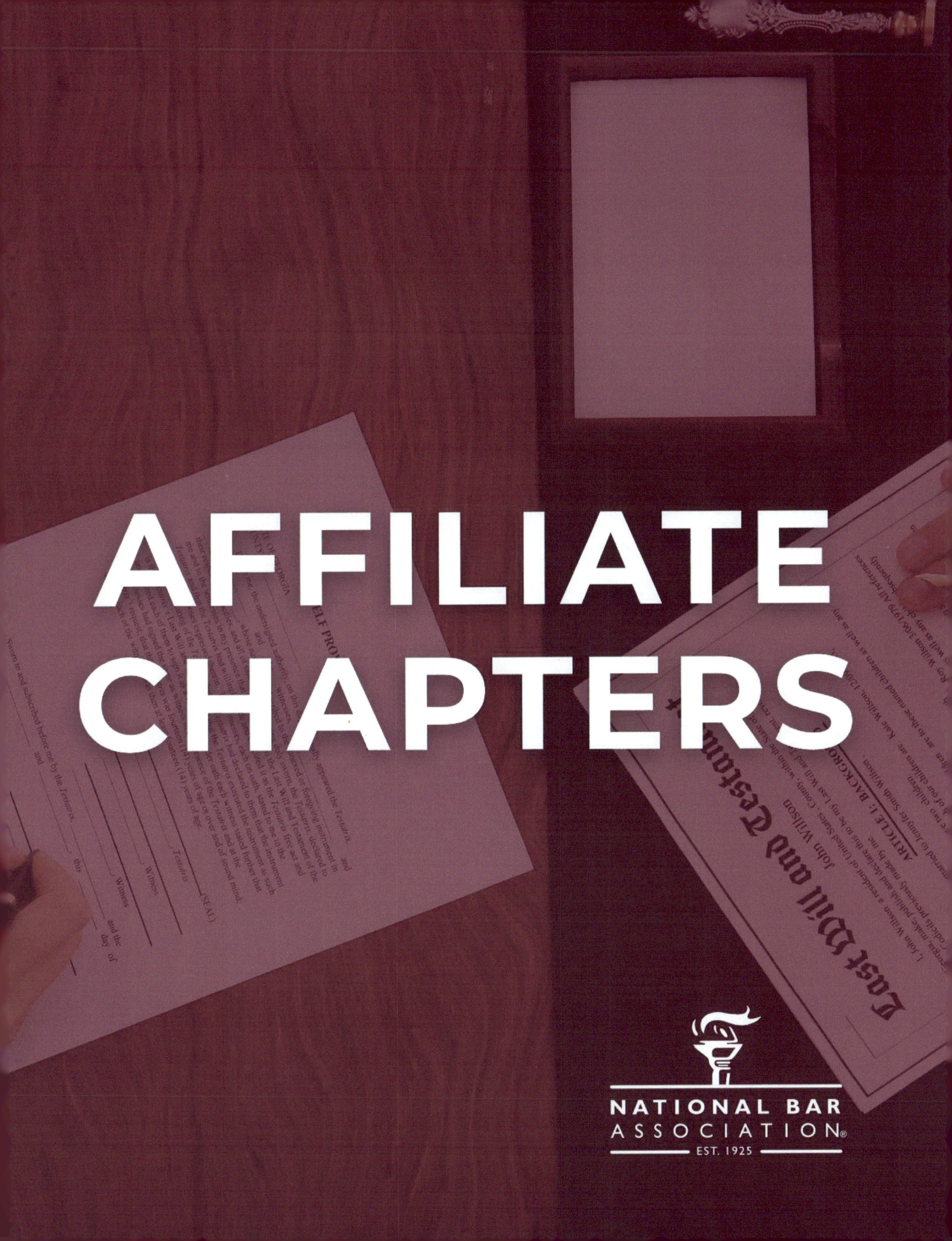

NATIONAL BAR ASSOCIATION
EST. 1925

National Bar Association Affiliate Chapters

African-American Lawyers Section (SBOT)

Ben F. Jones Chapter, NBA

Black Women Lawyers

Association of Michigan

Black Women Lawyers Association of Los Angeles

Black Women Lawyers Association of Northern California

California Association of Black Lawyers

Charles Houston Bar Association

Charles W. Anderson, Jr. Bar Association

Cook County Bar Association

D. Augustus Straker Bar Association

Delaware Barristers Association

Garden State Bar Association

Gate City Bar Association

Georgia Association of Black Women Attorneys (GABWA)

Greater Washington Area Chapter

Haitian American Lawyers Association of Illinois (HALA)

Houston Lawyers Association

Franklyn Bourne Bar Association

Jackson County Bar Association

JL Turner Legal Association

Justice Bar Association of Indiana Inc.

Clifford Davis Legal Association

Las Vegas Chapter, NBA

Loren Miller Bar Association

Louis A. Martinet – Baton Rouge

Louis A. Martinet – Lafayette

Marion County Bar Association

Metropolitan Black Bar Association

Mound City Bar Association

Napier Looby Bar Association

NBA South Africa Bar Association

New Mexico Black Lawyers Association

Norman S. Minor Bar Association

Ohio Black Judges

Oklahoma City Association of Black Lawyers (OKC-ABL)

Old Dominion Bar Association

The Botswana Bar Association

Virgil Hawkins National Bar Association

Washington Bar Association

Wolverine Bar Association

*Note: This summary reflects available information; not all NBA affiliates submitted updates or historical information.

NATIONAL BAR ASSOCIATION AFFILIATES

African American Lawyers Section of the State Bar of Texas	Akron Bar Association	Alabama Lawyers Association
Alliance of Black Women Attorneys of Maryland, Inc.	Amistad Long Island Black Bar Association	Arizona Black Bar Association
Austin Black Lawyers Association	Ballard Taylor Bar Association	Barristers Association of Philadelphia
Baton Rouge Chapter of Louis A. Martinet Legal Society	Ben F. Jones Chapter of the National Bar Association	Bernard S. Jefferson Law Society
Black Lawyers Association of Cincinnati	Black Lawyers of Shreveport	Black Women Lawyers Association of Los Angeles, Inc.
Black Women Lawyers Association of Michigan	Black Women Lawyers of New Jersey	Black Women Lawyers of Northern California
Botswana Bar Association	California Association of Black Lawyers	Charles Anderson Bar Association
Charles Houston Bar Association	Clifford Scott Green Bar Association	Cook County Bar Association
D. Augustus Straker Bar Association	Delaware Barrister Association	Donald James Sampson Bar Association
Earl B. Gilliam Bar Association	Floyd Skinner Bar Association	Garden State Bar Association
Gate City Bar Association	George Crawford Bar Association	Georgia Alliance of Black Women Attorneys
Greater New Orleans Louis A. Martinet Legal Society, Inc.	Greater Washington Area Chapter, Women Lawyers Division (GWAC)	Haitian American Lawyers Association of Illinois
Homer S. Brown Legal Association	Houston Lawyers Association	Hugh Goodwin Bar Association
Inland Empire Bar Association	Iowa National Bar Association	J. Franklyn Bourne Bar Association
J.L. Turner Bar Association	Jack Tanner Bar Association	Jackson County Bar Association
James Kimbrough Bar Association	John Langston Bar Association	John Rowe Chapter of the NBA
Justice Bar Association of Indiana	L. Clifford Davis Legal Association	Los Vegas Chapter of the NBA
Loren Miller Bar Association	Louis A. Martinet Legal Society of Lafayette	Louisville Black Lawyers Association
Macon B. Allen Bar Association	Magic City Bar Association	Magnolia Bar Association
Marion County Bar Association	Metropolitan Black Bar Association	Minnesota Association of Black Lawyers
Mound City Bar Association	Napier-Looby Bar Association	New Mexico Black Lawyers Association
Norman S. Minor Bar Association	Ohio Black Judges Association	Oklahoma City Bar Association
Old Dominion Bar Association	Oregon Chapter of the NBA	Rochester Black Bar Association
S.L. Hutchins Bar Association	Sam Cary Bar Association	San Antonio Black Lawyers Association
Springfield Association of Black Attorneys	South Africa Bar Association	South Carolina Black Lawyers Association
South Hampton Roads Bar Association	Tennessee Alliance of Black Lawyers	Thurgood Marshall Bar Association
Virgil Hawkins Florida Chapter of the NBA	W. Harold Flowers Bar Association	Washington Bar Association, Inc.
Westchester Black Bar Association	Wiley N. Manuel Bar Association	Wisconsin Association of African American Lawyers
Wolverine Bar Association		

As of March 2025

Black Women Lawyers Association of Northern California (BWLNC)

Honoring Legacy. Building Power.

Overview and Mission

Founded in 1979, the Black Women Lawyers Association of Northern California (BWLNC) is a 501(c)(6) membership organization dedicated to the advancement of Black women in the legal profession. BWLNC exists to support, empower, and elevate Black women attorneys and law students through mentorship, community building, professional development, and public service.

We proudly carry the legacy of our namesake, Patricia McKinley—a pioneering Black woman attorney in Northern California whose leadership and commitment to equity inspired the formation of an organization rooted in sisterhood and excellence. Her legacy continues to guide our work today.

Leadership and Legacy

For over four decades, BWLNC has been a catalyst for professional advancement and social justice. Our members serve as judges, law firm partners, general counsel, public servants, and law professors. We maintain an active presence in regional and national bar associations, policy discussions, and pipeline development initiatives.

Under the leadership of Past President Tiega-Noel Varlack, BWLNC launched civic engagement programming (Sistas Leading Change), deepened partnerships with other bar organizations, and expanded support for law students through new internship, mentorship, and scholarship initiatives.

Investing in the Future

BWLNC is committed to ensuring the success of the next generation of legal professionals. In 2024, we proudly launched the BWLNC Sports Law Scholarship, sending two Black women law students to the 44th annual Black Entertainment and Sports Lawyers Association (BESLA) Conference in Mexico. This scholarship reflects our mission to create access to high-impact spaces in underrepresented practice areas.

Our student ambassador program, bar exam support, and internship placements continue to serve students across Northern California's law schools, including Berkeley Law, Santa Clara, UC Law SF, Golden Gate, and more.

Signature Events and Community Impact

- The McKinley Awards Brunch, honoring exemplary legal professionals in the spirit of Patricia McKinley;
- BWLNC at 45, a formal celebration of our legacy and future;
- Cocktails and Candidates, promoting civic engagement and public service;
- Counsel & Cocktails, an intergenerational space for mentorship and connection.

Looking Ahead

BWLNC is entering a bold new chapter focused on expansion, visibility, and advocacy. We are committed to increasing scholarship funding, doubling the presence of Black women in legal leadership, and building strategic partnerships across the profession.

To learn more or support our mission, visit bwlnc.com.

Celebrating
OUR AFFILIATES

Greater New Orleans Louis A. Martinet Legal Society.

The Louis A. Martinet Legal Society was created in 1957 by 17 individuals for the purpose of challenging racial injustice through the legal system. The Society is named in honor of an African-American pioneer in the legal profession, Louis André Martinet, who was the first African-American graduate of Straight University Law School (now Dillard University) in 1876. He helped organize legal resistance to discriminatory laws in Louisiana and was a key strategist in the events that led to the landmark Supreme Court decision, Plessy v. Ferguson.

The Greater New Orleans chapter of the Louis A. Martinet Legal Society includes members throughout the practice and the bench. Our objectives are to encourage interchange of ideas, promote legal scholarship, advance the science of jurisprudence, promote the administration of justice, uphold the order and ethics of the courts and the profession of law, and promote the welfare of the legal profession in Louisiana.

Current officers include:

Charles Hamilton Houston – WBA Co-Founder and WBA 3rd President

George E. C. Hayes–WBA Co- Founder and WBA 1st President (w/T. Marshall and J. Nabrit)

Ollie May Cooper
formed First Women Law Partnership in U.S.

Isadore Letcher
formed First Women Law Partnership in U.S.

J. Clay Smith– WBA 28th President and Author, Emancipation: The Making of the Black Lawyer (1993)

William Lepre Houston – WBA 7th President and NBA 9th President

Victor Jones,
President

Michael Harrison,
President-Elect

Bianca Moore,
Immediate Past President

Zachary Simmons,
Treasurer

Shanice Smith-Banks,
Vice President of External Communications

Makala Graves,
Vice President of Internal Communications

Mollie Ponds;
Vice President of Membership

NATIONAL BAR ASSOCIATION®
EST. 1925

THE GATE CITY BAR ASSOCIATION
OF ATLANTA, GEORGIA

Congratulates the

NATIONAL BAR ASSOCIATION

on

100 YEARS OF

excellence, advocacy, and legacy

We celebrate your unwavering commitment to justice and the advancement of Black legal professionals

2025 EXECUTIVE BOARD

President: Christopher Bruce

President-Elect: Pierce Hand Seitz
Vice President: Cameron Hawkins
Immediate Past President: N. John Bey
Treasurer: Taylor A. Middleton
Secretary: Daedra Fenwick
Assistant Secretary: Brent Radcliff
Historian: Miguel Dominquez
Member At Large: Racquel McGee
Member At Large: William Boddie
Member At Large: Karlos Emmanuel
Member At Large: Shalamar Parham
Member At Large: Michelle Arrington

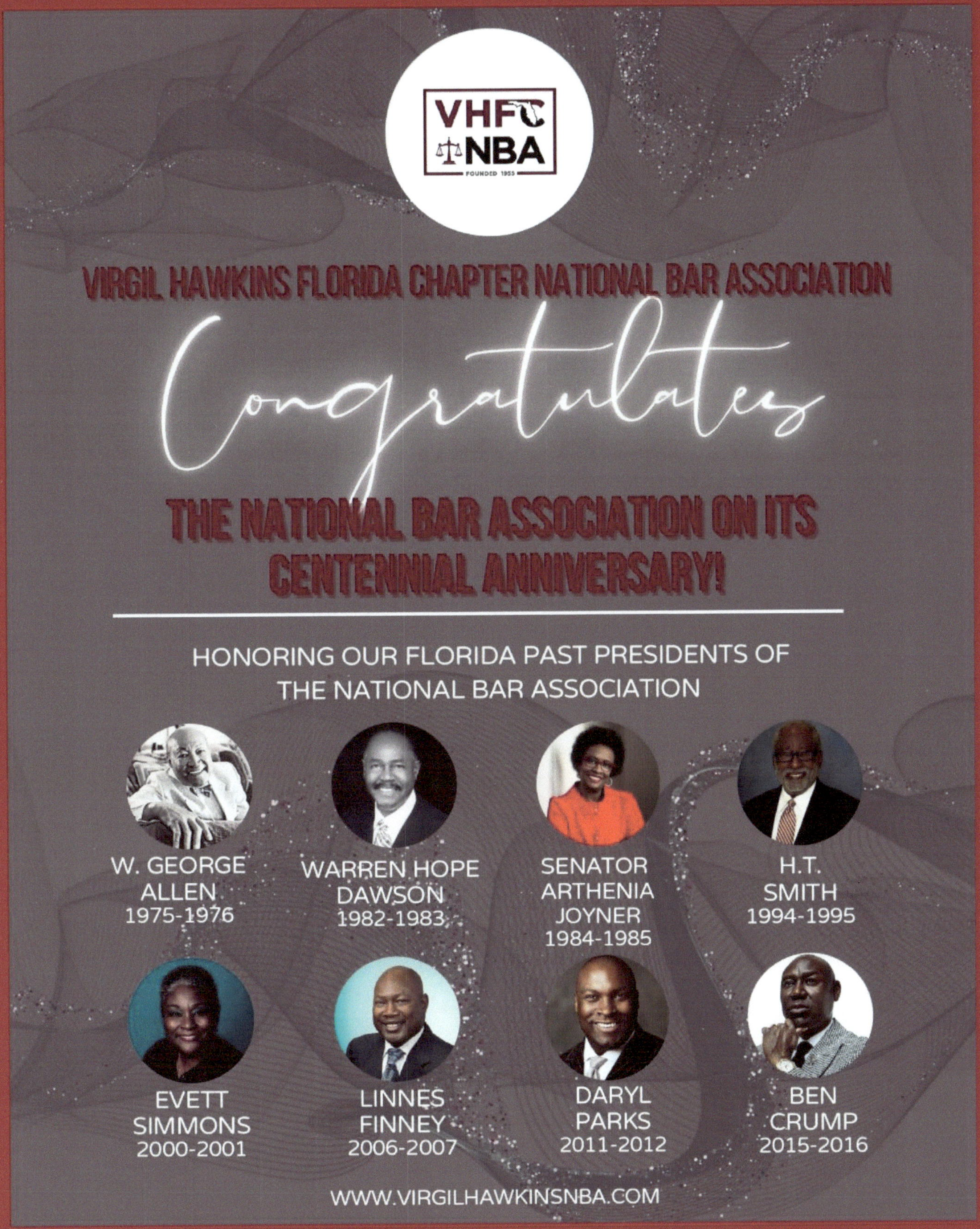
VHFC NBA
FOUNDED 1955
VIRGIL HAWKINS FLORIDA CHAPTER NATIONAL BAR ASSOCIATION
Congratulates
THE NATIONAL BAR ASSOCIATION ON ITS CENTENNIAL ANNIVERSARY!
HONORING OUR FLORIDA PAST PRESIDENTS OF THE NATIONAL BAR ASSOCIATION
W. GEORGE ALLEN 1975-1976
WARREN HOPE DAWSON 1982-1983
SENATOR ARTHENIA JOYNER 1984-1985
H.T. SMITH 1994-1995
EVETT SIMMONS 2000-2001
LINNES FINNEY 2006-2007
DARYL PARKS 2011-2012
BEN CRUMP 2015-2016
WWW.VIRGILHAWKINSNBA.COM

HLA'S HISTORY FOR NBA'S CENTENNIAL BOOKLET

The Houston Lawyers Association ("HLA"), an affiliate chapter of the National Bar Association, was founded in 1955 to address the needs of Black lawyers and the legal needs of the Black community in general. During this time, African American lawyers were excluded from joining the Houston Bar Association. In response, our founders—Robert W. Hainsworth, Aloysius M. Wickliff, Sr., Matthew W. Plummer, Sr., Francis Williams, Weldon H. Berry, and Roberson L. King—came together to form an organization that would serve as a platform for addressing racial injustice and advancing equality in the legal profession and beyond. Other attorneys who helped shape the legacy of HLA in our early years include W.M.C. Dickson; F.S.A. Whittaker; Hon. Henry E. Doyle, who was the first Black law student to enroll at a state law school in Texas and Texas's first Black law school graduate; and Congresswoman Barbara C. Jordan, who was HLA's first female president and the first African American elected to the Texas Senate since Reconstruction, the first southern African-American woman elected to the U.S. House of Representatives, and one of the first two African Americans elected to the U.S. House from the former Confederacy since 1901.

Our founders and early members were instrumental in dismantling systemic racial barriers during the mid-20th century. Their collective efforts directly shaped the legal profession and the broader Houston community through landmark challenges such as:

- Hainsworth v. Harris County Commissioners Court (1951): Advocating for the desegregation of the Harris County Law Library, which now bears Robert W. Hainsworth's name;
- Plummer v. Casey (1955): Securing equal access for Black attorneys in the Harris County Civil Courthouse cafeteria;
- Ross v. Houston Independent School District (1956): Challenging the refusal of the Houston Independent School District to fully integrate its schools following Brown v. Board of Education; and
- Wille v. Harris County, Texas (1959): Winning the fight to desegregate Sylvan Beach in La Porte, Texas.

In 1964, HLA successfully passed Resolution 8 at the State Bar of Texas Annual Meeting, advocating for non-discriminatory membership qualifications in local bar associations. This resolution marked another milestone in HLA's commitment to equality and inclusiveness within the legal profession.

The fight for justice persisted through subsequent decades. In the 1990s, HLA's advocacy reached the United States Supreme Court. In Houston Lawyers Association v. Attorney General of Texas, the Court ruled in favor of HLA, establishing that judicial elections are covered by Section 2 of the Voting Rights Act—a critical victory in the ongoing fight to protect voting rights and representation.

Today, HLA remains steadfast in its dedication to advancing justice, equality, and opportunity. Throughout the year, we host dynamic programs that educate, inspire, and foster connections among our members. Our initiatives include continuing legal education seminars, community outreach, mentorship, and advocacy efforts on issues such as economic justice, criminal justice reform, health equity, education, and affordable housing. With a commitment to empowering future generations of legal minds, we provide scholarships, mentorship opportunities, and resources for professional growth. Together, we honor the legacy of our founders by striving to create a more just and equitable society.

HLA
IN ACTION

The National Bar Association
International Affiliates Initiative

Written using excerpts as reported by NBA Vice President Ernestine Sapp, Visionary Creator of International Affiliates Initiative, included in Annual Report of NBA President Algenita Scott Davis, Presented at First Plenary Session of 1991 66th Annual Meeting Indianapolis. Indiana

Pursuant to the first ever formal enactment of an international outreach program by the National Bar Association, forty-three representatives of the NBA journeyed to the Motherland in June 1991. They traveled in implementation of the Association's objectives --- to advance the science of jurisprudence and promote professional and social intercourse among the members of the American and international bars --- and the 1990-1991 bar theme "Unity in the Transcentury 90's."

The initial international affiliates were located in the cities of Dakar, Senegal and Abidjan Cote D' Ivoire. To standing room only audiences, each Opening Session of the meetings in these cities featured the Ministers of Justice of the host countries in a glowing display of togetherness in advocacy of the rule of law. Initiating the program in Senegal was the Mayor of Dakar, Mayor Mammadou Diop, the Secretary General of the Supreme Court of Cote D'Ivoire and the President of the Senegalese Bar Association, Young Lawyers Division. The participants in the Abidjan Opening Session included the Minister of Tourism, the Minister for the Advancement of Women, the United States Ambassador, Kenneth Brown and the President of the Ivorian Bar Association, Gabriel Assamoa. Conference seminars covered two substantive law areas, "Equal Protection Under the Law; African and African American Experiences" and "Legal Framework for Building Business Relations," which allowed the sharing of specific information between the panelists from both African countries and the NBA. Publications and other information were shared on business opportunities. One highlight of the Conference was a special meeting with African law students and faculty to discuss and compare the requirements for the practice of law. This meeting resulted in the employment of a Senegalese law student in the office of an NBA member.

In the most moving experience of the ten-day journey, the delegates visited the Island of Goree, the principal location from which thousands of enslaved African persons were placed on board vessels bound for the Americas. A visit to the Ivorian capital city of Yamossuukro permitted them to behold the magnificence of the Foundation for Peace (Hall and Library of Congress), the two billion dollar Basilica Notre Dame, three recently constructed universities and several surrounding villages. The NBA Delegation was hosted by Senegalese and Ivorian officials in numerous meetings, elaborate receptions and luncheons and other special events to allow them to experience the full essence of local environments. The United States Embassy Center of Cultural Affairs in Cote D'Ivoire hospitably provided programming, planning and other meetings.

We were received as brothers and sisters – naturally. In the words of one of the members of the Senegalese Bar Association members, "We are you and you are us." .... Through this effort, the National Bar Association has taken another step to establish bridges of international interest and inter-support. We called upon our brothers and sisters in Cote D'Ivoire and Senegal to help us as we demanded the enactment of the Civil Rights Act of 1991. It was the supportive vote of Cote D Ivoire which permitted the United States of America to proceed with its actions in Kuwait. .... As we study their solutions to employment opportunities, we can seek to identify business, manufacturing and marketing opportunities from our African siblings with whom we share similar tastes, strong religious beliefs and intense familial devotion. It's natural. In ten short days, we side-stepped the language barrier to share our mutual experiences which have resulted through the years from racism, colonialism or both. We agreed to formalize the commitments of affiliation and unity in these transcentury nineties. It was all so natural. ...Warmth and enthusiasm cannot be described by mere words; sincerity can only be measured by the heart.

ARTICLE II. Objectives The objectives of the Association shall be to advance the science of jurisprudence, to improve the administration of justice, preserve the independence of the judiciary to uphold the honor and integrity of the legal profession, to promote professional and social intercourse among the members of the American and the international bars, to promote legislation that will improve the economic condition of all American citizens regardless of race, sex, or creed in their efforts to secure a free and untrammeled use of the franchise guaranteed by the Constitution of the United States, and to protect civil and political rights of the citizens and the residents of the United States. ARTICLE III. National Bar Association's

The J. Franklyn Bourne Bar Association, Inc.

The J. Franklyn Bourne Bar Association was established in 1977 by a courageous group of African American attorneys committed to advancing justice, equity, and professional excellence within Maryland's legal community. The Association was named in honor of the Honorable J. Franklyn Bourne, Jr., a trailblazing jurist whose distinguished career and perseverance in the face of racial discrimination inspired generations of Black attorneys across Prince George's and Montgomery Counties.

Judge Bourne, a graduate of Howard University School of Law, was a brilliant legal mind and a tireless advocate for civil rights. Despite his exceptional qualifications and legal acumen, he was denied membership in the Prince George's County Bar Association solely because of his race. Undeterred, Judge Bourne went on to become the first African American appointed to the District Court of Maryland for Prince George's County. His legacy is one of resilience, leadership, and an unwavering commitment to justice.

Naming the Association in Judge Bourne's honor was both a tribute to his pioneering accomplishments and a resolute affirmation that African American attorneys would no longer accept exclusion from the legal profession. The J. Franklyn Bourne Bar Association was formed to provide a professional and supportive home for Black attorneys in Prince George's and Montgomery Counties and to champion their rightful place in the legal and civic landscape.

Today, the Association represents more than 300 attorneys, judges, and legal professionals who live and/or work in Prince George's and Montgomery Counties. It is committed to legal excellence, community service, and the advancement of African Americans in the legal profession.

The Association's mission is to promote the continued presence and success of African Americans in the legal field; to defend, protect, and support the cultural, socio-economic, and political advancement of African American communities through the instrument of the law; to educate the public about their rights and responsibilities; to preserve the historical legacy of African American attorneys in the region; and to provide continuing legal education programs that foster the professional development of its members.

The J. Franklyn Bourne Bar Association carries out this mission through a wide range of impactful initiatives. The Association hosts expungement clinics, organizes community service projects, mentors young attorneys, and hosts an annual oratorical competition for high school students. It testifies before the Maryland General Assembly, offers pro bono legal services, raises thousands of dollars in scholarship funds for aspiring law students, and conducts continuing legal education programs throughout the year. The Association also partners with local and national organizations, supports civic engagement, and promotes the appointment and election of diverse members of the bench and bar. Through these efforts, the Association affirms its unwavering commitment to service, advocacy, and the upliftment of the African American community.

Through its enduring dedication to these principles and its deep sense of purpose, the J. Franklyn Bourne Bar Association continues to honor the legacy of its namesake while serving as a vital force for justice and equity in Maryland's legal profession.

Patricia (Pat Rosier
Email: patmrosier@aol.com

CENTENNIAL AFFILIATES

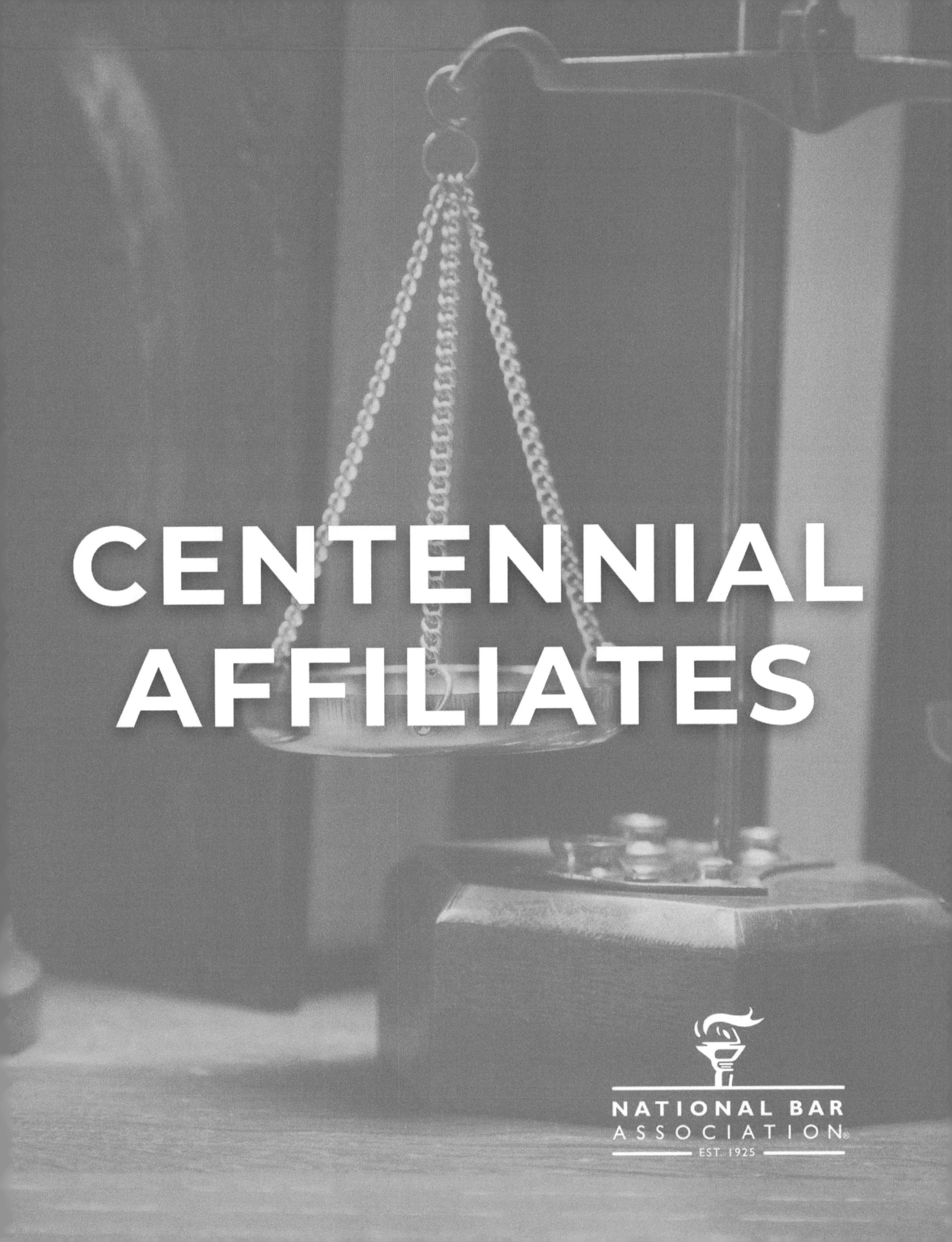

NATIONAL BAR ASSOCIATION®
EST. 1925

IGNITING JUSTICE
FOR 100 YEARS

NATIONAL BAR ASSOCIATION 100 YEARS

ANNUAL MEETINGS HOSTED BY CENTENNIAL AFFLIATES

CENTENNIAL AFFILIATES RECEPTION

Iowa National Bar Association
Des Moines, IA

- **1st Annual Meeting (1925)**

Cook County Bar Association
Chicago, IL

- **2nd Annual Meeting (1926)**
- **4th Annual Meeting (1928)**
- **19th Annual Meeting (1944)**
- **51st Annual Meeting (1975)**
- **61st Annual Meeting (1985)**
- **71st Annual Meeting (1996)**
- **100th Annual Meeting (July 2025)**

Marion County Bar Association
Indianapolis, IN

- **8th Annual Meeting (1932)**
- **24th Annual Meeting (1949)**
- **37th Annual Meeting (1963)**
- **Annual Meeting (1991)**
- **84th Annual Meeting (2009)**

Mound City Bar Association
St. Louis, MO

- **3rd Annual Meeting (1927)**
- **9th Annual Meeting (1933)**
- **Annual Meeting (1992)**
- **Annual Meeting (2016)**

Washington Bar Association
District of Columbia

- **6th Annual Meeting (1930)**
- **Annual Meeting (1988)**
- **Annual Meeting (2000)**
- **Annual Meeting -Virtual (2020)**

IGNITING JUSTICE
FOR 100 YEARS

NATIONAL BAR ASSOCIATION 100 YEARS

CENTENNIAL AFFILIATE MEMBERS WHO SERVED AS NBA PRESIDENTS

CENTENNIAL AFFILIATES RECEPTION

Iowa National Bar Association Centennial Affiliate members who served as President of NBA

George H. Woodson	1925 – 1926

Cook County Bar Association Centennial Affiliate members who served as President of NBA

C. Francis Stradford	1928 – 1929
George W. Lawrence	1935 – 1937
Earl B. Dickerson	1945 – 1947
Hon. William Peterson	1969 – 1970
Archie B. Weston, Sr.	1973 – 1974
Hon. Arnette R. Hubbard	1981 – 1982
Vanita Banks	2007 – 2008
Juan Thomas	2017 – 2018
Wiley S. Adams	2024 – 2025

Mound City Bar Association Centennial Affiliate members who served as President of NBA

Homer G. Phillips	1927 – 1928
Sidney R. Redmond	1939 – 1941
Hon. Scovel Richardson	1951 – 1953
Hon. Billy Jones	1967 – 1968
Mavis Thompson	2009 – 2010
Pamela J. Meanes	2014 – 2015

Washington Bar Association Centennial Affiliate members who served as President of NBA

William L. Houston	1937 – 1939
Thurman L. Dodson	1947 – 1949
Hon. Richard Atkinson	1955 – 1957
Hon. William Thompson	1957 – 1959
James W. Cobb	1971 – 1972
William A. Borders, Jr.	1980 – 1981
Thomas Duckenfield	1989 – 1990
Keith W. Watters	1995 – 1996
Michael S. Rosier	2001 – 2002
Kim M. Keenan	2004 – 2005
Patricia Rosier	2013 – 2014
Kevin D. Judd	2016 – 2017
Alfreda Robinson	2019 – 2020

CENTENNIAL AFFILIATE SPOTLIGHT CONT.

THE HISTORY OF WASHINGTON BAR ASSOCIATION

In December 1901, African American lawyers from throughout the State of Iowa met in the city of Des Moines, Iowa and organized a state bar association for African American lawyers. It was known as the Iowa Negro Bar Association (the "INBA") and George H. Woodson ("Woodson") was its first president. As reported in the December 4, 1901 edition of the *Des Moines Register, "It is gratifying to note that these young attorneys are making a place and a name in their profession worthy of emulation."* Woodson had been born to slave parents in Virginia and graduated in 1895 from Howard University Law School. By 1896, he had opened a law practice in Iowa, with offices in Des Moines, Oskaloosa, and Albia.

In 1905, S. Joe Brown (who had a partnership with Woodson) became the first African American attorney to appear before the Iowa Supreme Court. He successfully argued the first discrimination case before the Iowa Supreme Court in 1906.

For the next 24 years, the Iowa Negro Bar Association took bold steps with its advocacy and dedication to the protection of its community. For example, in 1908, the INBA formed a Legislative Committee to "watch the actions of the 33rd (Iowa) General Assembly so as to oppose measures hostile to the general welfare of the people of Iowa and particularly offensive to the Negro Race, who are striving against great injustice growing out of adverse sentiments, amounting in many instances to brutal, unchristian and cruel oppression..." *(Pg. 1 of The Iowa Bystander, Des Moines, 5 Nov. 1909).* (The Iowa Bystander was an African American weekly established in Des Moines in 1894 as the voice of Iowa's African American community.)

A headline in the Iowa Bystander proclaimed that "Iowa State Negro Bar Association Meets in 8th Annual Session – Legislative Committee Makes Important Report". In 1909, the Legislative Committee made a report to the president and members of the INBA at its 8th Annual Session held on October 28, 1909. The Report was set forth in the newspaper..."in plain violation of the express provisions of the constitution and statutes, equal public accommodation and all most every public accommodation is still openly and defiantly denied all of our people, the cultured, industrious, and religious along [sic] with the vulgar, sinful and depraved criminal class and that is the hard unreasonable part of, the discrimination which our people are made to suffer all over Iowa and the country." The Legislative Committee considered it a "duty to urge the INBA to continue and increase its vigilance in trying to guard the liberty of Iowa citizens wherever it be threatened or assailed , and especially the rights of the most humble and oppressed".

At the 23rd Annual Banquet of the INBA held on February 11, 1925, the program contained a discussion of the proposed National Bar Association and a report from the historian as to what a "real National Bar would mean to us". Per the program, attorneys from various cities Iowa, Chicago, Kansas and Washington, D.C. and other states were at the banquet.

CENTENNIAL AFFILIATE SPOTLIGHT CONT.
THE HISTORY OF IOWA NATIONAL BAR ASSOCIATION

A few months later, on August 1, 1925, five (5) prominent and successful INBA lawyers including S. Joe Brown, Charles P. Howard, Sr., James B. Morris, Gertrude E. Durden Rush and George H. Woodson, joined 7 of their colleagues from Chicago and Kansas City formed the NBA. Woodson, the first president of the INBA, became the NBA's first president in 1925.

The INBA is the largest association of African-American attorneys, judges, professors and deans in the State of Iowa. It is the oldest affiliate of the National Bar Association. Paxton J. Williams is the current president of the INBA. Over the years, the INBA has served as a network of communication and provides support for its members.

In July 2018, members of the INBA were present at the Public Dedication of *A Monumental Journey*, and were proud to oversee the fulfillment of its vision for the creation of a world class public art project by renown sculptor Kerry James Marshall which honors the legacy of the 12 African American lawyers who founded the NBA in Des Moines, Iowa. Members of the INBA provided the genesis of the establishment of the national memorial to celebrate the spirit of the NBA Founders. The vision and persistence of the Honorable Odell McGhee (ret.), a former president of the INBA (and a former NBA Board member) gave rise to the $ 2.1 million monument.

Over the years, many members of the INBA have assumed "firsts" within the larger Iowa legal community. For example, Vicky Long Hill, current Vice President of the INBA was the first African-American assistant city attorney with the City of Des Moines Legal Department. Judge Luther T. Glanton, Jr. and his wife, Attorney Willie Stevenson Glanton personified the word " power couple". Judge Glanton, born in 1910, in 1958, he became Iowa's first African American judge. In 1953, Attorney Glanton was the 2nd African-American female attorney Iowa. She was also the first African American female to serve in the State legislature. In 2008, Judge McGhee was named as the first African American President of the Iowa Judges Association. In 2010, one of is members, Iowa District Associate Court Judge Romonda D. Belcher (ret.) became the first female African American Judge in Iowa and in 2022, INBA past president Henry Hamilton became the first African American president of the Iowa State Bar Association.

HON. GEORGE H. WOODSON
IOWA NEGRO BAR ASSOCIATION
Account for 1924
BANQUET OF
NEGRO LAWYERS
DES MOINES, IOWA, FRIDAY, NO
INBA
Iowa National Bar Association
P.O. Box 283 *Ankeny, Iowa 50021
www.iowanationalbar.org
NEGRO LAWYERS.
State Bar Association Organized in Des Moines.
The negro lawyers of the state met in this city Friday and organized a State Bar Association. The organization was preceded by a banquet, with George H. Woodson as toastmaster. The following toasts were responded to: I. E. Williamson, of Des Moines, "Time and Experience at the Bar;" S. J. Brown, of Albia, "Scholarship in the Law;" George I. Holt of Des Moines, "How Can We Best Encourage Business Enterprises Among Negro Citizens;" J. B. Rush, of Des Moines, "Black Man Before the Law;" H. R. Wright, of Des Moines, "The Profession as I Have Found It."
Following the very interesting and instructive remarks in response to the toasts, the Negro Bar Association of Iowa was organized, with George H. Woodson, president; I. E. Williamson, vice-president; George I. Holt, secretary; S. J. Brown, treasurer. The members are George H. Woodson, of Muchakinock, S. J. Brown, of Albia, William Mott, of Davenport, Mr. Holden, of Ottumwa, I. E. Williamson, George I. Holt, H. R. Wright and J. B. Rush, of Des Moines. It is gratifying to note that these young attorneys are making a place and a name in their profession worthy of emulation.
The Bystander
WANTS NEGROES PROTECTED
Atty. Woodson Celebrates 25 Yrs. As Lawyer
Take Up Negro Problem, Southern
SUBSCRIBERS

COOK COUNTY
BAR AUXILIARY
COOK COUNTY
BAR
ASSOCIATION
Cook County Bar Association
COOK COUNTY BAR ASSOCIATION
ADVOCATES FOR JUSTICE
SINCE 1914
A resolution
adopted by The City Council
of the City of Chicago, Illinois
Presented by MAYOR RAHM EMANUEL on MAY 28, 2014
Whereas, in 1869 Lloyd G. Wheeler became the first Black man licensed to practice law in the State of Illinois, and, in 1894, Ida Platt became the first Black woman attorney licensed in Illinois. By 1896, 32 African Americans had been admitted to the Illinois bar and they began meeting informally to devise a legal strategy to protest against discrimination in hotels, theaters, restaurants, schools and the judiciary; and
WHEREAS, This informal collaboration among African American attorneys lasted until 1914, when a younger generation of Black lawyers decided to form the Cook County Bar Association ("CCBA") to improve, protect, and defend the lives and rights of all citizens in the Greater Chicago area. The CCBA is the oldest association of Black lawyers in the country; and
WHEREAS, Since the CCBA's inception, its members have served as advocates, judges and legal educators, and as elected and appointed representatives, participating at every level of government to fight injustice, to advocate on behalf of underserved communities, and to promote the interests of African American lawyers and judges; and
WHEREAS, Throughout its distinguished history, the CCBA has provided leadership, service and advocacy for African-American attorneys and to people residing in underserved communities; and
WHEREAS, The CCBA's myriad accomplishments include the work of its outstanding members, such as C. Francis Stradford, who co-founded the National Bar Association in 1925; Earl B. Dickerson, who represented the plaintiffs in Hansberry v. Lee, the seminal 1940 case protesting restrictive covenants in Chicago's housing markets; and William R. Ming, who served on the NAACP team litigating Brown v. Board of Education in 1954; and

CENTENNIAL AFFILIATE SPOTLIGH

THE HISTORY OF THE COOK COUNTY BAR ASSOCIATI

In 1869, Lloyd G. Wheeler became the first African American to be licensed to practice law in the State of Illinois. Ida Platt became the first African American female to be licensed in 1894. By 1896, 32 African Americans had been admitted to the Illinois bar. They began meeting informally to devise a legal strategy to protest against discrimination in public accommodations, i.e. hotels, restaurants, theaters and to address judicial elections and school desegregation. This informal collaboration continued amongst African American attorneys until December 18, 1914 when, denied membership to the American Bar Association and the Chicago Bar Association, a younger generation of African American attorneys met and organized the Cook County Bar Association ("CCBA") to improve, protect and defend the lives and rights of all citizens in the greater Chicago area.

On January 22, 1915, the newly formed association met and elected officers. Edward H. Wright was elected as its first president. From the beginning, members of the CCBA came to the defense of African American citizens who were arrested during the 1919 race riots. CCBA members initiated lawsuits to collect damages for property damage, personal injury and death resulting from the riots. CCBA members actively participated in local politics to obtain representation at all levels of government. They met with judges and court clerks to lodge complaints about the mistreatment of African American lawyers by court personne.

Wendell E. Green, C. Francis Stradford, Jesse N. Baker, William H. Haynes and George C. Adams were part of the CCBA delegation that traveled to Des Moines, Iowa in 1925 to help form the National Bar Association ("NBA"). Attorney Stradford later served as a president of the CCBA in 1926 and as the first CCBA president of the NBA in 1928.

Shortly after Charles Hamilton Houston was named as Dean of the Howard University Law School, he prepared a preliminary report on a survey of activities by Negro lawyers throughout the country which he sent to Dean Roscoe Pound of the Harvard Law School. In February 1928, he wrote of the CCBA, *"...the Chicago bar association, properly named as the Cook County Bar Association, is the most influential of all. It numbers 113 paid financial members and includes all but about ten of the Negro lawyers in active practice in Chicago. At its annual meeting of January 6, 1928, eighty-six members were actually present while proxies brought the total number of votes cast in the election to 108. The endorsement of the Association is sought by candidates for the bench and other elective officials connected with the administration of justice in Chicago......" Tentative Findings re Negro Lawyers, 1928.*

The CCBA has a long history of grooming its members to assume positions of leadership within the NBA. Starting with Attorney Stradford, eight (8) of its members are Past Presidents of the NBA. One of those, the Honorable Arnette R. Hubbard, was the first woman president of the CCBA and the NBA. The NBA's current president, Wiley S.
Adams, is an esteemed officer and board member of the CCBA. Many of its other members have held national offices within the NBA.

CENTENNIAL AFFILIATE SPOTLIGHT CONT.

THE HISTORY OF THE COOK COUNTY BAR ASSOCIATION

The CCBA has played host to at least five (5) annual meetings (1926, 1928, 1975, 1985, 1996 and now the Centennial Meeting in 2025). It has served as host for many other national meetings including Wiley Branton Symposiums and Gertrude Rush meetings.

Throughout its distinguished history, the CCBA and its members have provided leadership, service and advocacy for African American attorneys and the Chicago African American Community. Over the years, its storied members have been in the national legal and political spotlights. For example, Earl B. Dickerson, represented the plaintiffs in Hansberry vs. Lee, the seminal 1940 case protesting restrictive covenants in Chicago's housing markets and William R. Ming served on the NAACP team litigating Brown vs. Board of Education in 1954. The Hon. Harold Washington, a CCBA member, was elected in 1983 as the first African American mayor in the City of Chicago; in 1992, the Hon. Carol Moseley Braun was elected as the first African American female to the U.S. Senate; and in 2008, CCBA member, Senator Barak Hussain Obama was elected as President of the United States.

As Nicholas E. Cummings, the CCBA's current and 110th President notes on the CCBA's website, "for 110 years, the CCBA and its membership have been advocates for economic, social, political and racial justice for Black communities in the Chicagoland area. Over the course of this rich history, the CCBA and its members have worked to diversify our profession and advocated for legislation leading to one of the most diverse judiciaries in the country. If anyone knows the power of collective collaboration, it is the luminaries of this illustrious organization."

MCBA
MOUND CITY
BAR ASSOCIATION
1922

IGNITING JUSTICE
FOR 100 YEARS

NATIONAL BAR ASSOCIATION 100 YEARS

CENTENNIAL AFFILIATE SPOTLIGHT
THE HISTORY OF MOUND CITY BAR ASSOCIATION

On December 23, 1921, and again on January 6, 1922, the following notice appeared in the *St. Louis Argus* newspaper, the oldest continuous Black business in St. Louis, Missouri, announcing the inaugural meeting of Black attorneys in the city:

> "Believing that a closer relationship of the members of the Bar will redound to the benefit of the race and the profession, and with a view of bringing about this much needed result, the undersigned attorneys hereby cordially invite all Negro members of the bar to meet at Pythian Hall, 3137 Pine Street on January 7, 1922 at 8:00pm for the purpose of perfecting a Bar Association.
> Geo. L. Vaughn, Daniel W. Bowles, Homer G. Phillips, S.E. Garner, Geo. B. Jones, W.R. Hill, Jos. A. Smith, Robert N. Owens, Emanuel Williams, N.A. Mitchell, E.H. Taylor, Hutchins Inge, J.H Roberts and Freeman L. Martin."

The *Argus* reported on January 13, 1922, that the attorneys had met and organized the St. Louis Negro Bar Association. George L. Vaughn was elected president; Robert Owens, Vice-president; Albert Burgess, Treasurer; and George Jones, Secretary. The founding lawyers had graduated from a variety of law schools across the United States. Silas E. Garner graduated from Walden University's law department in 1908, and Homer G. Phillips was a 1903 graduate of Howard Law School. By 1924, there were twenty-eight Black lawyers in St. Louis.

The name of the St. Louis Negro Bar Association was changed to the Mound City Bar Association ("MCBA") on September 16, 1922. This change was consistent with the other Black professional organizations in St. Louis, such as the Mound City Medical Association and the Mound City Dental Association, which took the name "Mound City" after the Indian,mounds in North St. Louis.

St. Louis's long-standing connection with the National Bar Association began in 1927 when the NBA's annual meeting was held in St. Louis with over one hundred Black attorneys attending from across the United States and the Republic of Panama. St. Louis attorney and Mound City Bar Founder Homer G. Phillips was elected the third president of the NBA. NBA presidents from St. Louis include: Homer G. Phillips, 1927; Sidney Redmond, 1939-1940; Scovel Richardson, 1951-1953; Judge Billy Jones of East St. Louis, 1967-1968; Mavis T. Thompson, 2009-2010; and Pamela Meanes, 2014-2015. The National Bar Association met again in St. Louis in 1933 when it held its ninth convention in the city, as well as in 1992 and 2016.

Mound City Bar recognized its Centennial Anniversary with a public Reception at the Civil Courts Building on April 8, 2022. The event was postponed from January 2022 because of health concerns due to COVID-19. The afternoon concluded with a photograph taken of the membership in attendance to commemorate the occasion. Researching Mound City history, it was discovered there was no photograph of the membership. For the next Centennial, there will be one.

LAWYERS FORM TIDEWATER BAR ASSOCIATION

W. L. Davis, of Norfolk, President; B. H. Prue, of Newport News, Vice President D. H. Edwards, Secretary.

HOPE TO DEVELOP A STATE ORGANIZATION

JUSTICE
SHRBA
COMMUNITY
LEGACY
EST. 1923
South Hampton Roads Bar Association

Complete Text Of Bar Association's Resolution

Walter L. Davis

Complaint Filed

Lawyer Denied Dining Service At Va. Bar Meet

Tidewater Attorneys Protest "Humiliation"

LAWYERS TO DISCUSS POLL TAX PAYMENTS

No Action Taken On Fee Proposal

Overton, Jordan, Mason paved way for local Black lawyers

Lawyers

Students Enjoy 'Day In Court'

IGNITING JUSTICE
FOR 100 YEARS

NATIONAL BAR ASSOCIATION 100 YEARS

CENTENNIAL AFFILIATE SPOTLIGHT
THE HISTORY OF SOUTH HAMPTON ROADS BAR ASSOCIATION

Having been denied membership in the American Bar Association, in 1907 a group of African American attorneys formed the National Negro Bar Association (NNBA) in Little Rock, Arkansas. In August 1922, the NNBA held its 14th annual conference in Norfolk, Virginia, bringing many of the top legal minds from across the country to Norfolk. In October 1923, African American members of the local bar formed the Tidewater Bar Association (TBA). Founding members included TBA officers Walter L. Davis, President; R.H. Pree, Vice President; D.H. Edwards, Recording Secretary; V.C. Hodges, Corresponding Secretary; and A. Rainey, Treasurer. The TBA was renamed the Twin City Bar Association (TCBA), and for a brief period was also known as the Norfolk County Bar Association. Members of the TCBA worked collectively and collaboratively with organizations such as the NAACP Legal Defense Fund to challenge legalized segregation and discrimination that existed at the state and local levels, and to combat residential segregation, underfunded segregated schools, and disparities in pay for teachers at those schools. By 1933, the TCBA was instrumental in the effort to encourage African Americans to register to vote and in assisting residents in the community to become qualified voters. The TCBA also left its mark on the landscape of the local legal system and community.

In 1954, the Old Dominion Bar Association (ODBA), the statewide bar association for minority attorneys in Virginia, held workshops in Norfolk at the Young Park Recreational Center on civil rights procedures for local attorneys. The ODBA and TCBA met regularly to collaborate on this initiative. The TCBA also worked to attain fair and equitable treatment of all individuals in the courtroom. Toward this end, in 1954, twenty-three members of the TCBA, led by attorneys Hilary H. Jones, Jr. and W.T. Mason, Jr., endorsed a candidate for the Corporation Court of Norfolk. In 1955, several members of the TCBA unsuccessfully applied for membership in the Norfolk Portsmouth Bar Association, which at the time did not have any African American members. TCBA president Hilary H. Jones, Jr., and members Victor J. Ashe, C. Arnett Bibbins, Yolande H. Chambers, E. Armistead Dawley, Jr., T. Ione Diggs, J. Hugo Madison, Sr., William T. Mason, Jr. and James A. Overton were all denied membership. Nevertheless, the TCBA and its members continued to press on and to advocate for change.

TCBA eventually became known as South Hampton Roads Bar Association after seven cities and towns in and around Norfolk and the metropolitan area surrounding the Tidewater region of Virginia.

SHRBA held a gala in celebration of its Centennial in October 2023 recognizing its President- emeritus W.T. Mason, Jr. who died just a few months before the event. SHRBA continues to serve the South Hampton Roads legal community and the community at large.

A 1928 news article reports that some of the founders of the Marion County Lawyers Club were James T.V. Hill; Robert Lee Bailey, Freeman B.

1962 MCBA Hosted the 37 NBA National Bar Association Conference in Indianapolis.

At press time Thursday Atty. Rufus C. Kuykendall, general chairman of the National Bar Association confab, said due to civil rights actions in Albany, Ga., Rev. Dr. Martin Luther King will not speak here as earlier announced. He was replaced by another outstanding rights leader, Rev. Fred Shuttlesworth, formerly of Birmingham, Ala., but now pastor of Revelation Baptist Church, Cincinnati. Rev. Shuttlesworth was a prime figure in Alabama civil rights struggles and was forced to

A Hearty Welcome to Indianapolis...

NATIONAL BAR ASSOCIATION

Twenty-fourth Annual Convention

Thursday, Friday, Saturday, Sept. 15, 16, 17th

Headquarters: Walker Casino, Indiana Ave. & West St.

MARION COUNTY BAR ASSOCIATION OFFICERS AND MEMBERS

National Bar Association: Fighting for equality

National Bar Association meets in Indianapolis

MCBA
MARION COUNTY
BAR ASSOCIATION

Forest Littlejohn-Lawyers Club President: In 1932 the Marion County Lawyers Club hosted the 8 th National Conference of the NBA. Madam CJ Walker Casino, Movie Theater, Drug Store and Office Building: Corner of West Street and Indiana Avenue.

J.T.V. HILL

ROBERT L. BAILEY

Following are the members of the Marion County Lawyers Club commitee: Atty. R. L. Bailey, Chm. Atty. F. B. Ransom, Atty. C. H. Thurston, Atty. James B. Batty, and Atty. Robert Lee Brokenburr.

Welcome... Members National Bar Association!

SHOTGUN BLAST ENDS FATALLY

15c Indianapolis Recorder

IGNITING JUSTICE
FOR 100 YEARS

NATIONAL BAR ASSOCIATION 100 YEARS

CENTENNIAL AFFILIATE SPOTLIGHT
THE HISTORY OF MARION COUNTY BAR ASSOCIATION

The Marion County Bar Association was originally founded in 1925 as the Marion County Lawyers' Club. On October 27, 1942, the name was changed to the Marion County Bar Association or MCBA. The Marion County Bar Association was established as a direct result of exclusionary policies practiced by white contemporary associations.

Prior to 1900, there were very few Black lawyers practicing in the Indianapolis, Marion County, Indiana vicinity. Records show that the first Black Attorney admitted to the bar in Indianapolis was James T.V. Hill. Attorney Hill practiced law from 1882 to 1928 and was active in civic affairs. History also shows that James H. Lott began a legal practice and was a civic leader in the 1890's.

Injustices toward minorities in the early 1900's were at a high and unsavory peak. Nevertheless, in 1909 the State of Indiana witnessed the birth of the National Association for the Advancement of Colored People (NAACP) and the National Urban League. Between 1909 and 1912 several noted personalities from the Black Communities distinguished themselves. In 1910, Robert L. Brokenburr, a young law graduate for Howard University in Washington D.C., was admitted to the Indiana Bar. At the same time, Madame C. J. Walker, set up headquarters in Indianapolis. Madame Walker was destined to revolutionize the cosmetic industry. Madame Walker retained the legal services of Attorney Freeman B. Ransom who served the Walker Company for some thirty-five (35) years as General Manager and Legal Counsel.

The Marion County Bar Association has had a long history with the National Bar Association. The Eighth Annual Convention of the NBA was held in Indianapolis in 1932 and, again in 1949, 1963 and 1991.

A Centennial Gala is planned for October 2025.

Newly-elected officers of the Marion County Bar Association, 1983 **Credit:** Indianapolis Recorder Collection, Indiana Historical Society

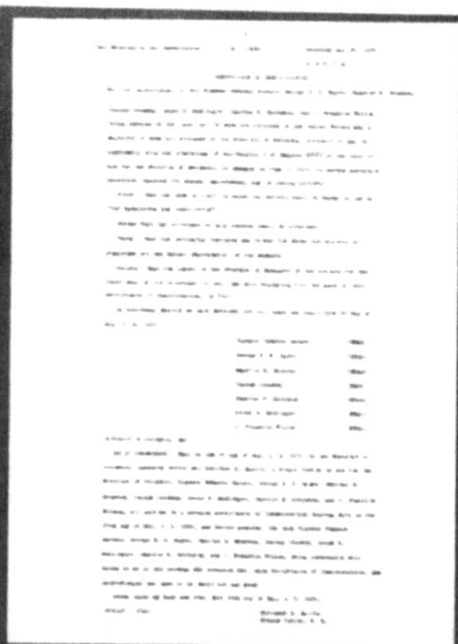

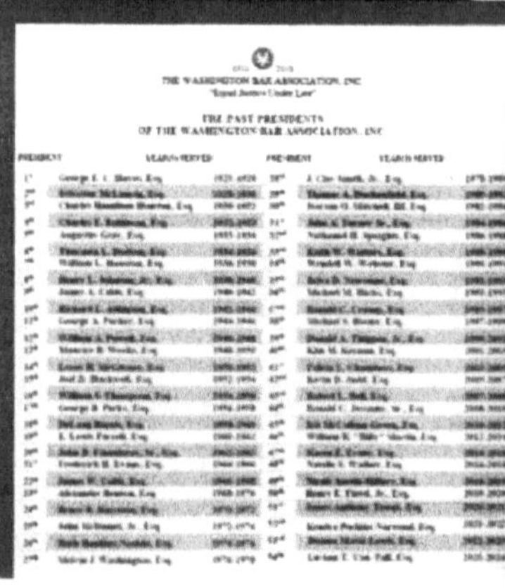
THE WASHINGTON BAR ASSOCIATION, INC

"Equal Justice Under Law"

THE PAST PRESIDENTS
OF THE WASHINGTON BAR ASSOCIATION, INC

IGNITING JUSTICE
FOR 100 YEARS

NATIONAL BAR ASSOCIATION 100 YEARS

CENTENNIAL AFFILIATE SPOTLIGHT
THE HISTORY OF WASHINGTON BAR ASSOCIATION

The deep roots and history of African American lawyers in Washington, D.C. dates back to the Reconstruction Period when in 1869, George Boyer Vashon was admitted to the bar of the District of Columbia. Later, in 1872, Charlotte E. Ray was admitted as the first African American female lawyer in both the District of Columbia and the country. Other African Americans were admitted over the years, and in 1916, recognizing the need to associate with each other in order to survive a profession that was dominated by an inhospitable white legal fraternity and a white judicial system that oft times tried to impede them, they formed the District of Columbia Colored Bar Association (the "DCCBA"). That group and their progeny laid the foundation for what would later become the Washington Bar Association ("WBA").

Out of the rising racial consciousness of the "roaring twenties" and the "New Negro Movement," the "WBA" was incorporated on May 26, 1925 by a new generation of young African American lawyers. These lawyers looked away from the pace and approach of the DCCBA and decided to totally commit themselves to the formation of a new kind of bar association with a dedicated mission of making the concept of "equal justice under law" a reality for all. The WBA's seven founders included Charles Hamilton Houston and others who became uncompromising, equal justice pioneers dedicated to using the law for the advancement of human rights and civil rights, equally, for all namely, George E.C. Hayes, J. Franklin Wilson, Isaiah Lisemby, Louis R. Mehlinger, Charles E. Robinson and Ulysses S. Garnes.

Attorney Hayes served as the first president of the WBA. Joshuah R. Turner is the current and 55th WBA President. To date, 13 members of the WBA have also served as president of the National Bar Association ("NBA"), starting with William Lepre Houston, the NBA's 9th President (1937 to 1939) ending with the NBA's 77th President, Alfreda Robinson (2019 to 2020). With the national headquarters of the NBA strategically located in the nation's capital, the WBA has served as host to numerous National Bar Association's Annual Meetings and countless Wiley Branton Symposiums, Mid-Year Meetings and other meetings.

Over the years, the WBA and its members have continued to be a force in the general welfare of the District of Columbia, pleading that the local and federal courts, the administrative staffs of the courts in that Circuit, the Office of the Corporation Counsel and the U.S. Attorney's Office for the District of Columbia were competently staffed and occupied by people of color, women, and fair minded personnel who were in touch with all the citizens of the District. Members of the WBA have contributed significantly to the development of effective equal justice theories, practices and precedents and pursued them all the way to the U.S. Supreme Court.

CENTENNIAL AFFILIATE SPOTLIGHT CONT.
THE HISTORY OF WASHINGTON BAR ASSOCIATION

It was the equal justice advocacy and practice of many WBA members and other Black lawyers that formed the jurisprudence that underpinned the Supreme Court's 1954 decisions of Brown vs. Board of Education (1954) and Bolling vs. Sharpe (1954). The past is oftentimes the best teacher for the present and the future. The 28th WBA Past President Dr. J. Clay Smith wrote the authoritative book entitled Emancipation: The Making of the Black Lawyer-1844-1944 (1993).

Further, the WBA has consistently provided leadership from its membership, founders and leadership regarding the significant roles played by the black lawyers in the development and improvement of the legal profession and democracy in America. The WBA continued its leadership and development into all aspects of the legal community in our nation's capital. It is expected to continue to have a role to ensure that constitutional guarantees are not further diluted, civil rights laws are properly enforced and that the rights, dignity and humanity of the citizens of the District of Columbia are protected. On January 18, 2025, a "Call to Commemoration –1925-2025" was issued at a WBA Centennial Year Kick Off Reception with the theme of a *Centennial Salue to the Washington Bar Association Founders, Leadership and its Legacy of Pursuing Equal Justice Under Law.*

For the past century, the equal justice record of the WBA demonstrates that the same challenges that faced Black people and Black lawyers at its founding in 1925, have remained in various guises throughout the years. True to its founding mission, the WBA has continued its leadership and development into all aspects of the legal community in our country and in the nation's capital. With continued dedication to its core equal justice mission, and legacy, the WBA will continue to ensure that constitutional guarantees are not further diluted, civil rights laws are properly enforced and that the rights, dignity and humanity of the citizens of the District of Columbia, and the nation, are protected.

In keeping with this perpetual equal justice thrust, mission and legacy, on January 18, 2025, in Washington, D.C., Charles Hamilton Houston III was the Keynote Speaker at the WBA Centennial Year Kickoff Reception in the George E.C. Hayes Fellowship Hall where a "Call to Commemoration–1925-2025" was issued with the theme: *Centennial Salute to the Washington Bar Association Founders, Leadership and its Legacy of Pursuing Equal Justice Under Law.*

(Prepared with the assistance of Robert L. Bell, WBA Historian and 43rd WBA Past President, 2007 to 2008).

- - - 0 - - -

Ex

The Washington Bar Association) No. 17950 Recorded May 26, 1925

At 2:23 P. M.

CERTIFICATE OF INCORPORATION

We, the undersigned, to wit Ulysses Simpson Garnes, George E. C. Hayes, Charles H. Houston,

60 Isaiah Lisemby, Louis R. Mehlinger, Charles E. Robinson, and J. Franklin Wilson, being persons of full age, all of whom are citizens of the United States and a majority of whom are citizens of the District of Columbia, pursuant to and in conformity with the provisions of Sub-Chapter 3 of Chapter XVIII of the Code of Law for the District of Columbia, as amended to June 7, 1924, do hereby associate ourselves together for mutual improvement, and do hereby certify:

First. That the name or title by which the society shall be known in law is "THE WASHINGTON BAR ASSOCIATION":

Second That the existence of said society shall be perpetual.

Third, That the particular business and object for which the society is organized are the mutual improvement of its members;

Fourth: That the number of the Trustees or Managers of the society for the first year of its existence, to wit, the year beginning with the date of this Certificate of Incorporation, is five.

In testimony whereof we have hereunto set our hands and seals this 25 day of May, A. D. 1925.

Ulysses Simpson Garnes (SEAL)
George E. C. Hayes (SEAL)
Charles H. Houston (SEAL)
Isaiah Lisemby (SEAL)
Charles E. Robinson (SEAL)
Louis R. Mehlinger (SEAL)
J. Franklin Wilson (SEAL)

DISTRICT OF COLUMBIA, SS:

BE IT REMEMBERED, That on the 25 day of May, A. D. 1925, in the District of Columbia, appeared before me, Mortimer M. Harris, a Notary Public in and for the District of Columbia, Ulysses Simpson Garnes, George E. C. Hayes, Charles H. Houston, Isaiah Lisemby, Louis R. Mehlinger, Charles E. Robinson, and J. Franklin Wilson, all parties to a certain certificate of Incorporation bearing date on the 25th day of May, A. D. 1925, and hereto annexed, the said Ulysses Simpson Garnes, George E. C. Hayes, Charles H. Houston, Isaiah Lisemby, Louis R. Mehlinger, Charles E. Robinson, and J. Franklin Wilson, being personally well known to me as the persons who executed the said Certificate of Incorporation, and acknowledged the same to be their act and deed.

Given under my hand and seal this 25th day of May, A. D. 1925.

(NOTARIAL SEAL)

Mortimer M. Harris
Notary Public, D. C.

- - - 0 - - -

1925 2025

THE WASHINGTON BAR ASSOCIATION, INC.

"Equal Justice Under Law"

THE PAST PRESIDENTS
OF THE WASHINGTON BAR ASSOCIATION, INC.

PRESIDENT		YEAR(S) SERVED	PRESIDENT		YEAR(S) SERVED
1st	George E. C. Hayes, Esq.	1925-1928	28th	J. Clay Smith, Jr., Esq.	1978-1980
2nd	Sylvester McLaurin, Esq.	1928-1930	29th	Thomas A. Duckenfield, Esq.	1980-1982
3rd	Charles Hamilton Houston, Esq.	1930-1932	30th	Iverson O. Mitchell, III, Esq.	1982-1984
4th	Charles E. Robinson, Esq.	1932-1933	31st	John A. Turner Sr., Esq.	1984-1986
5th	Augustus Gray, Esq.	1933-1934	32nd	Nathaniel H. Speights, Esq.	1986-1988
6th	Thurman L. Dodson, Esq.	1934-1936	33rd	Keith W. Watters, Esq.	1988-1990
7th	William L. Houston, Esq.	1936-1938	34th	Wendell W. Webster, Esq.	1990-1991
8th	Henry L. Johnson, Jr., Esq.	1938-1940	35th	Belva D. Newsome, Esq.	1991-1993
9th	James A. Cobb, Esq.	1940-1942	36th	Michael M. Hicks, Esq.	1993-1995
10th	Richard L. Atkinson, Esq.	1942-1944	37th	Ronald C. Crump, Esq.	1995-1997
11th	George A. Parker, Esq.	1944-1946	38th	Michael S. Rosier, Esq.	1997-1999
12th	William A. Powell, Esq.	1946-1948	39th	Donald A. Thigpen, Jr., Esq.	1999-2001
13th	Maurice R. Weeks, Esq.	1948-1950	40th	Kim M. Keenan, Esq.	2001-2003
14th	Leroy H. McGivney, Esq.	1950-1952	41st	Felicia L. Chambers, Esq.	2003-2005
15th	Joel D. Blackwell, Esq.	1952-1954	42nd	Kevin D. Judd, Esq.	2005-2007
16th	William S. Thompson, Esq.	1954-1956	43rd	Robert L. Bell, Esq.	2007-2008
17th	George B. Parks, Esq.	1956-1958	44th	Ronald C. Jessamy, Sr., Esq.	2008-2010
18th	DeLong Harris, Esq.	1958-1960	45th	Iris McCollum Green, Esq.	2010-2012
19th	E. Lewis Farrell, Esq.	1960-1962	46th	William R. "Billy" Martin, Esq.	2012-2014
20th	John D. Fauntleroy, Sr., Esq.	1962-1963	47th	Karen E. Evans, Esq.	2014-2016
21st	Frederick H. Evans, Esq.	1964-1966	48th	Natalie S. Walker, Esq.	2016-2018
22nd	James W. Cobb, Esq.	1966-1968	49th	Nicole Austin-Hillery, Esq.	2018-2019
23rd	Alexander Benton, Esq.	1968-1970	50th	Henry E. Floyd, Jr., Esq.	2019-2020
24th	Bruce R. Harrison, Esq.	1970-1972	51st	James Anthony Towns, Esq.	2020-2021
25th	John McDaniel, Jr., Esq.	1972-1974	52nd	Kendra Perkins Norwood, Esq.	2021-2022
26th	Ruth Hankins-Nesbitt, Esq.	1974-1976	53rd	Dionna Maria Lewis, Esq.	2022-2023
27th	Melvin J. Washington, Esq.	1976-1978	54th	LieAnn T. Van-Tull, Esq.	2023-2024

WBA FOUNDERS: Ulysses Simpson Games, George E. C. Hayes, Charles Hamilton Houston, Isaiah Lisemby, Louis Rothschild Mehlinger, Charles E. Robinson and J. Franklin Wilson

CELEBRATING 100TH ANNIVERSARY!

"Centennial Salute to WBA's Founders, Leadership and Its Legacy of Pursuing Equal Justice Under Law.

PAST CONVENTIONS

NATIONAL BAR ASSOCIATION
EST. 1925

NATIONAL BAR CONVENTIONS SINCE 1980

⏳ 1980s

1989 – Oakland / San Diego
1988 – Washington, DC
1987 – New York, NY
1986 – Denver, Colorado
1985 – Oakland, California
1984 – Atlanta, GA
1983 – San Antonio, TX
1982 – Detroit, MI
1981 – New Orleans, LA
1980 – Dallas, Texas

⏳ 1990s

1999 – Philadelphia, Pennsylvania
1998 – Memphis, Tennessee
1997 – Minneapolis, Minnesota
1996 – Chicago, Illinois
1995 – Baltimore or Philly
1994 – Seattle, Washington
1993 – Boca Raton, Florida
1992 – St. Louis, Missouri
1991 – Indianapolis, Indiana
1990 – Houston, Texas

⏳ 2020s

2025 – Chicago, IL
2024 – Las Vegas, Nevada
2023 – Minneapolis, Minnesota
2022 – Memphis, Tennessee
2021 – VIRTUAL
2020 – VIRTUAL

⏳ 2000s

2009 – San Diego, California
2008 – Houston, Texas
2007 – Atlanta, Georgia
2006 – Detroit, Michigan
2005 – Orlando, Florida
2004 – Charlotte, North Carolina
2003 – New Orleans, Louisiana
2002 – San Francisco, California
2001 – Dallas, Texas
2000 – Washington, DC

⏳ 2010s

2019 – New York, NY
2018 – New Orleans, LA
2017 – Washington, DC
2016 – St. Louis, Missouri
2015 – Los Angeles, California
2014 – Atlanta, Georgia
2013 – Miami, Florida
2012 – Las Vegas, Nevada
2011 – Baltimore, Maryland
2010 – New Orleans, Louisiana

PAST PRESIDENTS

NATIONAL BAR ASSOCIATION
EST. 1925

NBA PAST PRESIDENTS

2020s

2023–2024 Dominique D. Calhoun
2022–2023 Lonita K. Baker
2021–2022 Carlos Moore
2020–2021 Tricia "CK" Hoffler

2010s

2019–2020 Alfreda Robinson
2018–2019 Joe Drayton
2017–2018 Juan R. Thomas
2016–2017 Kevin D. Judd
2015–2016 Benjamin L. Crump
2014–2015 Pamela J. Meanes
2013–2014 Patricia Rosier
2012–2013 John E. Page
2011–2012 Daryl D. Parks
2010–2011 Hon. Demetrius D. Shelton

2000s

2009–2010 Mavis T. Thompson
2008–2009 Rodney G. Moore
2007–2008 Vanita Banks
2006–2007 Linnes Finney, Jr.
2005–2006 Reginald M. Turner, Jr.
2004–2005 Kim M. Keenan
2003–2004 Clyde E. Bailey, Sr.
2002–2003 Malcolm S. Robinson
2001–2002 Michael S. Rosier
2000–2001 Evett L. Simmons

***Note: This summary reflects available information; not all NBA Past Presidents submitted updates or historical information.**

1990s

1999–2000 Harold D. Pope
1998–1999 Beverly McQueary Smith
1997–1998 Randy K. Jones
1996–1997 U. Lawrence Bozé
1995–1996 Keith W. Watters
1994–1995 H.T. Smith
1993–1994 Paulette Brown
1992–1993 Hon. Allen J. Webster, Jr.
1991–1992 Sharon McPhail
1990–1991 Algenita Scott Davis

1980s

1989–1990 Thomas A. Duckenfield
1988–1989 James O. Cole
1987–1988 Dr. Walter L. Sutton, Jr.
1986–1987 Thomas J. Broome
1985–1986 Fred D. Gray
1984–1985 Arthenia L. Joyner
1983–1984 Hon. Dennis W. Archer
1982–1983 Warren Hope Dawson
1981–1982 Hon. Arnette R. Hubbard
1980–1981 William A. Borders, Jr.

1970s

1979–1980 Robert L. Harris
1978–1979 Junius W. Williams
1977–1978 Mark T. McDonald
1976–1977 Hon. Carl J. Character
1975–1976 W. George Allen
1974–1975 Charles Howard
1973–1974 Archie B. Weston, Sr.
1972–1973 O.T. Wells
1971–1972 James W. Cobb
1970–1971 Hon. Edward F. Bell

1960s

1969–1970 Hon. William E. Petersen
1967–1968 Hon. Billy Jones
1965–1967 Hon. Revius O. Ortique
1963–1965 Theodore Coggs
1961–1963 Robert Lillard

NATIONAL BAR ASSOCIATION
EST. 1925

1950s

1959–1961 Elmer C. Jackson
1957–1959 Hon. William Thompson
1955–1957 Hon. Richard Atkinson
1954–1955 Harold Bledsoe
1953–1954 W. Harold Flowers, Sr.
1951–1953 Hon. Scovel Richardson

1940s

1949–1951 James R. Booker
1947–1949 Thurman L. Dodson
1945–1947 Earl R. Dickerson
1943–1945 Charles W. Anderson
1941–1943 Euclid Louis Taylor

1930s

1939–1941 Sidney R. Redmond
1937–1939 William L. Houston
1935–1937 George W. Lawrence
1933–1935 Eugene W. Rhodes
1931–1933 Jesse S. Heslip

1920s

1929–1931 Raymond P. Alexander
1928–1929 C. Francis Stradford
1927–1928 Homer G. Phillips
1926–1927 Charles Calloway
1925–1926 George H. Woodson

NBA President

Junius Williams Esq. 1978-79

-The year of Affirmative Action **-A Speech At The United Nations**

The opinion page

Year of Affirmative Action

Black lawyers urged to help 'oppressed'

TIMES

US LAWYERS CONDEMN RHODESIAN POLLS

- **Youngest Person Elected NBA President**
- **First NBA President to speak at the United Nations, in support of Independence for Zimbabwe, Southern Africa**
- **The NBA Paper on Zimbabwe became an Official UN Document**
- **Founder and 1st. Chair of the modern day Young Lawyers Division**
- **Convened 1st NBA Mid Year Convention (NYC, 1979)**

. . . With Good Friends Forever

JUDGE ARNETTE HUBBARD

NATIONAL BAR ASSOCIATION
PRESIDENT 1981- 1982

"LAW CREATED DISCRIMINATION. LAWYERS CAN DISMANTLE IT."

Arnette Hubbard broke the glass ceiling for women in bar leadership when she became President of the National Bar Association (NBA) in 1981. Of her election Hubbard said:

"The support of women in the NBA who had long worked to break the glass ceiling, especially including the Women Lawyers Division, was critical to victory in a contested election. For women who will succeed me, I dare not fail."

Early in her presidency, she established the National Bar Institute and served as its first Chair. She also initiated the creation of the NBA Medical Legal Committee, made up of lawyers who were also licensed medical doctors. From that committee came the Quadrennial Conference on Health, Law, and Economics.

Renowned civil rights lawyer Fred Gray was appointed as a presidential advisor and led many of the NBA's voting rights efforts. Hubbard traveled the country supporting NBA Affiliate Chapters and advocating for legal equality.

The National Bar Association was incorporated in 1925 by one woman, Attorney Gertrude Darden Rush, and eleven men. During her presidency, Hubbard established the Gertrude Rush Award which remains one of the association's most prestigious honors.

President Hubbard represented the NBA at high levels of government and diplomacy. She led a delegation to meet with U.S. Secretary of State George Schultz. That meeting indirectly led to her securing voting rights for an exiled anti-apartheid leader in Johannesburg, South Africa, for the 1994 All Race Election.

She testified before the U.S. Senate Judiciary Committee in support of Sandra Day O'Connor's nomination to the U.S. Supreme Court—her words preserved in the 1981 Congressional Record. She also met with White House Counsel Fred Fielding to raise concerns about the lack of diversity and transparency in federal judicial appointments. She later joined the President for the Law Day proclamation ceremony from the Rose Garden balcony.

Admitted to the bar in 1969, Hubbard practiced law for decades. She was appointed in 1997 and elected in 1998 as Judge of the Circuit Court in Chicago, Illinois. She retired In December 2022 after 20 years presiding over civil jury trials in the Law Division.
"I am rewiring, not retiring," she said.

Senator Arthenia Joyner

National Bar Association President 1984-1985

A woman whose relentless pursuit of justice began with the Woolworth Sit-Ins in high school, two arrests and incarcerations while in college and continues to this day...

- **Longest Serving Black Woman Lawyer in Florida's History - 56 years**
- **First Black Woman Member of the Hillsborough County Bar Association**
- **First Black Lawyer in Polk County, Florida; First Black Woman Lawyer in Hillsborough County, Florida**
- Co-Founder of NBA Women Lawyers Division (1972)
- Chair of Tampa for Shirley Chisholm's Presidential Campaign (1972)
- Treasurer of the NBA (1973-1983)
- While President of the NBA, arrested for protesting President Reagan's Position on Apartheid in South Africa (1985)
- NBA Board of Directors (1973-1990); Commercial Law Section Chair for 2 terms
- Chair, Jesse Jackson's Presidential Campaigns (1984, 1988)
- Co-Coordinator for Hillsborough County of Lawton Chiles' Gubernatorial Campaign (1990)
- Co-Coordinator for Hillsborough County of Bill Clinton's Presidential Campaign (1992)
- First Black Gubernatorial Appointee to the Hillsborough County Aviation Authority (1991-1995);First Black Chair (1993-1995)
- Gertrude Rush Award Recipient (1994)
- Presidential Appointment to the U.S. Delegation to the International Conference on Population and Development in Cairo, Egypt (1994)
- U.S. Delegation to the United Nations 4th World Conference on Women in Beijing, China (1995)
- Elected to Florida House of Representatives (2000-2008) and Florida Senate (2008-2016)
- First Black Female Florida Senate Minority Leader (2014-2016)
- Equal Justice Award Recipient (2001)
- NBA Prayer Breakfast Named her in honor (2015)
- Hillsborough County Board of County Commissioners names library in her honor (2018)
- C. Francis Stradford Award Recipient (2021)
- Hillsborough County Bar Association Outstanding Lawyer Award and Justice & Diversity Award (2021)
- Leroy Collins Lifetime Achievement Award Recipient from Leadership Florida (2023)
- Virgil Hawkins Florida Chapter's Public Service Award established in her name (2024)

FRED D. GRAY, SR.
A LAWYER'S LAWYER

Civil Rights Champion

Presidential Medal of Freedom Award 2022

Fred D. Gray is one of the nation's leading civil rights attorneys. At age twenty-four, he was the lawyer for Rosa Parks, Martin Luther King Jr., and the Montgomery Bus Boycott, which began the modern Civil Rights Movement. His other cases and clients include the Freedom Riders, the Selma-to-Montgomery March, numerous school desegregation and voting rights lawsuits, and many others.

Algenita SCOTT DAVIS, ESQ.

48th President, National Bar Association
VISIONARY. ADVOCATE. INNOVATOR OF OPPORTUNITY.

With every role she has held—attorney, advocate, executive, educator—Algenita Scott Davis has lived the principles of equity, empowerment, and public service.

Her presidency of the National Bar Association in 1990 marked a transformative era. Under the theme, **"Unity in the Transcentury Nineties,"** Davis championed collaboration across generations and geographies, launching the NBA's International Affiliates Summit—a visionary movement connecting Black legal professionals worldwide. From Dakar to Abidjan, her leadership placed the NBA on a global stage, forging lasting international ties that continue to flourish three decades later.

Her trailblazing journey includes more than 30 positions within the NBA—from Vice President of Affiliates to Secretary, Regional Director, and founder of structural reforms that advanced the association's mission. Her courage helped guide critical institutional stances, including the landmark vote opposing the Thomas nomination.

But her impact extends far beyond the bar.

As General Counsel of the Port of Houston Authority, and later as Senior Vice President of JPMorgan Chase, Davis shaped policy and investment in underserved communities. She led the funding and development of subdivisions, shopping centers, and institutions that today anchor neighborhoods across Houston and the state of Texas.

Her signature is seen in over $500 million in public infrastructure, housing for thousands, and the revitalization of historic areas. As Chair of multiple Redevelopment Authorities and Boards—including Texas Southern University's facilities corporations—her leadership is synonymous with transformation. A native of Houston's Fifth Ward, she is one of two 1967 Phillis Wheatley classmates to lead the NBA. Whether teaching at Texas Southern University or leading Houston Habitat for Humanity, the proud Howard University Law graduate combined legal intellect with unmatched civic devotion.

Her life's work continues to illuminate the path for future generations of lawyers, leaders, and community builders.

Attorneys Attends NBA Confab

"Justice is not only a profession—it is a mission."

—Algenita Scott Davis

U. Lawrence Boze'

54 TH PRESIDENT OF THE NATIONAL BAR ASSOCIATION 1996-1997

- Established the **Legislative Division of the NBA** in 1997
- Hosted luncheon, with **Past-President Fred Gray**, on May 16,1997 for the "eight surviving black men" involved in the **Tuskegee Syphilis Study**. Thereafter, invited to the East Room of the White House to witness President Bill Clinton as he delivered a nationally televised Presidential apology to these eight surviving black men.
- Created the **Roland Harmon Brown International Award of Merit** with the approval of the Brown family.
- Instituted the **Heman Sweatt Luncheon** during the 1997 Mid-Year Conference held in Houston, Texas.
- **Delegate to the 1997 African-African-American Summit** in Harare, Zaire by written invitation of President Bill Clinton. The delegation flew to Zaire on Air Force 2, led by **Reverend Jessie Jackson** and Secretary of Transportation, **Rodney Slater** along with the **Little Rock 8, Dorothy Height** and **Coretta Scott King**.

- Along with **Texas State Senator Royce West** and **Tom Joyner**, created a NBA sponsored legal question and answer program on Tom Joyner's syndicated radio show. Prominent members of the NBA would answer legal questions in their respective areas of legal expertise for radio listeners across the country. Questions were pre-submitted legal questions, read and vetted by law students from Howard, Georgetown and other law schools before being addressed on the radio show.
- Implemented the tradition of the Past President Medallion.
- Texas Board of Law Examiners, appointed by the Texas Supreme Court 1997-2009, only black member of the board and elected to Vice Chair in 2008.

NBA CONVENTION CHICAGO, IL 1996

NU BETA ALPHA CHAPTER

"Forging Alliances In The Uncompromising Fight For Justice And Equality"

Evett Louise Simmons, Esquire
58th President of the National Bar Association

Evett L. Simmons is managing member of Simmons, Finney & Winfield, LLC, a minority-women owned law firm, with offices in Florida and Georgia. She launched her Firm after 18 years of employment as a shareholder and Chief Diversity Officer at Ruden McCloskey which merged with Greenspoon Marder. She received her Undergraduate Degree from Florida Southern College, her Law Degree from Mercer University Walter F. George School of Law, and an Honorary Doctor of Laws from Suffolk University.

For years, Ms. Simmons has practiced primarily estate planning, probate, and guardianship law. She is rated AV Preeminent by Martindale-Hubbell and listed nationally as a Lawyer of Distinction.

Ms. Simmons was the 58th President of the National Bar Association (NBA) and its first President in the new millennium. In 2022, she was admitted into the NBA Hall of Fame. She currently chairs the NBA's Centennial Celebration Commission. In Florida, she was past President of the Florida Chapter of the National Bar Association and chaired the convention when the NBA came to Boca Raton; she served on The Florida Bar Board of Governors. She was the first woman appointed by The Florida Bar to the Judicial Qualifications Commission, a Commission that disciplines judges in Florida; the first African American to Chair The Florida Bar Continuing Legal Education Committee; and served on The Florida Bar Standing Committee on Diversity and Inclusion. She also was active in the American Bar Association (ABA) where she chaired the ABA President's Council on Diversity in the Profession, served as a member of the ABA Diversity Center, was a delegate for the NBA in the ABA House of Delegates, and was an on-site inspector to law schools pertaining to ABA accreditation. Locally, she was the first woman President of the Port St. Lucie Bar Association and the first African American to open a law office in Port St. Lucie.

As President of the NBA, she established the NBA Crump Law Camp and the Evett L. Simmons Mock Trial Competition. For over 20 years, high school students from across the country came to Washington, DC to participate in the Law Camp at Howard University and developed life changing skills.

Ms. Simmons is a Fellow of the American Bar Foundation, a member of The Florida Bar Foundation, and a member of the American Law Institute. For over 20 years, she has served on the Board of Trustees for Florida Southern College in Lakeland, Florida and Chairs the Diversity, Equity and Inclusion Council. In 2013, FSC named the Multicultural Center after her in recognition of her accomplishments.

Since 1992, Ms. Simmons has been President of Unity Property Development Corporation, Inc. which is a multimillion-dollar minority real estate development company owning several commercial and residential properties in Florida.

Boards and organizations on which she has served include Phi Mu Fraternity, Fort Pierce Alumnae Chapter Delta Sigma Theta Sorority, Inc. (past President); PACE Center for Girls of the Treasure Coast; United Way of St. Lucie County; St. Lucie County Chamber of Commerce, Omicron Delta Kappa, Phi Alpha Delta, and Lay Delegate for First United Methodist Church of Port St. Lucie.

Ms. Simmons' awards include the NBA's Gertrude E. Rush Award to honor those who have demonstrated spirit and commitment to mankind; the NBA Sankofa Award for contributing to the legal pipeline; Lawyers of Distinction recognizing excellence in Probate Law, PACE Believing in Girls Embrace Growth & Legacy Award; Mercer University School of Law Alumni of the Year Award; Florida Southern College Alumni Achievement Citation; St. Lucie County United Way Volunteer of the Year Award); The Florida Bar 19th Judicial Circuit Pro Bono Award, and induction into the Fernandina Beach High School Hall of Fame inaugural class.

Ms. Simmons has lectured in probate, guardianship, estate planning and diversity. Her publications include *Inside the Minds, Building and Encouraging Law Firm Diversity, published in 2014 by Thomson Reuters/ Aspatore; A Special Bowl of Oatmeal; The Sunday Before Christmas; Sun Up to Sun Down Revisited Again; and Black History Poems.*

CONGRATULATIONS!

NATIONAL BAR ASSOCIATION

ON YOUR
CENTENNIAL ANNIVERSARY

Congratulations to the National Bar Association on reaching this extraordinary centennial milestone. For 100 years, the NBA has been a powerful force for justice, advocacy, and representation, uplifting Black legal professionals and our communities with unwavering commitment. May the next century build upon this proud legacy with even greater impact.

PAULETTE BROWN

51st President

1993 - 1994

MICHAEL S. ROSIER

59th President of the NATIONAL BAR ASSOCIATION (2001-2002)
"PARTNERS IN PROGRESS - Together We Can Make A Difference"

- **First International Meeting to Italy**
  Hosted by NBA Ambassador at Italian Embassy and met/visited Italian courts and jurists
- **Led NBA delegation to audience at Vatican with the Pope**
- **Led NBA to Cuba to meet with Fidel Castro with Howard University Medical Association**
- **LED NBA and continued its programs and events during the turbulent times Following terrorist attack on the United States on September 11, 2001**
- **Invited to official visit at Ground Zero with New York Government officials**
- **Co-Founder of the Small Firms/Solo Practitioners Division**
- **Partnered with other organizations such as the NAACP, National Medical Association, National Dental Association, and others to address injustices**
- **Listed in Ebony Magazine as a 100 Most Influential Black American**
- **Participant on nationally televised series, "Power of Attorney"**
- **Commencement speaker at Florida A & M University's 2001 Graduation**
- **Led the NBA's efforts for a Moratorium on the Death Penalty**

JAMS Congratulates

Kim M. Keenan, Esq.

Recognizing Her Service As The 62nd National President of the National Bar Association

2004-2005 – Presidential Year:

- Organized the large election protection coalition for a presidential campaign
- Raised over $1M in Corporate Sponsorship
- Created the Cora T. Walker Corporate Partnership Award
- Created the Johnnie Cochran Legends Award
- Testified before Maryland legislature to successfully rename the BWI Airport to the Thurgood Marshall Airport

Recipient of the:

- C. Francis Stratford Award
- Gertrude Rush Award
- Sankofa Award
- Scroll of Distinction Award from the Women Lawyers Division

Kim M. Keenan, Esq., joined the JAMS Washington, D.C. panel in 2020, after an impressive career as a nationally known trial lawyer, mediator and in-house counsel, as well as a recognized leader among multicultural social justice organizations. Ms. Keenan has earned a reputation as a smart, skilled negotiator adept at crafting realistic and sustainable results while always maintaining a calm and balanced demeanor. Currently, she is a founding Director of the Digital Progress Institute, a bi-partisan nonprofit focused on advocating for digital inclusion for every American.

JAMS

Local Solutions.
Global Reach.

2007-2008

National Bar Association President

Vanita M. Banks

65th President of the NBA

"EBONY POWER 150"
Most Influential Blacks in America

President Vanita Banks Capitol Hill Meeting with Senator Richard Durbin, Majority Leader Senator Harry Reid, President-Elect Rodney Moore, Chief Counsel Associate Dean Alfreda Robinson and Juan Thomas, Spring, 2008

Decades of NBA Leadership

- In Fall 2007, President Vanita Banks led a delegation to the White House to advocate for justice for the Jena 6, African American judicial nominees and cabinet officials.

- International Affiliates Meeting: On May 11, 2008, she led a delegation of 60 lawyers, judges and doctors from 12 states to Toronto where she advocated for diversity and inclusion in Bay Street Law Firms. From Toronto, Canada, the Delegation traveled to Havana and Trinidad Cuba during the U.S. embargo on a humanitarian mission to promote civil society, and to build bridges of cooperation and professional affiliation.

- She hosted the Inaugural and largest to date Congressional Black Caucus Foundation Reception at which she presented Awards to 35 members of the Congressional Black Caucus. She emphasized that it is critical that the NBA, the legal conscience of our nation collaborate with the Congressional Black Caucus, the conscience of Congress.

- Under her leadership, the NBA published a Diversity Scorecard of the 27 largest law firms in Illinois.

- She advocated against ABA bar passage Rule 301-6 that would result in an adverse impact on law school accreditation.

- President Banks continues to be actively engaged with the NBA. She serves on the NBA Board of Governors and is Chair of the Civil Trial Advocacy Section, which hosts a full day Boot Camp during the annual Convention and other litigation programs. President Banks sponsors the prestigious NBA Sankofa Award that she conceived with Allstate Insurance Company. Allstate has been an NBA sponsor for 27 consecutive years.

On Capitol Steps with U.S. Representative Stephanie Tubbs Jones, September 25, 2007

President Vanita Banks with Presidential-Candidate Barack Obama, 2008

Past President Vanita Banks delivering Commencement Address at Southern Illinois University Law School in Carbondale, IL, 2009

Gertrude E. Rush Honorees featured in Jet Magazine, Spring 2008.

CONGRATULATIONS
NATIONAL BAR ASSOCIATION ON ITS CENTENNIAL ANNIVERSARY

NOTABLE ACHIEVEMENTS

Led the organization through previous dire financial obligations.

Represented the NBA at the 50th Anniversary of the March On Washington to an audience of over 250,000 people and televised to over 5,000,000 viewers with a call to action to become modern Freedom Riders, to overcome and challenge the stand your ground laws in various states.

Created the NBA Law Academy featuring the Constitution Day Program in partnership with the American Constitution Society. To date, NBA lawyers have taught over 600,000 students about the U.S, Constitution.

Led the NBA to Morocco, pursuant to an invitation by its King to visit and work with the Court of Cassation.

Led the NBA to Brazil to work with grassroot activists in attaining justice and equal rights.

Created a task force to educate and advise about human trafficking, its effects and solutions to eradicate it.

Led NBA members to Botswana to discover trade and business opportunities.

Created the NBA Expungement Project to help affected members of the public regain valuable freedoms and opportunities by removing minor criminal offenses from their records.

Co-founder of the NBA Small Firms / Solo Practitioners Division.

Under my leadership, membership increased culminating in one of the most well attended conventions in Atlanta, Georgia.

PATRICIA MOORE ROSIER

71ST PRESIDENT
2013-2014
"Standing Our Ground For Justice"

ALFREDA ROBINSON

NATIONAL BAR ASSOCIATION 77TH PAST PRESIDENT 2019-2020

Congratulations to the National Bar Association as we proudly celebrate 100 Years of extraordinary service to our Communities and Nation!

It was a distinct honor and pleasure to serve as the National Bar Association President from July 2019 to July 2020. It was a remarkable year despite the COVID-19 pandemic. I had an extraordinary Presidential Lead Team of exceptionally talented, committed, and experienced lawyers and professionals that fully embraced and executed my vision and presidential theme of "Moving Forward Boldly." Therefore, despite COVID restrictions, we were prepared and pivoted as needed to have a very successful Presidential Year.

My Presidential Year was the first almost entirely remote NBA year (seven months) due to the COVID pandemic. I had no roadmap or precedent to adopt or follow. Notwithstanding COVID-19, we leaned in by "Moving Forward Boldly" each day. There were many highlights during that year, including, but not limited to:

1. Achieving an all time NBA highest sponsorship record, that included a single payment of $500,000 by a single sponsor, and matching gifts of approximately $300,000 from others.
2. Planning and executing successfully the first completely remote NBA Convention, when other comparable nonprofits cancelled their annual meetings. It was one of the most financially successful conventions.
3. Hosting the First NBA Black Women's Equity Day nationwide, for which we received a D.C. Mayor Commendation and a D.C. City Council Commendation.
4. Leading the NBA Black Lives Matter National Protest in June 2020, held in the District of Columbia, about which the Washington Post newspaper Editorial Board declared: "Black Lives Matter May Be The Salvation of Democracy."

I thank NBA members for the privilege of having served. Alfreda

Lonita K. Baker

80th

National Bar Association

President

2022-2023

#purplereign

DOMINIQUE D. CALHOUN

81st President

At the 97th Annual Convention, Calhoun was elected president of the National Bar Association, becoming only the sixth Texan and the third youngest individual to hold the position at the time. As president, he prioritized restoring vital relationships with the White House and championing judicial diversity and independence. He represented the NBA before the United Nations in Switzerland, advocating for civil and political rights on a global stage. His administration forged strategic partnerships, expanded international engagement, and achieved one of the most financially successful years in the Bar's history. Calhoun's presidency blended vision with action, legacy with innovation, and diplomacy with determination. As the NBA embarks on its second century, his leadership serves as a call to lead boldly, advocate fearlessly, and build a more just world. Here's to the future — and the next 100 years!

Partnership

Federal Advocacy

Bar Collaboration

International Engagement

EXECUTIVE DIRECTOR EMERITUS

NATIONAL BAR ASSOCIATION®
EST. 1925

EXECUTIVE DIRECTOR EMERITUS

John Crump, JD, CMP, CAE

Executive Emeritus of the National Bar Association (NBA), John Crump received his BA degree in 1967 and his Juris Doctor in 1970 from Texas Southern University and embarked on a 30-year career of service to the bar and the legal profession. From the start, he distinguished himself as a visionary leader of the NBA, increasing its membership and helpin it make an impact by lending monetary support to civil rights attorneys pursuing discrimination cases. Under Crump's leadership, the NBA continued to be a powerhouse for civil rights.

The American Bar Association (ABA) noted Crump's contribution to the NBA and the legal profession, presenting him a Lifetime Achievement Award at its mid-year meeting February 6, 2010, "in recognition of outstanding service to the bar, the profession, and the ABA's goal of eliminating bias and enhancing diversity.

A champion of diversity in the legal profession, Crump always believed that if America is to become a country of inclusion, the legal system must lead the way. To this end, he set out to find a way to motivate young students to seek careers in the legal profession. In 2001, he established the NBA Crump Law Camp to introduce 14–17-year-olds in the 9th through 11th grades to the American Judicial System. Housed at Howard University, the two-week residential program provides students a rigorous academic agenda, exposure to the courts, and lectures by top legal professionals in the nation's capitol. The Crump Law Camp has become the centerpiece of the NBA's effort to "grow lawyers of color" and a model for other bar associations.

As a testament to Crump's commitment to diversity, the Council on Legal Education Opportunity presented him the Diversity Pioneer Award on its 40th anniversary in 2008. Diversity & the Bar Magazine (January/February 2009) chronicled his NBA career and highlighted his contribution to the NBA's development and character. Aso citing his contribution to the NBA, the Washington Bar Association presented him its 2009 president's Recognition Award.

Recipient of numerous awards from civic, professional, and educational organizations throughout his career, Crump says that serving as NBA executive director for three decades was more than a job or title, it was a commitment.

He is married to the former Edythe Traylor, they have one son, Jason, and two granddaughters, Jalyn and Jasmine.

EXECUTIVE EMERITI OFFICERS

NATIONAL BAR ASSOCIATION®
EST. 1925

National Bar Association
EMERITI OFFICERS

ANDREA PAIR BRYANT. SECRETARY EMERITA

July 19. 1942 -March 24, 2012

ANDREA PAIR BRYANT was born in 1942 in Baltimore. Maryland. She attended Howard and Morgan State where she was initiated into Delta Sigma Theta Sorority. Inc. A leader extraordinaire of the National Bar Association, she was vested with the title of Secretary Emerila, after serving as assistant Secretary of the NBA Board of Governors from 1983 to 1988 and Secretary from 1988 to 2000. Among her many other NBA positions. Andrea was Chair of the Intellectual Property Law Section, an officer in the Women Lawyers Division and served on the Board of the National Bar Institute, where she was Chair of its Grant Committee,

JOSEPH H. HAIRSTON. TREASURER EMERITUS

May 8^.1922 -December 23. 2019

JOSEPH H. HAIRSTON with the name Joe Henry Hairston was born in a log cabin in 1922 in Axton. Virginia and grew up in Connellsville. Pennsylvania. Before becoming a lawyer, he was a military man. He joined the Army in 1940, served as an Officer with the 92"'"^ Infantry Division in the Italian Campaign of World War II and became the U.S. Army's first Black helicopter pilot.

Following retirement from the Army, Joe earned two law degrees, becoming an attorney for the federal government and serving as a Division Director in the Internal Revenue Service.

He was a key participant in the Civil Rights Movement, serving as a member of the Reverend Dr. Martin Luther King Jr.'s security detail during the 1963 March on Washington for Jobs and Freedom.

Joe was committed to service, particularly to the National Bar Association as its longest serving Treasurer. He. often, personally kept the doors open when the cash flow was short. Joe was also the parliamentarian and offered classes at the NBA conventions on being a parliamentarian.

C. FRANCIS STRADFORD AWARD

NATIONAL BAR ASSOCIATION
EST. 1925

C. FRANCIS STRADFORD AWARD

The National Bar Association's highest award which is given annually during its convention is the C. Francis Stradford award, in recognition of eminent attorneys and judges within the African American community. This award is named after one of its founders, Cornelius Francis Stradford, who was a pioneering civil rights attorney who paved the way for many African Americans in the legal field. Additionally, he co-founded the Cook County Bar Association.

Stradford was the lead counsel in representing the African American community in a litigation case involving the race riots of Tulsa, Oklahoma, in 1921. His many accomplishments, including his unwavering dedication to securing full and equal protection under the law for the African-America community, have, and will continuously give rise to, and serve as an inspiration for his community.

The following criteria are employed in selecting the C. Francis Stradford Award recipients:

- **Leadership, Honor, Integrity, and Fairness**
- **Community Involvement and Activism**
- **Charity and/or Pro Bono work**
- **Youth Involvement and/or Mentorship Programs**

Over the years, many distinguished attorneys have received this award such as Willie E. Gary, Alfreda Robinson, Fred D. Gray, Theodore V. Wells, Jr., Patricia Rosier, Keith Watters, Kim Keenan, John Page, Pamela Meanes and Vanita Banks to name just a few.

GERTRUDE RUSH AWARD RECIPIENTS

NATIONAL BAR ASSOCIATION
EST. 1925

NATIONAL BAR ASSOCIATION ANNUAL GERTRUDE E. RUSH AWARD DINNER

Saturday, May 22, 1982

Sheraton Washington Hotel
Cotillion Ballroom

National Bar Association

FOUNDERS

*George C. Adams
*Jesse N. Baker
*S. Joe Brown
*Charles H. Calloway
*Wendell E. Green
*William H. Haynes
*Charles P. Howard, Sr.
*L. Amasa Knox
*James B. Morris
*Gertrude E. Rush
*C. Francis Stradford
*George H. Woodson

OFFICERS
1981–1982

Arnette R. Hubbard, *President*
Warren H. Dawson, *President-Elect*
Harrison Gregg, Jr., *Vice President*
Frank Seales, Jr., *Vice President*
Dwight Tillery, *Vice President*
Vince Monroe Townsend, *Vice President*
Walter L. Sutton, Jr., *Secretary*
Arthenia L. Joyner, *Treasurer*

THE NATIONAL BAR ASSOCIATION
Founded 1925

During the first quarter of the twentieth century, twelve Black Americans, with a mutual interest in and dedication to justice and civil rights for all, helped structure the struggle of the Black race in America. The National Bar Association (NBA), formally organized in Des Moines, Iowa on August 1, 1925, was conceived by such legal pioneers as George H. Woodson, S. Joe Brown, Gertrude E. Rush, James B. Morris, Charles P. Howard, Sr., Wendell E. Green, C. Francis Stradford, Jesse N. Baker, William H. Haynes, George C. Adams, Charles H. Calloway, and L. Amasa Knox.

The purpose of the National Bar Association is ". . . to advance the science of jurisprudence, uphold the honor of the legal profession, promote social intercourse among the members of the bar, and protect the civil and political rights of all citizens of the several states of the United States."

Legions of Black lawyers affiliated with the NBA ushered the rule of law through the turbulent 1920's and 1930's and remain in the vanguard working for justice in the 1980's.

When the NBA was organized in 1925, there were fewer than 1,000 Black lawyers in the nation, and at that time, only one of every 86 Blacks belonged to the Association. By 1945, there were approximately 250 dues-paying members — nearly 25% of the Black members of the bar. Over the past 57 years, the NBA has grown enormously in size and influence. Our network of over 8,500 lawyers, judges, law faculty and administrators, and students has made significant strides. Our affiliate chapter network now numbers 48.

Today, the NBA Board of Governors formulates the Association's policies. It consists of the officers, ten regional directors, five former NBA presidents, eleven members-at-large, five division representatives, one representative from each of the special interest sections, and seven affiliate chapter representatives, which address problems, needs and goals of minority lawyers.

HONORARY DINNER COMMITTEE

Dr. J. Clay Smith, Jr., *Chairman*
William T. Coleman, Esq.
Daryl F. Grishman
Walter J. Leonard, Esq.
The Honorable Wade H. McCree
Ruby B. McZier, Esq.
Reverend Claude J. Murphy
June Acie Rhinehart, Esq.
Otis M. Smith, Esq.
Andrew L. Thomas, M.D.

DINNER COMMITTEE

Frank Seales, Jr., Esq., *Chairman*
Thomas A. Duckenfield, Esq.
Carolyn Y. Howard, Esq.
Belva D. Newsome, Esq.
Gloria Sulton, Esq.
John A. Turner, Jr., Esq.
Leroy Wilson, Jr., Esq.

THE OCCASION

After 57 years as a force in the struggle for justice and equality, the National Bar Association pauses to recognize a woman who dedicated her life to these ideals. Gertrude E. Rush, the only woman co-founder of the National Bar Association was born ahead of her time. She did not, however, wait for times to change. Instead, she acted as a catalyst for change, setting goals for herself and those who worked alongside her.

The times dictated that a woman of such strength and intellect would be a pioneer — the first Black woman to practice law in the state of Iowa. The label "first Black woman" carried with it a responsibility. A responsibility to one's race to continue to achieve. Mrs. Rush lived up to this responsibility, excelling in several arenas: law, community service, education, and religion.

She was a gifted woman. Her ability to mobilize others made her a leader in the Des Moines community. She founded social service organizations to meet the needs of Des Moines' Black community and was equally involved in several projects simultaneously. A widow, Mrs. Rush kept busy by giving of herself. She developed her own talents as she inspired others to be creative.

The zeal with which she approached her civic duties was reflected in her contributions to the religious community. Having been raised in the Baptist tradition, Gertrude Rush was a disciple for our times. Her life serves as an example for all. I thank you for joining me this evening to honor this truly unique individual.

Arnette R. Hubbard, Esq.
President
National Bar Association

PROGRAM

Master of Ceremonies .... Wiley A. Branton, Dean
Howard University School of Law

Processional, Introduction of Dais Guests

Invocation .... Rev. Robert L. Pruitt
Metropolitan AME Church

Call to Dinner

Music .... Gregg Lamont Trio

Tribute to Recipients .... Dr. J. Clay Smith, Jr.
Presentation of Awards .... Arnette R. Hubbard
President, NBA

Sadie T. Alexander, *Esquire*
Gwendolyn Brooks, *Poetess*
Arthur D. Shores, *Esquire*
Edward B. Toles, *Judge*

Lift Every Voice and Sing

Benediction .... Rev. Robert L. Pruitt

MENU

Fresh Melon Wedge

Esquire Salad, Hearts of Romaine and Spinach Leaves with Tomato Wedges, Bacon Bits, Egg Slices, and Toasted Croutons, Gourmet Dressing

Club Steak, Maitre d'Hotel
Oven Roasted Potatoes
Asparagus au Beurre
Broiled Tomato

Baked Alaska with Chocolate Sauce

Rolls and Butter

Coffee, Tea, Sanka, or Milk

GERTRUDE E. RUSH, Esquire
1880-1962

Gertrude E. Rush, the only woman co-founder of the National Bar Association was born on August 5, 1880 in Navasota, Texas. She attended Parson Kansas High School from 1895 to 1899 and was graduated with a Bachelors degree from Des Moines College in 1914. After teaching school for many years, Mrs. Rush began the study of law under the tutelage of her husband, James B. Rush. In 1918, just 25 days after Mr. Rush's death, Mrs. Rush passed the Iowa Bar examination, becoming the first Black woman to practice law in that state. Mrs. Rush practiced law in Des Moines at 907 Walnut Street.

Through her participation in civic groups, Mrs. Rush assumed a leadership role in the Des Moines community. She was president of the Iowa State Federation of Colored Women's Clubs (1911-15), a charter member of the Des Moines Health Center, chairperson of the Mother's Department and the Legislative Department of the National Association of Colored Women, and secretary of the Des Moines Comfort Station Commission (1924-26). In 1912, Mrs. Rush formed the Charity League, a welfare organization for Blacks, which influenced the appointment of a "colored" probation officer in the Juvenile Court of Des Moines. Mrs. Rush was a founder of the Parliamentary Law and Culture Club and helped organize the Des Moines chapter of the National Association for the Advancement of Colored People.

A devoted church worker, Gertrude Rush was a member and trustee of Corinthian Baptist Church. Mrs. Rush also wrote music and lyrics for religious hymns. Two of her songs were published: "If You But Knew" (1905), and "Jesus Loves Little Children" (1907). She served as attorney for the Women's Auxiliary of the National Baptist Convention and chaired the Baptist Convention's Citizenship Department. Mrs. Rush died on September 5, 1962.

Gertrude E. Rush preached and practiced the gospel through coalition building. She used her God-given talents and professional skills to better the conditions of Black Iowans. Her life is a symbol of the quest by minorities in the legal profession of full participation in the American system of jurisprudence.

Excerpts from *Gertrude E. Rush: Co-Founder of the NBA*, by Dr. J. Clay Smith, Jr., *The National Bar Bulletin*, Vol. 13, Nos. 6 and 7, June/July, 1981.

GERTRUDE E. RUSH

Past Recipients

1982
Sadie T. Alexander, Esquire
Gwendolyn Brooks, Poetess
Arthur D. Shores, Esquire
Honorable Edward B. Toles

1983
Thomas L. Berkley, Esquire
Honorable Jane M. Bolin
Virgil D. Hawkins, Esquire
Arnette R. Hubbard, Esquire

1984
Honorable George W. Crockett
Cora T. Walker, Esquire
Lt. General Julius Wesley Becton, Jr.

1985
Honorable Shirley A. Chisholm
Reverend Jesse L. Jackson
Honorable William S. Thompson
Honorable Maynard H. Jackson
Honorable Charles B. Rangel

1986
James Allen Parker, Esquire
Joe L. Reed, Educator
Honorable L. Douglas Wilder

1987
Honorable Willie L. Brown Jr.
Donald Lee Hollowell, Esquire
Honorable Lucia T. Thomas

1988
Honorable Louis A. Bedford, Jr.
Honorable Ruth Hankins-Nesbitt
Honorable W. Harold Flowers, Sr.
Honorable Percy E. Sutton

1989
Ronald H. Brown, Esquire
Honorable Parren J. Mitchell
Honorable John H. Stroger, Jr.

1990
Honorable David N. Dinkins
Honorable Perlesta A. Hollingsworth
Donald M. Temple, Esquire
Faustine C. Jones-Wilson, Ph.D.
Althea T.L. Simmons, Esquire

1991
Reverend Dr. Benjamin F. Chavis
Comer J. Cottrell, Jr.
Honorable Revius O. Ortique, Jr.
Ruby Burrows McZier, Esquire
Honorable Carrie P. Meek

1992
Brig. General Clara L. Adams-Ender
Arthur L. Johnson, Ph.D.
Fredda Witherspoon, Ph.D.
Warren Hope Dawson, Esquire
Elaine R. Jones, Esquire

1993
Honorable Vince M. Townsend
Roland W. Burris, Esquire
Honorable Maxine Waters
Honorable Dwight Tillery
Honorable Theresa Hughes
Reverend Cecil L. Murray, Rel. D.

1994
Honorable Donald Payne
Honorable William F. Hall, Jr.
Professor Lani Guinier
Arthenia L. Joyner, Esquire

1995
Algenita Scott Davis, Esquire
Honorable Joseph W. Hatchett
Jesse J. McCrary, Jr., Esquire
Honorable Leander J. Shaw, Jr.

1996
Johnnie L. Cochran, Jr., Esquire
Thomas A. Duckenfield, Esquire
Juanita Jackson Mitchell, Esquire
Honorable Hazel R. O'Leary
Dr. J. Clay Smith, Jr.
Honorable Wayman F. Smith, III

1997
Wade J. Henderson, Esquire
Honorable Barbara C. Jordan
Honorable Kweisi Mfume
Frank Seales, Jr., Esquire
Honorable Rodney E. Slater
Dr. Walter S. Sutton, Jr.

GERTRUDE E. RUSH

Past Recipients

1998
Honorable Sharon Sayles Belton
Reverend George Benjamin Brooks, Sr.
Dr. Authur Fletcher
Major General (Ret.) Kenneth D. Gray
Robert L. Johnson
Honorable Benjamin J. Travis

1999
Honorable Kenneth N. Browne
Honorable Veronica Simmons McBeth
Honorable Gregory W. Meeks
Honorable George Bundy Smith
Honorable Sonia Sotomayor

2000
Honorable John Conyers
Elliott S. Hall
Honorable Alexis Herman
Honorable Anne Diggs Tayior

2001
L. Marilyn Crawford, Esquire
Tom Joyner
Honorable Janet Reno
H. T. Smith, Esquire

2002
Honorable Robert M. Bell
Honorable Roger L. Gregory
Honorable Joseph C. Howard, Sr.
Honorable Peggy A. Quince

2003
Charlye O. Farris, Esquire
Robert J. Grey, Jr., Esquire
Honorable Harriet M. Murphy

2004
Alice G. Bullock, Esquire
Frankie Muse Freeman, Esquire
Honorable John R. Lewis
Ernestine S. Sapp, Esquire

2005
Linda Spradley Dunn, Esquire
Mabel D. Haden, Esquire
Oliver W. Hill, Sr., Esquire
Hon. Stephanie Tubbs Jones
Honorable Robert C. Scott
Honorable Annice M. Wagner

2006
R. Larry Brown
Honorable Earnestine H. Dorse
Honorable Benjamin L. Hooks
Honorable H.T. Lockard
Ruby R. Wharton, Esquire

2007
Evett L. Simmons, Esquire
Charles J. Ogletree, Jr.,
Henry Latimer, Esquire
Louis Gossett, Jr.
Dr. Johnnetta B. Cole

2008
Lerone Bennett, Jr.
Honorable Williams Cousins, Jr. (Ret.)
Honorable Emil Jones, Jr.
Linda Johnson Rice
Honorable Ann Claire Williams

2009
Honorable Joyce London Alexander Ford
Jeff L. Greenup, Esquire
Honorable Barbara Lee
Honorable Theodore T. Jones

2010
Paulette Brown, Esquire
Margaret Bush Wilson, Esquire
Willie E. Gary, Esquire
Honorable Charles Shaw
Cleota Proctor Wilbekin, Esquire

2011
Barbara R. Arnwine, Esquire
Robert L. Harris, Esquire
Honorable Thelton E. Henderson
G. William "Billy" Hunter, Esquire
Eva Paterson, Esquire

2012
Honorable Alice Bonner
Tony Dungy
Bishop C. Holifield, Esquire
Marilyn J. Holifield, Esquire
Honorable Mary S. Scriven
Carolyn House Stewart, Esquire
Honorable Karla Foreman Wright

GERTRUDE E. RUSH

Past Recipients

2013
Kim K.W. Rucker, Esquire
Karol Corbin Walker, Esquire
Thomas J, Sabatino, Jr., Esquire
Honorable Allen J. Webster, Jr.
Brad Smith, Esquire
Michael A. Lawson, Esquire

2014
Honorable Wayne K. Cuny Curry
Honorable Angela D. Alsobroak
Vanita M. Banks, Esquire
Honorable Eric Holder, Jr.
Honorable Michele D. Hotten
Allie B. Latimes, Esquire
Honorable Gloria L. Lawlah
Keith W. Watters, Esquire
Honorable Robert L. Wilkins
Honorable Alexander Williams, Jr.

2015
Honorable Emmanuel Cleaver
Bryan Stevenson, J.D.
Honorable Ronnie L. White
Barbara A. Washington, CSEP

2016
Yolanda Cash Jackson, Esquire
Honorable Alcee Hastings
Eugene Pettis, Esquire
Juliet Roulhac, Esquire
Honorable Emerson Thompson

2017
Professor John C. Brittain
Vice Admiral James W. Crawford
Kim M. Keenan
Joyce Ann Hanks Moorehead
William H. Billy Murphy
William "Bill" C.E. Robinson
Grace Speights
Honorable Emmet G. Sullivan

2018
James Montgomery, Esquire
Mavis Thompson, Esquire
Diane Nash, Esquire
Dr. Jeremiah Wright, Jr.
Lawrence Kennon, Esquire

2019
Honorable Harrison Greg, Jr.
Sonya D. Hoskins, Esquire
Honorable Bernette Joshua Johnson
Sadiqa N. Reynolds

2020
NBA Past President Daryl D. Parks, Esquire
Honorable Eleanor L. Ross
Honorable Clarence Copper
Avarita L. Hanson, Esquire
Honorable Justice Robert Benham
Juanita P. Baranco, Esquire
NBA Vice President Nathaniel Lee, Esquire

2021
Thomas G. Sampson, Sr.
M. Gino Brogdon, Sr
David Green
Dawn M. Jones
Tanya Clay House, Esquire
Leslie Fields
Bruce Jackson

2023
J. Michael Brown
Honorable Denise G. Clayton
Benjamin Crump
Honorable Bernice Donald
Laura Douglas
Senator Gerald Neal
Marilyn Mosby
Senator Reginald Thomas

2024
Ricky Anderson, Esquire
Honorable Jasmine Crockett
Honorable L. Clifford Davis
Vanessa D. Gilmore
Harry L. Johnson, Sr., Esquire
Cynthia (Cynt) Marshall

2025
Honorable Romoda Belcher
Roxanne Barton Conlin
Honorable Odell McGhee
Juan R. Thomas, Esquire

FRED D. GRAY HALL OF FAME INDUCTEES

NATIONAL BAR ASSOCIATION
EST. 1925

Hall of Fame Inductees

1986
John Adams, Jr., Esq.
Hon. Elreta Alexander-Ralston
Dr. Sadie T. M. Alexander, Esq.
Joseph J. Attwell, Esq.
Lawrence B. Bailey, Sr., Esq.
Hon. Richard L. Baltimore, Jr.
Thomas L. Berkeley, Esq.
Louis Berry, Esq.
Theodore M. Berry, Esq.
Hon. Jane Bolin, Esq.
Hon. Amos Bowman, Esq.
Harry O. Bright, Esq.
Oscar C. Brown, Esq.
Wyatt C. Brownlee, Esq.
Edward M. Byrd, Esq.
Fred J. Carnage, Esq.
Charles V. Carr, Esq.
Hon. Robert L. Carter
Thomas P. Clarke, Esq.
Hon. George W. Crockett, Jr.
Jesse O. Dedmon, Jr., Esq.
Earl B. Dickerson, Esq.
Hon. Edward R. Dudley
Hon. Joseph E. Dyer
Hon. Dennis Edward, Jr.
Fred H. Elliot, Esq.
Hon. W. Harold Flowers, Sr.
Hon. Walter H. Gladwin
Harry H.C. Gibson, Esq.
Truman K. Gibson, Esq.
Everett I. Hall, Esq.
Houston H. Hall, Esq.
Hon. Oliver Hill
Hon. Elmer C. Jackson, Jr.
Hon. Bernard Jefferson
Hon. Billy Jones
John T. Jones, Esq.
Hon. Sidney A. Jones
Hon. Robert Lillard
Hon. Mercer M. Mance
Hon. Thurgood Marshall
Hon. William A. McClain
William T. McKnight, Esq.
James A. McLendon, Esq.
Louis Rothschild Mehlinger, Esq.
Archie Mills, Esq.
Coleman C. Moore, Esq.
Alvin H. Moss, Esq.
George B. Nesbitt, Esq.
W. Lawrence Oliver, Esq.
Hon. Hubert B. Pair
Aaron H. Payne, Esq.
Hon. William E. Peterson
Hon. Cecil F. Poole
Henry E. Quales, Sr., Esq.
Willard B. Ransom, Esq.
Hon. R. J. Reynolds
Hon. Spottswood W. Robinson, III
Hon. Jawn A. Sandifer
Arthur D. Shores, Esq.
Charles C. Spaulding, Esq.
Hon. Harold A. Stevens
Herman L. Taylor, Esq.
L. E. Thomas, Esq.
Hon. Lucia T Thomas
Hon. William S. Thompson
Hon. Edward B. Toles
Vince M. Townsend, Jr., Esq.
Samuel W. Tucker, Esq.

1987
No inductees

1988
Herbert L. Dudley, Esq.
Vanue B. Lacour, Esq.
John W. Langford, Esq.
James J. Sansom, Jr., Esq.
Cora T. Walker, Esq.

1989
John Adams, Jr., Esq.
William S. Mayfield, Esq.
R J. Reynolds, Esq.
Hon. Clinton W. White

1990
Frankie Muse Freeman, Esq.
Melton M. Lewis, Esq.
Hon. H. T. Lockard
John Hamlin Rennick, Esq.
Hon. Nathan B. Young

1991
Irving P. Andrews, Esq.
Louis A. Bedford, Jr. , Esq.
Lawrence W. Carroll, Esq.
Hon. Harry A. Cole
Nathaniel S. Colley, Esq.
John T. Dixon, Esq.
Hon. Richard C. Erwin
Hon. Marion W. Garnett
Harry E. Groves, Esq.
Mabel D. Haden, Esq.
Ruth E. Hankins-Nesbitt, Esq.
Hon. James L. Harris
Hon. Evelyn F. Johnson
Hon. Glenn T. Johnson
Hon. George N. Leighton
John Morton-Finney, Esq.
Hon. James B. Parsons
Hon. William E. Peterson
Robert C. Power, Esq.
Hon. D. Adolphus Rivers
Hon. Juanita Kidd Stout
Hon. William S. Thompson
Francis Williams, Esq.
Robert L. Witherspoon *

1992
Harvey E. Beech, Esq.
Hon. Clyde S. Cahill
Curtis C. Crawford, Esq.
Stuart J. Dunnings, Jr., Esq.
Wilson Gray, Esq.
Hon. Billy Jones *
Annie Brown Kennedy, Esq.
Harold L. Kennedy, Jr., Esq.
J. Kenneth Lee, Esq.
Hon. Theodore McMillan
Charles R. Oldham, Esq.
Daniel G. Sampson, Esq.

1993
Oscar W. Adams, Esq.
Phillip L. Burton, Esq.
Carl A. Earles, Esq.
Wendell G. Freeland, Esq.
Hon. Sara J. Harper

1994
Hon. Solomon Baylor
Louis Berry, Esq.
Hilbert L. Bradley, Esq.
Hon. Carl J. Character
Eddie M. Cole, Esq.
James Romeo Corley, Esq.
Hon. William Cousins, Jr.
Hon. Calvin H. Hall
W. Theophilus Jones, Esq.

Hall of Fame Inductees

Thornton J. Meacham, Jr., Esq.
Willard B. Ransome, Esq.
Charles M. Stokes, Esq.
J. Warren Watson, Esq.
Avon N. Williams, Esq.

1995
Frederick M. Douglass, Esq.
Robert V. Franklin, Esq.
Willie S. Glanton, Esq.
Hon. Albert J. Grant
Fred D. Gray, Esq.
Hon. John R. Hargrove, Sr.
Oscar E. Jones, Esq.
Lena K. Lee, Esq.
Hon. Edith Miller
William H. Murphy, Sr., Esq.
Hon. Odas Nicholson
Lawrence Olivier, III, Esq.
Hon. Matthew J. Perry
L. Steven Robinson, Esq.
George L. Russell, Esq.
Hon. Louis Stokes
Hon. Jack E. Tanner
Jay B. White, Esq.
Charles E. Williams, Esq.
Robert A. Wright, Esq.

1996
Hon. Lewis W. Clymer
Hon. George D. Covington
Alfonso C. Fuller, Esq.
Lawrence E. Kennon, Esq.
Caesar Cooleridge Latimer, Esq.
Hon. John T. Letts
Alphonse Lewis, Esq.
James D. Montgomery, Esq.
Earl L. Neal, Esq.
Hon. James Lopez Watson

1997
Hon. Weldon H. Berry, Sr.+
Hurbert H. Bryant, Esq.
Hon. L. Clifford Davis
A. Glenn Epps, Esq.
Hon. Addeliar D. Guy *
Douglas Hall, Esq.
Roberson L. King, Esq. *

1998
Hon. Richard Bancroft
Hon. Paul L. Brady
Earl Carl, Esq. *
Hon. Earl B. Gilliam
Herbert H. Henderson, Esq.
The Reverend Benjamin L. Hooks, Esq.
Hon. Charles V. Johnson
Hon. Robert N. C. Nixdr
Hon. Revius Ortique, Jr.
Hon. Paul Webber, III

1999
Hon. Howard E. Belk
Hon. Clarence D. Bolden
Charles W. Bowser, Esq.
William H. Brown, III, Esq.
Hon. Arthur L. Burnett, Sr.
Hon. Jesse H. Butler
Mahala Ashley Dickerson, Esq.
Hon. Clifford S. Green
Jeff L. Greenup, Esq. he
Hon. A. Leon Higginbotham, Jr.*
James E. Jones, Esq.
Allie B. Latimer, Esq.
Hon. Theodore R. Newman, Jr.
Raleigh R. Rawls, Esq.
Hon. Handy Williams

2000
Simon L. Cain, Esq.
Clinton W. Chapman, Esq.
James Cobb, Sr., Esq.
Harvey McCormick, Esq.
John McDaniel, Esq.
P. Tureaud, Esq.
Hon. William Wallace
O. T. Wells, Esq

2001
Hon. Charles H. Anderson
Thomas James "CJ" Cunningham, Esq.
Charlye O. Farris, Esq.
Joseph H. Hairston, Esq.
Ollen B. Hinnant, II, Esq.
Hon. Horace T. Ward

2002
Hon. Willie L. Brown, Jr.
Hon. George D. Carroll
Leroy W. Daggs, Esq.
Hon. John Dearman
Donald L. Hollowell, Esq.
Hon. Nathaniel R. Jones
Carl B. Metoyer, Esq.
Hiawatha T. Roberts, Esq.
Hon. Roosevelt Robinson
Hon. Benjamin Travis'
Hon. Marcus O. Tucker

2003
W. George Allen, Esq.
Hon. Nils Raymond Douglas
Hon. Elrich Allen Eastman
Hon. Loils Edward Elie
John O' Connor Moss, Jr., Esq.
Mark T. McDonald, Esq.
Hon. James Nathaniel Reese

2004
Sylvia X. Allen, Esq.
Hon. Taylor L. Baker, Jr.
Calvin L. Brown, Esq.
Julius L. Chambers, Esq.
Hon. Sammie Chess, Jr.
Hon. Henry E. Frye

2005
James A. Crumlin, Sr. Esq.*
Hon. Josephn W. Hatchett
Jack H. Olender, Esq.
Hon. Leander Shaw, Jr.
Delano S. Stewart, Esq.
Hon. Horace Wheatley

2006
Hon. Christopher C. Brown
Hon. Geraldine Bledsoe Ford*
Hon. Harold Hood
Hon. Damon J. Keith
Peter J. Randolph, Esq.
Hon. Anna Diggs Taylor

2007
Hon. Clarence Cooper
Warren Hope Dawson, Esq.
Hon. Louise Thornton Hornsby
Senator Leroy Johnson
Cornell Leverette Moore, Esq.
Howard Moore, Esq.
Hon. John H. Ruffin, Jr.

2008
Hon. Alice A. Bonner
Joan A. Burt, Esq.
William J. Durham, Esq.
Hon. Theodore Johns
Hon. Raymond Jordan
Hon. Gabrielle Kirk McDonald
Hon. Eileen R. Peterson
Bobby Stafford, Esq.

2009
Hon. Reuben V. Anderson
Hon. Fred L. Banks, Jr.
Leo A. Branton, Jr.
Rev. Frank E. Breckenridge, Esq.
Ben E. Espy, Esq.
Walter L. Gordon, Esq.
Hon. Arnette R. Hubbard
Hon. Arthenia L. Joyner
Glenwood P. Roane, Sr., Esq.
Hon. George Bundy Smith
Myzell Sowell, Esq.
Junius Williams, Esq.

Hall of Fame Inductees

2010
Nelson Atkins, Esq.
Irwin Evans, Esq.
Dr. Norman C. Francis
Constance Slaughter-Harvey, Esq.
Justice Bernette J. Johnson
Hon. Harriett M. Murphy
Hon. John Peavy
Hon. Inez Smith Reid
Solomon Seay, Esq.
Dr. Walton Sutton, Jr.
Hon. Walter Williams

2011
Hon. Robert M. Bell
Hon. Arrie W. Davis
William Murphy, Jr., Esq.
David B. Allen, Esq.
John S. Wood, Esq.
Alvin O. Chambliss, Jr., Esq.
Hon. Thelma Wyatt Cummings Moore
Edward Gray, Esq.
James Coles, Esq.
Leroy Wilson, Jr., Esq.
Taylor Fields, Esq.

2012
James Matthew Douglas, Esq.
Hon. Harrison Gregg, Jr.
Oliver Lofton, Esq.
James O. Porter, Esq.
Hon. Allen Webster, Jr.

2013
Hon. Patricia Banks
Shirley Stewart Farmer, Esq.
Hon. Donald J. Floyd
Robert L. Harris, Esq.
Raymond Howard, Jr., Esq.
Hon. Benjamin H. Logan
Hon. Veronica Morgan-Price
H. T. Smith, Esq.
Clyde Williams, Jr., Esq.

2014
Hon. Robert Benham
Rep. Sanford D. Bishop, Jr.
Willie E. Gary
Jo M. Glasco, Esq.
Elihu M. Harris
Shirley A. Henderson
George Holland, Sr.
Charles S. Johnson, III
Janice Orr, Esq.
Hon. Freddie Pitcher, Jr.
Thomas G. Sampson

2015
Algenita Scott Davis, Esq.
Thomas J. Broome, Esq.
Hon. Zinetta Arceneaux Burney
Hon. Candice D. Cooper
Anne L. Fredd, Esq.
A. Martin Wickliff, Jr. Esq.
Alfred Henry Rhodes, Esq.
A. Dwight Pettit, Esq.
Hon. Charles Scarlett
William H. Hastie, Jr. Esq.
Hon. Veronice S. McBeth
Hon. Craig Strong
Hon. Irma J. Brown

2016
Hon. Morris Overstreet
Hon. Bonnie Joye Fitch
Hon. Johnnie Hardwick
Hon. Wayman Flynn Smith, III
James Neely, Esq.
Hon. Booker Shaw
Hon. Bruce F. Weekes
Gilbert King, Jr. Esq.
MacArthur Drake, Esq.
Eleanor Darden Thompson, Esq.
Kaydell Wright-Douglas, Esq.

2017
John Burris, Esq.
Hon. Prince Cartwright
Hon. Carr L. Darden
Hon. Gerald Bruce Lee
Debra Matlock, Esq.
Otis McGee, Esq.
Hon. Peggy A. Quince
Hon. Justice Rucker
Hon. Mary Maxwell Thomas

2018
Linda Copeland Drake, Esq.
Hon. Ernestine Steward Gray
Hon. L. Priscilla Hall
Johnnie Landon, Esq.
Wayne J. Lee, Esq.
Hon. Ivan L. R. Lemelle
Prof. Emerita Beverly McQueary Smith
Hon. Gerald A. Neal
Hon. Gammiel Gray Poindexter
Ernestine Stubblefield Sapp, Esq.
Hon. Carl E. Stewart
Carolyn House Stewart, Esq.
Lorenzo Williams, Esq.

2019
James Townsley Breedlove, Esq.
Paulette Brown, Esq.
Honorable Anne-Marie Clarke
Regina Darby
Honorable Joyce London Alexander Ford
Iris McCollum Green, Esq.
Elton Lester, Esq.
Melvin McWilliams, Esq.
Wilma J. Pinder, Esq.
Kenneth G. Standard, Esq.
Honroable Sharon Strickland
Nina Wells, Esq.
Theodore Wells, Esq.
Honorable Anne Claire Williams

2020
Donald A. Thigpen, Jr.

2021
Avarita Hanson
James Michael Haygood
George Knox
Judge Bobbi Tilmon
Judge Gary Jackson

2022
Hon. Yvette Mansfield Alexander
Lawrence Boze Esq.
Rodney Ellis Esq.
William Harold Flowers, Jr. Esq.
Hon. Al Green
Hon Mary Ellen Hicks
Nelson Marion Jones, III Esq.
Hon Shelia Jackson Lee
Joyce Ann Gates Mitchell, Esq.
Hon. Denise Sweet Owens
Michael S. Rosier, Esq.
Patricia Moore Rosier Esq.
Frank Seales, Jr. Esq.
Ray L. Shackelford, Esq.
Evett L. Simmons, Esq.
Paula Sellars Tillman, Esq.
Honorable Emerson R. Thompson, JR.
Jacqueline A. Walker, Esq.
Hon. Carolyn Wright-Sanders
Royce West Esq.

2023
Hon. Clayton Graham
Norma Hutcheson
Grace Speights
V. Lynn Whitfield

2024 Fred D. Gray
Hall of Fame Inductees

Richard Austin

Hon. Willie E.B. Blackmon

Randy K. Jones, 55th President of the National Bar Association

Belinda D. Stith

Benjamin F. Wilson

NATIONAL BAR ASSOCIATION
EST. 1925

2025 Fred D. Gray
Hall of Fame Honorees

Honorable Cynthia J. Ayers (Posthumous)

Clyde E. Bailey, Sr. (Posthumous)

Vanita M. Banks, NBA President (2007–2008)

Honorable Robert L. Bell

Margo Bouchet

Honorable Steven Brister, J.M.C.

Honorable Sharon V. Burrell

Honorable L. Clifford Davis (Posthumous)

Beverly F. Druitt, Esq.

Honorable Mablean Ephriam

Charlye O. Farris (Posthumous)

Linnes Finney, Jr., NBA President (2006–2007)

Jenice Golson-Dunlap

Honorable Marcella Holland

Jason Holt

Honorable Gregory Eugene Jackson

Nathaniel Lee

Valerie D. Lewis

Hon. Denise Langford Morris

Harold Pope, NBA President (1999–2000)

William C.E. Robinson

Vickie Turner

Honorable Monte Watkins

THE NATIONAL BAR ASSOCIATION CRUMP LAW CAMP

NATIONAL BAR
ASSOCIATION®
EST. 1925

IN THE BEGINNING:
Growing Our Own Lawyers

The National Bar Association Crump Law Camp was established in 2000 under the leadership of Past President Evett L. Simmons as a means of addressing the declining enrollment of minorities in law schools, particularly African Americans, The Board of Governors named the Law Camp after Executive Director John Crump to recognize his twenty-five (25) years of service with the Bar.

Sadly, African Americans represent only about four (4%) of the total number of lawyers and judges in the United States. Hispanics, Asian-Pacific and Native Americans jointly comprise about an additional eight (8%) percent. Yet, the United States is not that many years away from becoming a country whose majority is comprised of minorities.

To instill confidence in the legal system, a legal profession of diverse lawyers and judges invested with the responsibility of interpreting and enforcing the laws of this country is critical for governing a multi-cultural, multi-ethnic society. In her acceptance speech. Past President Simmons made it clear that "if we lose our youth, we lose our race; therefore, it was incumbent upon the NBA as well as the other bars of color to be in the business of 'growing' lawyers who will one day be leaders in the profession." John Crump added that "If America is to become a true melting pot, the legal system must lead the way. This can only be done when diverse groups of people bring their cultural, ethnic, and social backgrounds into the equation."

Toward that end, on July 8, 2002, the NBA commenced its first National Bar Association-Crump Law Camp at Howard University in Washington, D.C. Thirty-two high school students, primarily African Americans, learned, worked and played together with the goal of going to college, then to law school to become lawyers. Dean Ruby Sherrod served as its first Executive Director.

The Law Camp was designed with an academic component and an experiential learning component. In the academic component, students are introduced to the legal system by judges, lawyers, and law professors. The experiential learning component featured trips to museums, monuments, and the US Supreme Court. Students also attended and observed court proceedings.

After the lectures, students prepared for the highlight of the academic component, which was the acclaimed Evett L. Simmons Mock Trial Competition. This competition provided each student with a full range of courtroom experience that culminated in making oral arguments before a panel of judges. The final four (4) winners competed at the National Bar Association's annual convention. The winner received a laptop donated by Past President Simmons.

The Law Camp ends with graduation and the recital of the Law Camp Creed which was written by Past President Simmons for the Law Campers to recite and follow:

NATIONAL BAR ASSOCIATION CRUMP LAW CAMP CREED

We are tomorrow's lawyers.

We are diversity in action.
We are evidence that the future of.
The legal profession will reflect .
The diversity of our country.

We are students of faith-

Faith in God, our creator and protector:
Faith in family, our foundation and support:
Faith in community, uplifting each other;
Faith in self that we can achieve what we believe.

We are students of hope-

Hope that God will be pleased with our choices;
Hope that we will receive a good education;
Hope that we leave this world a better place;
Hope that we will be happy and responsible.

We are the future of our family.

We are the future of our country.
We are the future of the NBA.
We are the National Bar Association
Crump Law Camp Scholars.

IN THE BEGINNING:
The Crump Law Camp

The mission of the National Bar Association (NBA) is to advance the science of jurisprudence, preserve the independence of the judiciary, and uphold the honor and integrity of the legal profession. Founded in 1925, it represents 67,000 lawyers, judges, law professors, and law students in the United States and around the world. While fulfilling its core mission, the NBA sought to increase the number of minorities in the legal profession by encouraging young students of color to attend college and law school. It was determined that the most efficient way to achieve this was to establish a law camp for high school students. The NBA Crump Law Camp was established in July 2001. The goal was to provide the students a comprehensive introduction to the American judicial and legal system in the nation's capitol.

The Camp was designed with an academic component and an experiential learning component. In the academic component students are introduced to the legal system by judges, lawyers, and law professors. After the lectures, students prepare a mock trial—the highlight of the academic component. The Evett L. Simmons Mock Trial Competition is held the final week of the camp. The final four winners compete at the National Bar Association's annual convention. The experiential learning component features trips to museums, monuments, and the US Supreme Court. Students also attend court proceedings, where they observe arraignments.

In partnership with the Howard University School of Law, the National Bar Association recruited high school students in grades 9-11. The goal of the camp was to attract students with diverse backgrounds throughout the United States and provide them with an enjoyable, comprehensive introduction to the challenge of a legal education.

The Camp has attracted applicants from 32 states, the US Virgin Islands, and the District of Columbia. Approximately 34-36 students are selected for the program. The students reside at Howard University. The Camp was held virtually during the Pandemic. At the end of the two-week program, the students are given a survey to gather feedback. Overall, students have found both the academic and non-academic program enjoyable and informative. Upon graduation students are administered the Crump Law Camp Creed.

According to John Crump, for whom the camp is named, " If America is to become a true melting pot, the legal system must lead the way. This can only be done when diverse groups of people bring their cultural, ethnic, and social backgrounds into the equation. Although the camp has an open enrollment policy and is available to all students, its emphasis is on empowering students of color."

YOUTH PROGRAMS

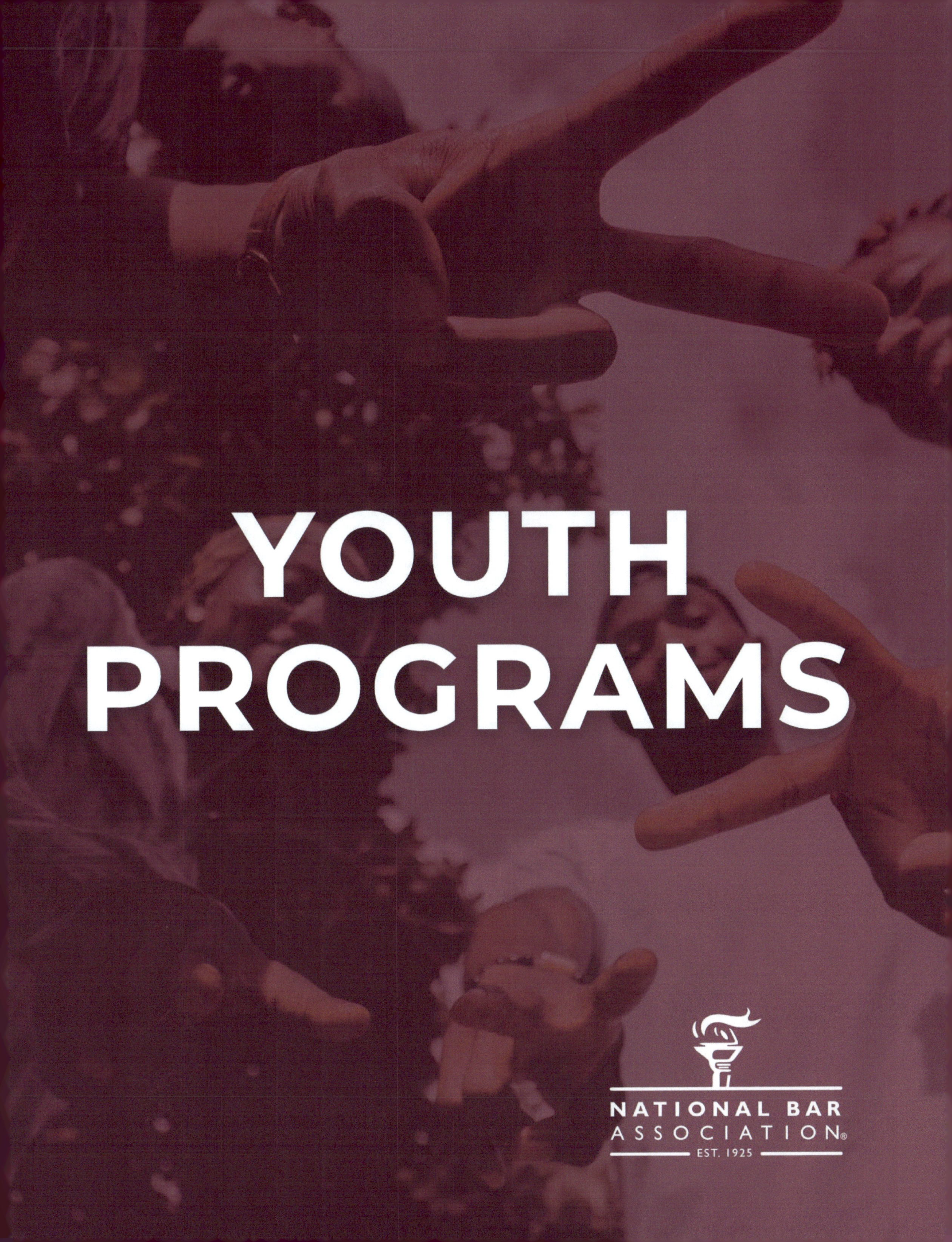

NATIONAL BAR ASSOCIATION®
EST. 1925

National Bar Association Crump Law Camp | Virtual

The National Bar Association Crump Law Camp was established to provide students entering the 9th through 11th grades (ages 14 to 17) with an introduction to the American judicial system. Three other national minority bars—the Hispanic National Bar Association, the Native American Bar Association, and the National Asian Pacific Bar Association- have generously supported the camp as well. By providing incentive, motivation, and direction to aspiring law students of color, the National Bar Association Crump Law Camp helps prepare the nation's future lawyers, judges, and protectors of the judicial system. The inaugural two-week camp was held during the summer of 2001 at Howard University School of Law, supported by a grant from the Ford Motor Company Fund. Thirty-two students of diverse backgrounds and ethnicities descended upon the Howard University campus, where they were introduced to law school and learned some of the skills required to be an effective lawyer.

Linnes Finney, Jr. National Bar Association Youth Day

Held during the Annual Convention, this day-long program provides high school students with a chance to learn about careers in the legal profession. This program aims to increase the number of diverse students applying to and being admitted to our nation's law schools by providing them with resources and knowledge about what it takes to become a lawyer. Participants attend various workshops on the application/admissions process, trying cases, and legal profession options. The students will also participate in mock trial competitions. The program culminates with an awards presentation.

The Dr. Martin Luther King, Jr. Drum Major for Justice Advocacy Competition

This contest is designed to motivate high school students to excel in education. The Competition encourages students to express their views on a pre-selected topic and focuses on the ability of the students to communicate orally and in writing. The Competition is also designed to give young people experience in public speaking and reviewing legal documents as well as provide an opportunity for them to obtain some financial support to continue their education.

Youth Symposia and Seminars CAMP

During the 2010-2011 bar year the National Bar Association published a pamphlet entitled, "How the Law Treats You Differently When You Turn 18." This publication was a part of the National Bar Association's "Lifting as We Climb" series and is intended to inform, not advise, persons about certain rights and responsibilities they gain when they turn 18. During some bar years, a Youth Empowerment Symposium was held at various National Bar Association meetings. This symposium featured an in-depth look at the National Bar Association publication "How the Law Treats You Differently When You Turn 18," an informative session on bullying and teen dating violence and civic education in the nation's schools, and a seminar related to deconstructing the school-to-prison pipeline.

The Evett L. Simmons Mock Trial Competition

Traditionally, the program is held on Tuesday or Wednesday during the Annual Convention. The Evett L. Simmons Mock Trial Competition is the highlight of the National Bar Association Crump Law Camp. All students at the Law Camp participate in the Evett L. Simmons Mock Trial Competition. The finalist attends the convention and competes for a laptop computer. The students are rising 9th, 10th, and 11th graders. The first competition took place under Past President Simmons' Presidency. The 14th Annual Competition took place during the 89th Annual Convention and Exhibits.

Law Academy: Constitution Day

Constitution Day is a nationally recognized holiday that commemorates the signing of the U.S. Constitution on September 17, 1787. Educators throughout the U.S. are encouraged to teach students about one of the most important and influential events in American history, which established the many rights and freedoms "We the People" enjoy today.

The National Bar Association celebrates Constitution Day, on September 17, with educational programs in classrooms throughout the United States. Volunteer attorneys discussed the Constitution with junior high school students. The National Bar Association 2013 Pilot occurred in select cities around the country.

Diversity Task Force

This committee is responsible for planning and implementing programming which will increase diversity in the legal profession and assist law students with making a successful transition to the practice of law. During this bar, this task force was charged with the following three initiatives: i) Pilot program: National Bar Association Law Student Rep at 12-13 law schools across the country; ii) developing a Bridge the Gap Seminar for newly admitted attorneys; and iii) planning a collegiate Mock Trial Competition.

The Youth Achievers Breakfast

The Youth Achievers' Breakfast, formally renamed the Minnie P. Spaulding Youth Achievers' Breakfast, is a NABBS-sponsored event where the National Bar Association's Youth Enrichment Program and a local youth group perform, receive a fully prepared breakfast, and receive an attendance award recognition for attending the event before a bus trip/tour. Recently, this event was either scheduled Wednesday or Thursday due to the tight National Bar Association schedule. Historically, the event was held the morning of the youths' final day before the youth field trip and/or community service project.

NBA's Associate Advancement Academy for Excellence

The National Bar Association (NBA), Arnold & Porter, and the Arnold & Porter Foundation are committed to addressing retention issues in the nation's largest law firms (e.g., the AmLaw 200 law firms). To that end, the NBA has entered into a partnership with Arnold & Porter and the Arnold & Porter Foundation (collectively, "A&P") to develop and implement a program specifically intended to facilitate the retention and advancement of current and potential NBA members in AmLaw 200 firms. As part of the partnership, NBA is proud to announce the development of the NBA Associate Advancement Academy for Excellence! The NBA Associate Advancement Academy for Excellence is a tailored career advancement experience for associates within the first 3 years of practice in an AmLaw 200 firm, developed with the support of NBA's Minority Partners in Majority Firms Division, Young Lawyer Division, Commercial Law Section and Corporate Law Section.

About the NBA's Associate Advancement Academy for Excellence

The NBA's Associate Advancement Academy for Excellence ("NBA Advancement Academy" or "Academy") is specifically intended to facilitate the advancement and retention of current and future NBA members in the nation's largest law firms. The Academy, which will run annually from July 1st to June 30th of each year, includes educational, networking, mentoring, and pro bono/community service components tailored to advance the careers of attorneys within the first 3 years of practice in an AmLaw 200 firm.

Academy participants, ("NBA Associate Advancement Academy for Excellence Fellows" and "Fellows"), will participate in monthly educational and networking sessions, monthly mentoring check-ins with a law firm partner mentor and corporate counsel mentor, respectively, and various NBA events throughout the year. In particular, Fellows will be expected to commit to the following:

- Attend a monthly virtual professional development session
- Mentoring check-ins with NBA law firm partner mentor and corporate mentor
- Attendance at the following NBA Events:

The 2024-2025 cohort will include 20 associates, with no more than two associates from any one firm.

The Academy will cover a range of topics integral to successful advancement in law firm practice, including the following:

- Anatomy of a Big Law Firm
- Navigating a Law Firm and Capitalizing on Firm Professional Staff
- Legal Research & Writing Skills
- Accounting 101 & Corporate Basics
- The Art of Business Development
- The Clients: In-House Legal Perspectives
- Building your Brand-Externally
- Building your Brand-Internally
- The NBA & Using Your Legal Skills to Benefit the Black Community
- Wellness (physical and mental)
- Doing Well While Doing Good (successfully integrating pro bono/service into firm practice and as a tool for training and building your brand)

NATIONAL BAR INSTITUTE

NATIONAL BAR ASSOCIATION®
EST. 1925

The National Bar Institute:
Four Decades of Vision, Leadership, and Legacy

Introduction

The National Bar Institute (NBI) extends its heartfelt congratulations to the National Bar Association (NBA) on the monumental achievement of its 100th anniversary—a century marked by unwavering dedication to justice, advocacy, and the empowerment of African American attorneys supporting the African American community and human rights for all.

The NBI stands as the proud philanthropic arm of the NBA dedicated to advancing legal education, equality, and service. Founded in 1982, amid the NBA's long-standing commitment to advocacy, the NBI was envisioned as a means to channel resources and support into the next generation of legal leaders. Over the decades, the NBI has grown into a pillar of the NBA family by championing scholarships, educational programs, and initiatives that promote justice and opportunity nationwide. Through its work, the NBI has become synonymous with the sustained advancement of justice and the development of leaders devoted to equality under the law.

Founding and Mission

The National Bar Institute was established in 1982 out of a visionary drive to strengthen the future of African American legal advocacy. On June 17, 1982, three trailblazing attorneys – Mary Alice Gresham (later Bullock), Carolyn Y. Howard, and Frank Seales, Jr. – officially incorporated the NBI as a 501(c)(3) non-profit organization. These founders, who formed NBI's first Board of Directors, aimed to create a charitable arm of the NBA dedicated to educating the public on pressing legal issues, expanding access to quality legal education, and improving legal services for underserved communities of color.

The early 1980s context of retrenchment in civil rights enforcement underscored the urgency of the NBI's mission. By establishing a tax-exempt organization, leaders of the NBA ensured a vehicle to channel resources into scholarships, community legal education, and public-interest initiatives. This founding vision – "to ensure quality legal educational opportunities for all and enhance the quality of legal services for people of color and the poor" – set a profound tone for the NBI's trajectory.

National Bar Institute Charter Members (1982)

The Charter Members included the following: Dennis Archer, Lawrence R. Bailey, Jr., Samuel E. Bentley, James Booker, Harris C. Bostic, Thomas J. Broome, Lenore H. Cameron, Aldrinette M. Chapital, Carl J. Character, Winfred T. Colbert, James O. Cole, Hyacinth Collins, Doreen L. Cook, T. J. Cummingham, Esther D. Curtwright, Bonnie Fitch, Fred D. Gray, Harrison Gregg, Jr., Shelvin Hall, Robert L. Harris, Rosalind Hebert, Marilyn Holifield, Earle C. Horton, Carolyn Y. Howard, Arnette R. Hubbard, Thomas L. Jones, Arthenia L. Joyner, Grace W. Madison, Richard Madison, William S. Mayfield, Joyce Mitchell, Coleman C. Moore, Grady B. Murdock, Hon. Ted R. Newman, Jr., John D. Ogletree, Jr., Benjamin J. Pigot, Michael Pitts, Thelma L. Quince, Francis P. Rice, Oddie Richard, Jacquelyn R. Rucker, Ronald Samuels, Martha Algenita Scott-Davis, Frank Seales, Jr., Linwood Slayton, H. T. Smith, Gloria Sulton, Walter L. Sutton, Jr., Hon. Lucia T. Thomas, Hon. William S. Thompson, Dwight Tillery, Edward B. Toles, Emanuel A. Towns, Oscar Trivers, Caroleigh C. Tuitt, Cora T. Walker, Renee Jones Weeks, Dolores P. Wilson, LeRoy Wilson, Jr., and the Fort Worth Black Bar Association.

Growth and Financial Impact

ver four decades, the NBI has grown tremendously, expanding both its financial capacity and its reach. The NBI has awarded approximately $1.1 million in grants and received more than $1.2 million in donations.

Under the leadership of NBA Past President H.T. Smith, the NBI established the Endowment 2000 campaign to provide financial support to the legal, educational and social strategies of the NBA and the NBI. The initial goal to raise $1 million became a reality in February 2021 as a result of hard work and investment strategies of the NBI Board of Directors.

Signature Programs and Educational Initiatives

Central to NBI's legacy is its support for legal education and youth engagement. Through fellowships, scholarships, and national competitions, the NBI has empowered a pipeline of African American legal talent across the country. These programs not only provide financial assistance, but also open doors to mentorship, professional networks, and leadership training.

Law Student Fellowship Program (2001–2022)

- The Law Student Fellowship Program awarded $337,500 to 74 second-year law students committed to social justice. These fellowships reduced financial burdens, allowing students to pursue impactful careers in law. Alumni of the program have gone on to become civil rights attorneys, law professors, and corporate counsel, embodying the fellowship's goal of seeding the legal profession with leaders committed to equity and access.

Law Scholars Program (2021–Present)

- Launched with a $300,000 Amazon grant, the Law Scholars Program supports HBCU law students through multi-year scholarships, bar prep, and leadership development. Scholars engage in essay writing and mentorship, enhancing their preparation for legal careers. As of 2025, the program has supported three cohorts of 35 scholars.

Affiliates Scholarship & Bar Passage Success Program (2023–Present)

- This program engages NBA Regions and Affiliates in nominating students for bar preparation and scholarships. Top-choice students receive scholarships and bar exam prep support. A second group of students also receive bar exam and prep counseling. In two years, the program has awarded $75,000 and impacted all twelve (12) NBA Regions.

Martin Luther King, Jr. Drum Major for Justice Advocacy Competition (2001–Present)

- The competition gives high school students experience in public speaking and reviewing legal documents, while obtaining financial support to continue their education. Since 2000, more than $290,000 in scholarships have been awarded to 112 students. The final competition is held each year during the NBA Annual Convention.

NBA Crump Law Camp (2001–Present)

- Founded at Howard University with a grant from the Ford Motor Company, the Crump Law Camp introduces 9th through 11th grade students to the legal system through an on campus residential experience. Nearly 800 students have attended the camp. The Law Camp's namesake is John Crump, Emeritus Executive Director of the NBA, who oversaw its operations for 32 years. The camp has earned recognition from the American Bar Association and inspired many participants to pursue legal careers.

Council on Legal Education Opportunity (CLEO) Support

- NBI has long supported CLEO's mission of preparing diverse students for law school. Its financial backing helps under-represented students access a legal education—a testament to NBI's commitment to systemic equity.

Partnerships and Legacy Initiatives

The NBI has preserved African American legal history and promoted cultural awareness by funding projects such as:

- A grant to NBA Past President Elmer C. Jackson to assist in writing and publication of A Search for Equal Justice by African American Lawyers, a historical examination of the NBA.
- The video production of Portrait of the National Bar Association, proposed by NBA Past President Randy K Jones and managed by NBA Past President Junius Williams.
- The Jacob Lawrence Art Project working with the renowned artist under the leadership of former NBI Chair Ernestine Sapp.

Leadership and Governance

The NBI Board is comprised of thirteen (13) Directors, twelve (12) of whom are elected by the NBI membership. The NBA President-Elect also serves as a Director. The Board elects a Chair, Vice Chair, Treasurer and Secretary. This structure fosters alignment between NBI and NBA leadership and ensures consistency in executing the mission.

Distinguished past chairs have included: Hon. Arnette R. Hubbard (NBA Past President), Fred D. Gray (NBA Past President), Robert L. Harris (NBA Past President), J. Clay Smith, Frank Seales, Jr., Ernestine S. Sapp, H. T. Smith (NBA Past President), Dana Petersen Moore, and Harold D. Pope (NBA Past President).

The 2024-2025 Board of Directors are: Dr. Walter L. Sutton, Jr. (Chair), Regina K. Dillard (Vice Chair), Sonya D. Hoskins (Secretary), Frank Seales, Jr. (Treasurer), Ashley L. Upkins (NBA President-Elect), David Green, Norma Hutcheson, Antoinette 'Toni' M. Jackson, Stephanie D. Jones, Alfreda Robinson, Belinda D. Stith, Vickie E. Turner, and Kwamina Williford.

A Vision for the Future

The NBI looks forward with purpose--continuing to expand access, support diverse legal talent, and uplift a profession that mirrors the nation it serves. Its focus on legal education, youth and alumni engagements with national outreach, ensures that justice will have a bold and enduring voice in every generation. As the NBA celebrates its centennial, the NBI's role as the NBA's philanthropic and educational engine ensures that the next century will be as impactful as the last.

The National Bar Institute:

Four Decades of Vision, Leadership, and Legacy

About

In the struggle for social change and progress in the legal profession, the National Bar Institute (NBI) serves as a means to advance the understanding and practice of law among African Americans and other diverse minority groups.

Founded in 1982 by members of the National Bar Association, the oldest and largest professional organization of lawyers and judges of color in the world, the NBI shares the same passion and commitment for advancing minorities in the legal profession by promoting education, advocacy and action to ensure civil and human rights, and equal justice for all.

In fulfilling its mission, the NBI has established objectives that call for supporting students and legal education programs, and issues that broadly impact human and civil rights.

Since its founding, the NBI has established and implemented successful programs including the following:

- Law Student Fellowships awarded to academically promising 2L law students with a proven commitment to social justice.
- Grants for regional high school seniors and their chaperones to attend the National Bar Association (NBA) convention to participate in the Martin Luther King, Jr. Drum Major for Justice Advocacy Competition.
- Financial support to the National Black Law Students Association (NBLSA); NBA Women's Lawyers and Young Lawyers Divisions, and the Council for Legal Education Opportunity (CLEO).
- The Clyde E. Bailey, Sr. and Rapheal M. Prevot, Jr. Annual Golf Tournament.

NATIONAL ASSOCIATION OF BENCH & BAR SPOUSES

NATIONAL BAR ASSOCIATION®
EST. 1925

NABBS, INC.
National Association of Bench and Bar Spouses,

Celebrating the NBA: A Century of Legacy, Leade rship, Service, and Impact

NABBS, Inc. and the NABBS Foundation congratulate the National Bar Association on 100 Years of Excellence

As the National Bar Association celebrates its momentous 100th Anniversary, the National Association of Bench and Bar Spouses, Inc., along with the NABBS Foundation, joyfully extend our warmest congratulations. We are honored to stand with you in commemorating a century of trailblazing leadership, enduring advocacy, and unwavering dedication to justice.

From its founding, the NBA has served as a powerful force for progress—amplifying the voices of Black legal professionals and advancing civil rights across the nation. As the oldest and largest organization of Black lawyers, judges, and legal scholars, the NBA has led with integrity and courage through every challenge, shaping the course of American law and preparing future generations to lead with purpose.

Since our founding in 1951, NABBS has proudly walked alongside the NBA—supporting its mission through service, fellowship, and advocacy. Governed by our National Executive Board and strengthened by the work of regional representatives and local chapters, NABBS remains deeply committed to uplifting the legal profession and the communities it serves.

Our membership includes spouses and surviving spouses of attorneys and judges from across the United States and abroad—many of whom are accomplished professionals in their own right. Lawyers, educators, physicians, executives, artists, and public servants comprise our vibrant network, which fosters connection, celebrates culture, and reflects the unity of the NBA family.

For nearly 75 years, NABBS has left a meaningful mark on the lives we touch—sponsoring legal clinics, building strong family support systems, advancing Law Day events, and offering enriching workshops for our members. NABBS also developed and coordinated what is now known as the NBA's Youth Enrichment Program (YEP), creating lasting experiences for participants through activities like the Youth Achievers Breakfast. Additionally, NABBS organized and hosted its popular fashion shows, with proceeds supporting law school scholarshipsfor deserving students.

Together with the NBA, NABBS continues to stand at the intersection of service and purpose— advancing initiativesthat uplift legal families and empower communities across the nation. Our legacy is built on shared values and a collective commitment to justice, education, and the elevation of future leaders.

NABBS *Foundation*

National Association of Bench and Bar Spouses Foundation

As NABBS expanded in reach and vision, so too did our commitment to deeper service. In 1994, that vision gave rise to a powerful philanthropic arm: the NABBS Foundation, a 501(c)(3) charitable organization.

The NABBS Foundation furthers our mission through charitable efforts focused on education, health, and community well-being. Through strong partnerships with NABBS, Inc., the National Bar Association, the National Bar Institute, law firms, and institutions of higher education, the Foundation continues to extend our reach and deepen our impact.

Signature programs include:

- Dorothy Atkinson Legal Education Scholarship – supporting high-achieving, underrepresented law students since 1969. We are especially grateful to the National Bar Institute for its generous support in sustaining and growing this vital scholarship.

- Bonnie P. and Grace Laws Wheatley Breast Cancer Forum – promoting awareness, early detection, education, and sharing the latest breast cancer protocols.

- Dr. Annie Lawrence Brown Health Initiatives – encouraging wellness and preventive care in our communities.

- Dr. Cleota P. & Harvey Wibekin Coalition for the Homeless Fund – providing support to unhoused individuals and programs that help prevent homelessness.

- Presidents' Endowment Fund – ensuring the long-term sustainability of NABBS Foundation programs, honoring the service of past leaders, and funding scholarships, health initiatives, and civic outreach.

In alignment with the NBA's enduring mission, the NABBS Foundation proudly continuesto serve as a bridge between advocacy and action—strengthening communities, promoting equity, and creating opportunities that uplift the legal profession.

Together, NABBS, Inc. and the NABBS Foundation join in celebration of the National Bar Association's 100 years of extraordinary leadership and legacy. We are honored to share in this historic moment and remain steadfast in our commitment to supporting the people, principles, and progress that define this incredible journey.

With great pride and in celebration,

Taylora O'Bryant Gary
President, NABBS, Inc.

Katherine Wright Davis
President, NABBS Foundation

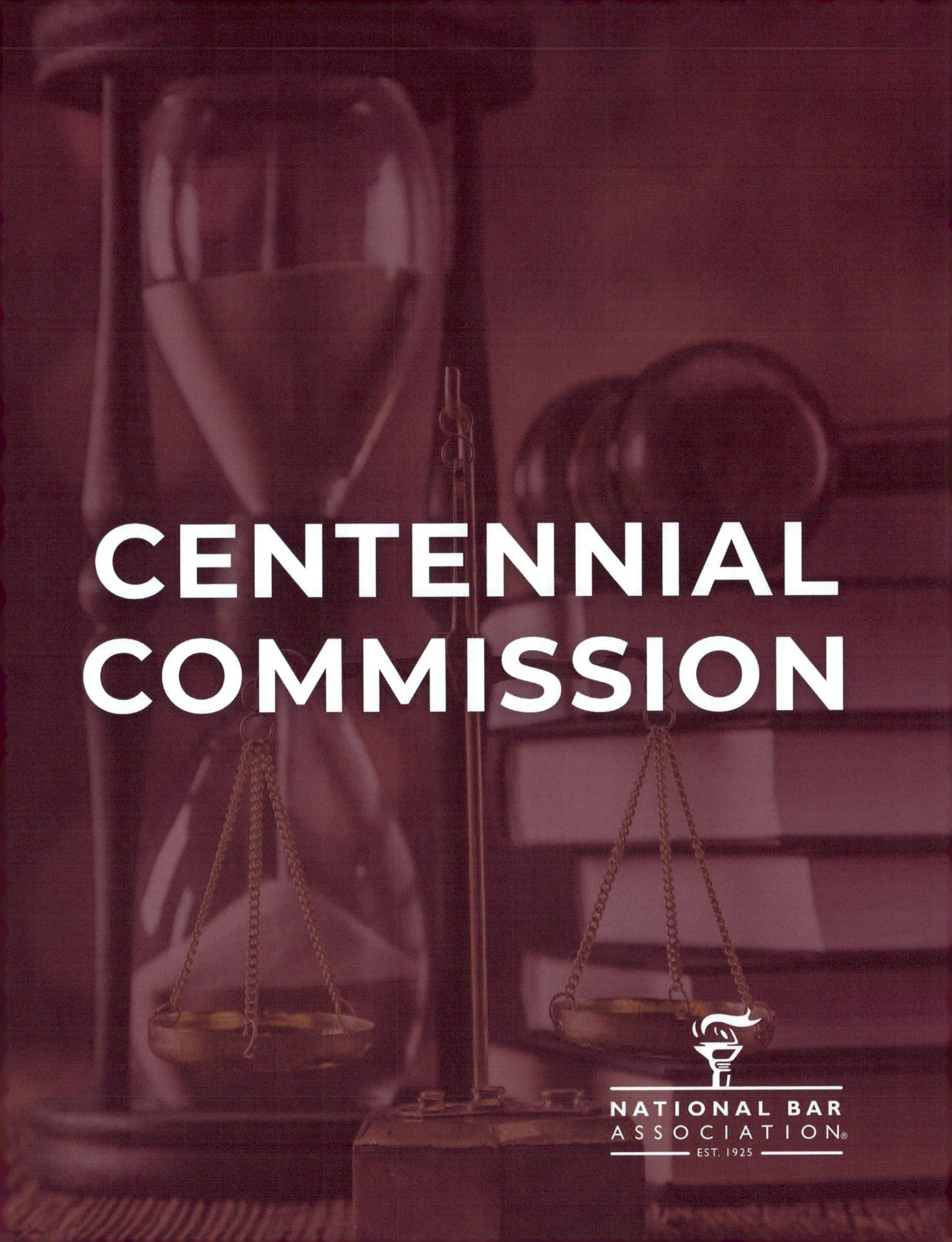

CENTENNIAL COMMISSION

NATIONAL BAR ASSOCIATION
EST. 1925

CENTENNIAL COMMISSION MEMBERS

Ben Crump, Honorary Chair
Evett L. Simmons, Chair
Paulette Brown, Co-Chair
Arthenia Joyner, Co-Chair
Keith Watters, Co-Chair
Wiley Adams, NBA President
Ashley Upkins, NBA President-Elect
Vanita Banks
Antoinette Barksdale
Dominique Calhoun
Anne Marie Clarke
John Crump
Ellen Douglass
Joseph "Joe" Drayton,
Cenceria Edwards
Monique Edwards
Iris McCullough Green
Henry Hamilton
Robert Harris
Tricia "CK" Hoffler
Sonya Hoskins
Carolyn Howard
Arnette Hubbard
Antoinette "Toni" Jackson
Maria John
Kevin Judd
Kim Keenan
Tamara Lawson
Alfreda Robinson
Michael Rosier
Patricia Rosier
Algenita Scott
Demetrius Shelton
H.T. Smith
Juan Thomas
Bernard Tolliver
Kimberley Ann Ward
Zenobia Waters
Junius Williams
Elizabeth Winfield

LEGACY SOCIETY

NATIONAL BAR ASSOCIATION

EST. 1925

NATIONAL BAR ASSOCIATION CENTENNIAL LEGACY SOCIETY MEMBERS

Chairman's Club

Ben Crump, Past President NBA

Vice Chairman's Club

AccessLex Institute

Platinum

Hoffler and Associates, PC (Tricia "CK" Hoffler, Past President)
James E. Ross
Lowenstein Sandler LLP
Microsoft
Simmons, Finney & Winfield (Evett L. Simmons & Linnes Finney Jr., Past Presidents)

Gold

Wiley S. Adams, NBA President
Sia Baker Barnes, President, The Florida Bar
Paulette Brown, Past President NBA & ABA
Dominique D. Calhoun, Past President
Hon. Anne-Marie Clarke
Jennifer Fisher
J. Wyndal Gordon
Amanda Heath
Hon. Arnette R. Hubbard, Past President
Antoinette "Toni" Jackson
Senator Arthenia Joyner, Past President NBA
Gray,Langford, Sapp, McGowan, Gray & Nathanson (Fred Gray, Past President NBA and Alabama Bar)
Hon. Cecil Patterson
A. Nick Pittman
Sandra E. Roper
Michael Rosier and Patricia Rosier, Past Presidents NBA
Belinda Stith
Ashley L. Upkins, NBA President Elect
Zenobia Waters, The Waters Firm PC

Silver

Lamont Bailey
Lonita K. Baker, Past President
Vanita Banks, Past President
Antoinette Barksdale
Hon. Romonda D. Belcher
Robert L. Bell
Hon. Gail Bereola
Hon. Alice A. Bonner
Sheila S. Boston
U. Lawrence Boze, Past President
Hon. Sharon V. Burrell
James Carter, NBA Vice President
Ellen E. Douglass
Linda C. Drake
Beverly F. Druitt
Danielle Dunn
Hon. Cenceria Edwards
Monique Edwards
Henry Floyd
Trudi McCollum Foushee
Phyllis Gillespie
DeMonica Gladney
Iris McCollum Green
Arlene Knighten Guerin
Hon. Henry Hamilton, III
Ronald J. Harper
Hon. Alfreda Harris
Robert L. Harris, Past President
Hon. Amanda N. Heath
Sonya D. Hoskins
Veronica James
Kevin D. Judd, Past President
Carthenia Jefferson
Maria C. John
Kim Keenan, Past President
Dean Cynthia Nance
Daryl Parks, Past President
Hon. Errol H. Powell
Tonya Primus
Alfreda Robinson, Past President
Ernestine S. Sapp
Frank Seales, Jr.
Grasford Smith
H.T. Smith, Past President & Past NBI Chair
Southern University
Charlyn Stanberry
Gloria R. Sulton
Walter Sutton, Past President & NBI Chair
Hon. Mavis Thompson, Past President
Karol Corbin Walker
Yuri Walker, NBA Treasurer
Kimberley A. Ward, NBA Vice President
Keith Watters, Past President
Bryce West
Hon. Royce West
Ethel Isaacs Williams
Junius Williams, Past President

CONGRATULATORY MESSAGES

NATIONAL BAR ASSOCIATION®
EST. 1925

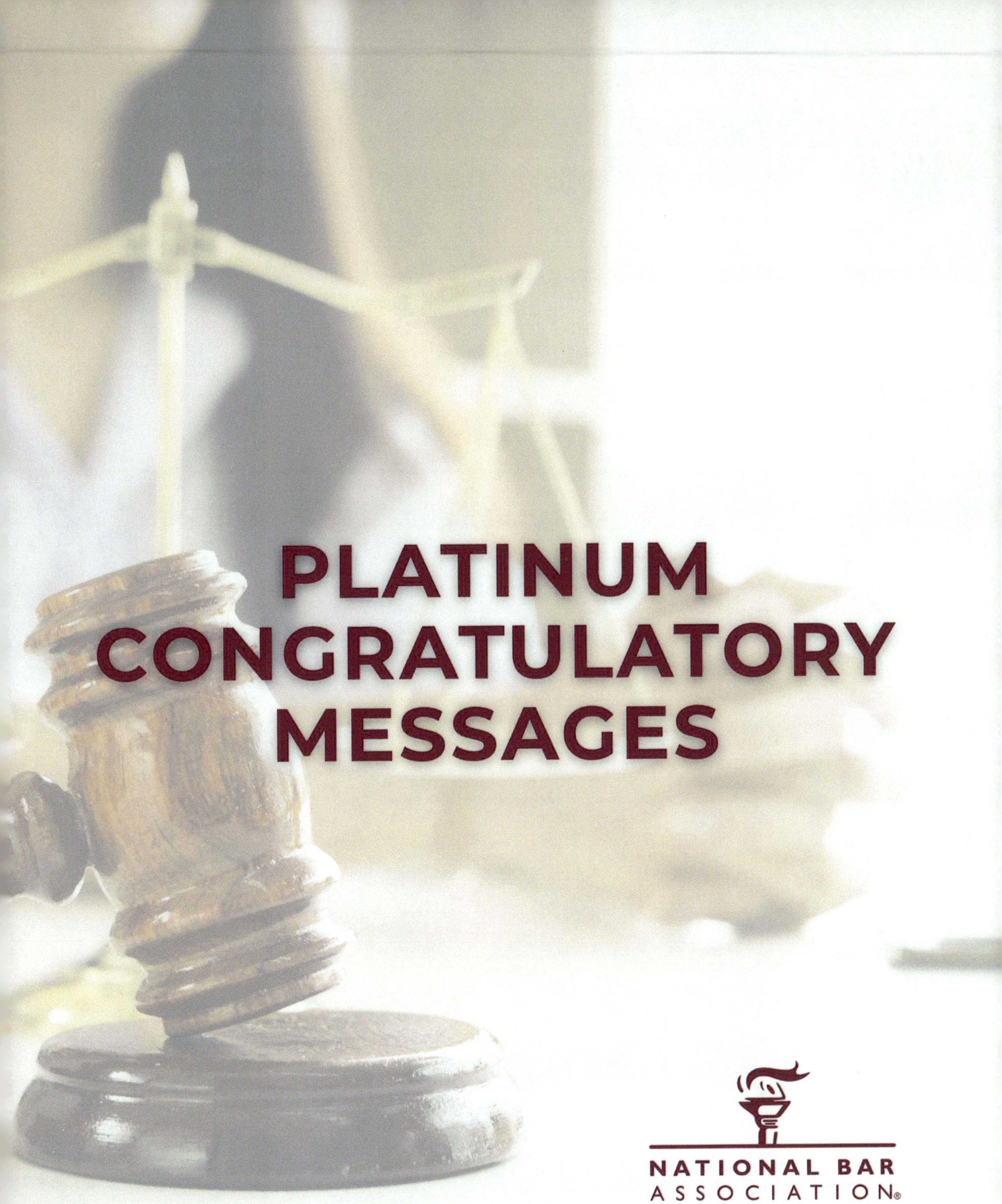

PLATINUM CONGRATULATORY MESSAGES

NATIONAL BAR ASSOCIATION®
EST. 1925

Congratulations to the National Bar Association for 100 years of fighting for human rights and equality!

Achieve Bigger, Better, Faster results with Ben Crump as your attorney.

Crump is the unique and trusted lawyer whose voice and reach can exponentially magnify settlements and verdicts. To drive a bigger outcome, put Ben on your case

"Ben Crump may be the hardest working attorney in the country."

NEW YORK MAGAZINE

MAJOR RESULTS

LA sexual abuse cases:	$4 billion
Flint water crisis:	$600 million
Product liability cases:	$450 million
Concert venue injury cases:	$427 million
Car accident verdicts:	$411 million
Banking discrimination cases:	$250 million
Randy Cox:	$45 million
George Floyd:	$27 million
Breonna Taylor:	$12 million

To explore opportunities with Ben, contact him and his team:
800-568-8111 | BenCrump.com

BEN CRUMP
TRIAL LAWYER FOR JUSTICE

I stand on the shoulders of those who came before me. Our steadfast commitment to excellence and justice for all is instilled in me and their sacrifices did not go unnoticed.

Ben Crump Law PLLC
633 Pennsylvania Ave NW
Washington, D.C. 20004
(800) 688-7111
www.BenCrump.com

GOLD CONGRATULATORY MESSAGES

NATIONAL BAR ASSOCIATION®
EST. 1925

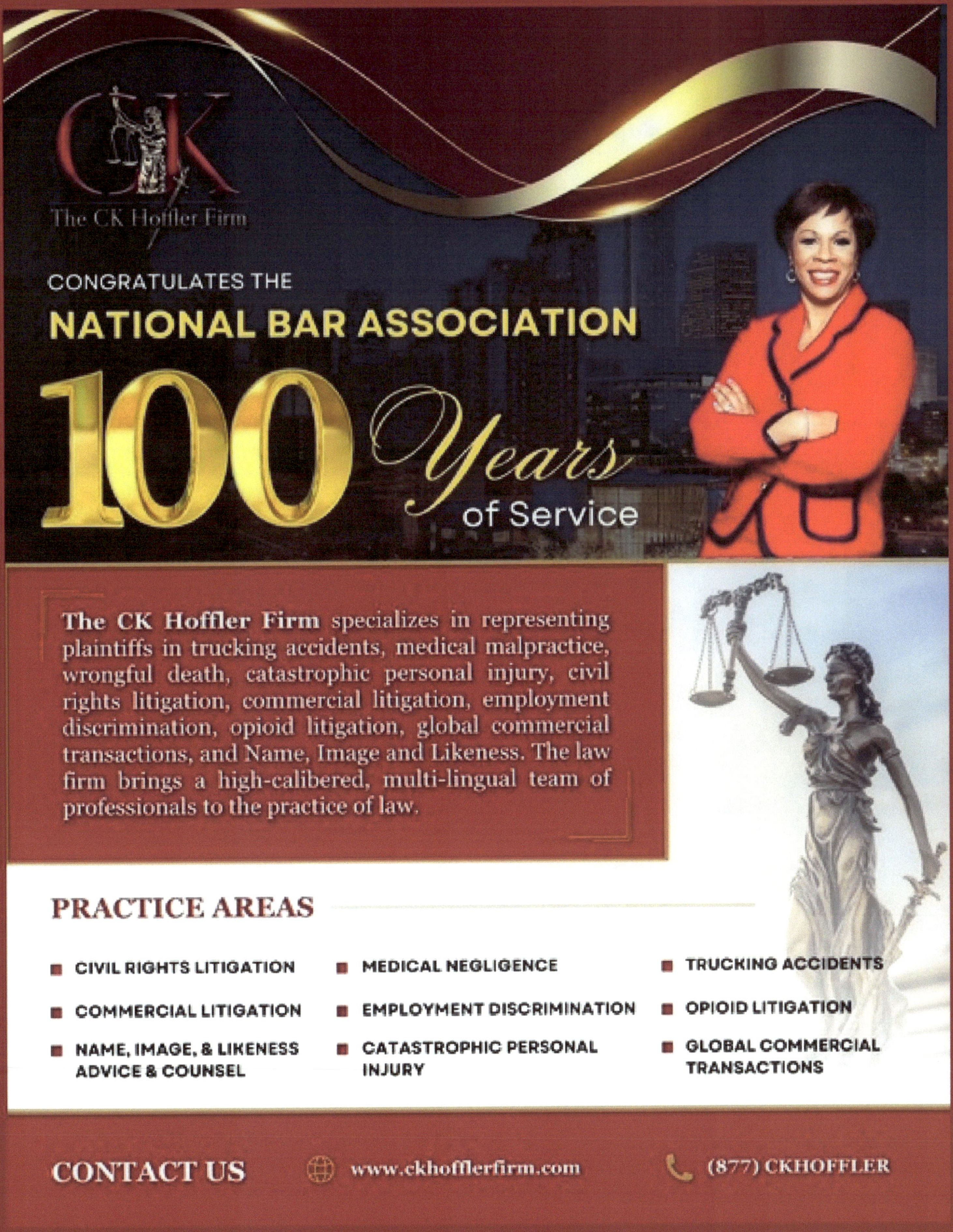
The CK Hoffler Firm
CONGRATULATES THE
NATIONAL BAR ASSOCIATION
100 Years
of Service
The CK Hoffler Firm specializes in representing plaintiffs in trucking accidents, medical malpractice, wrongful death, catastrophic personal injury, civil rights litigation, commercial litigation, employment discrimination, opioid litigation, global commercial transactions, and Name, Image and Likeness. The law firm brings a high-calibered, multi-lingual team of professionals to the practice of law.
PRACTICE AREAS
CIVIL RIGHTS LITIGATION
MEDICAL NEGLIGENCE
TRUCKING ACCIDENTS
COMMERCIAL LITIGATION
EMPLOYMENT DISCRIMINATION
OPIOID LITIGATION
NAME, IMAGE, & LIKENESS ADVICE & COUNSEL
CATASTROPHIC PERSONAL INJURY
GLOBAL COMMERCIAL TRANSACTIONS
CONTACT US
www.ckhofflerfirm.com
(877) CKHOFFLER

Congratulations to the National Bar Association for 100 Years of Service!

It has been an incredible honor to serve as the Chair of the Entertainment, Sports & Arts Law Section and contributing to the meaningful work of the National Bar Association. I appreciate the dedication, collaboration, and passion that each of you bring in advancing the National Bar Associations' shared mission.

I am looking forward to working with our Honorable Judges, Lawyers, and Law Students, as well as their families and friends as we continue on our journey toward justice.

Ricky Anderson, Esq.
Attorney Ricky Anderson PLLC
4265 San Felipe Street, Suite 1100
Houston, Texas 77027
(713) 929-6463
Ricky@AttorneyRickyAnderson.com

ΩΨΦ

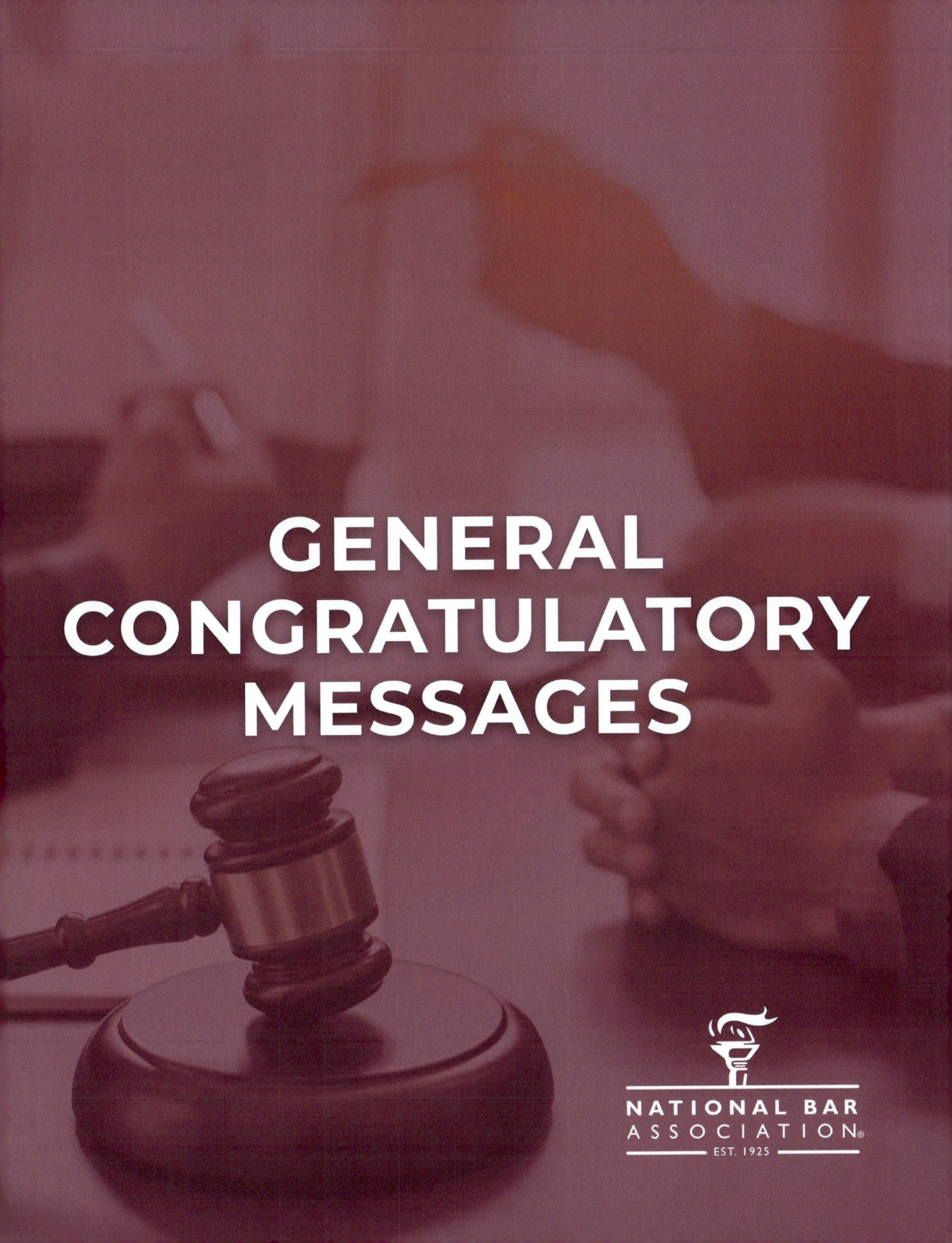

GENERAL CONGRATULATORY MESSAGES

NATIONAL BAR ASSOCIATION®
EST. 1925

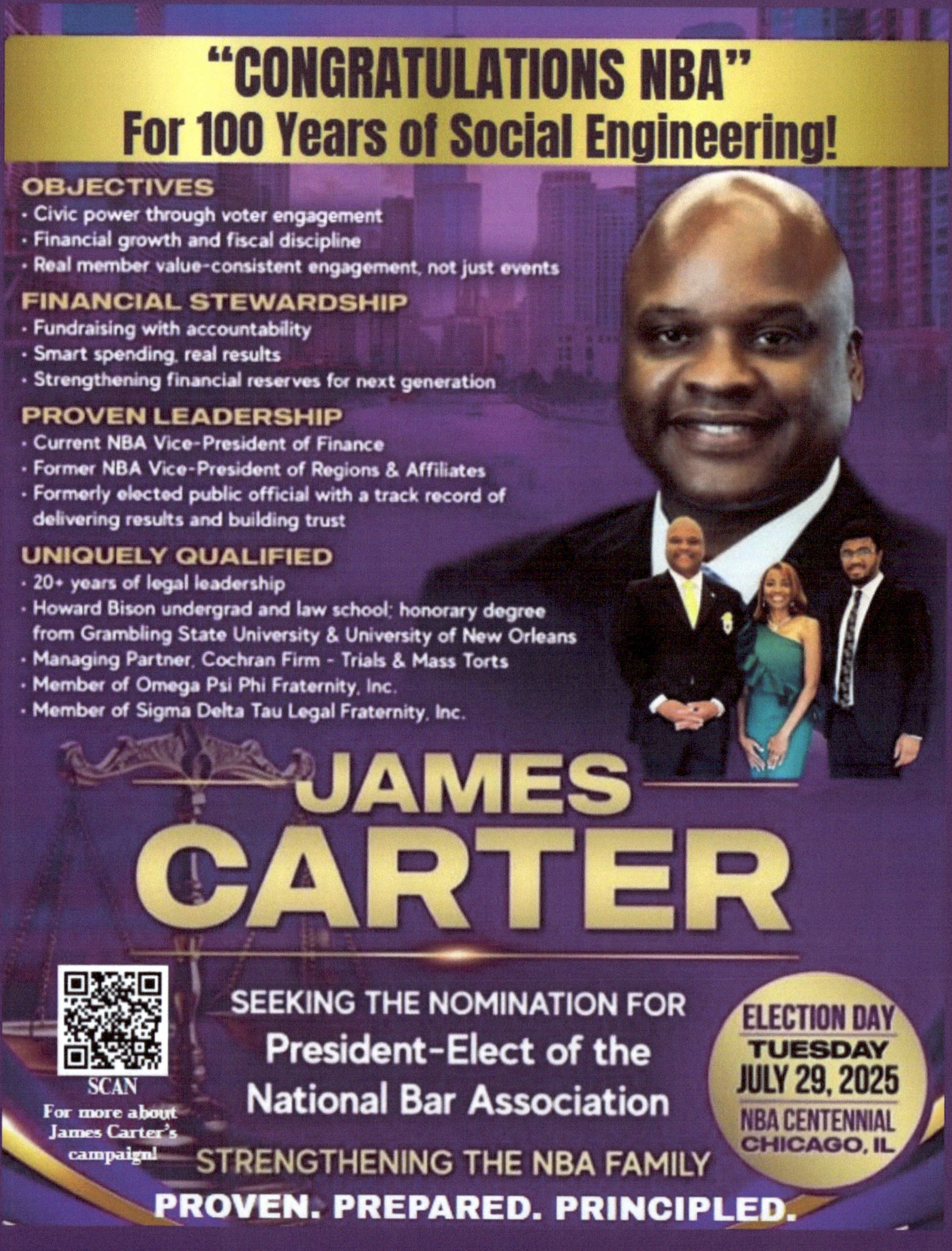

"CONGRATULATIONS NBA"
For 100 Years of Social Engineering!
OBJECTIVES
• Civic power through voter engagement
• Financial growth and fiscal discipline
• Real member value-consistent engagement, not just events
FINANCIAL STEWARDSHIP
• Fundraising with accountability
• Smart spending, real results
• Strengthening financial reserves for next generation
PROVEN LEADERSHIP
• Current NBA Vice-President of Finance
• Former NBA Vice-President of Regions & Affiliates
• Formerly elected public official with a track record of delivering results and building trust
UNIQUELY QUALIFIED
• 20+ years of legal leadership
• Howard Bison undergrad and law school; honorary degree from Grambling State University & University of New Orleans
• Managing Partner, Cochran Firm - Trials & Mass Torts
• Member of Omega Psi Phi Fraternity, Inc.
• Member of Sigma Delta Tau Legal Fraternity, Inc.
JAMES
CARTER
SCAN
For more about James Carter's campaign!
SEEKING THE NOMINATION FOR
President-Elect of the
National Bar Association
ELECTION DAY
TUESDAY
JULY 29, 2025
NBA CENTENNIAL
CHICAGO, IL
STRENGTHENING THE NBA FAMILY
PROVEN. PREPARED. PRINCIPLED.

**THE LAW OFFICE OF ROSALIND R. RAY CONGRATULATES
THE NATIONAL BAR ASSOCIATION, INC. - 100 YEARS & COUNTING**

Attorney Rosalind R. Ray
Boston University & Howard University

**Walter I. Ray, Jr. &
Rosemary W. Ray**
Past Administrators
Howard University Grads

Walter I. Ray, III, J.D.,
Morehouse College & Howard University

MY FRIEND
I will be your friend,
Into eternity, Above and beyond,
A centuries to-days, Or to-morrows.
Impenetrable my faith,
Against the balance, of right or wrong,
Or duty faint eye may see,
In judgement or chicanery.
MY FRIEND, I will never disown,
As long as I have breath, Our bond remains perpetual,
Inextricably bound To the pageantry of death.
©- 2005 Walter I. Ray, Jr.

**That's what the National Bar is to
THE LAW OFFICE OF ROSALIND R. RAY, OUR FRIEND**

The continued strides of the National Bar Association toward ***JUSTICE, PEACE, LOVE, UNITY and DEVOTION*** *did not go unnoticed! It has been such a blessing to be a part of an organization whose members constantly strive to right wrongs and encourage people from all walks of life to continue to do what is just, equitable and right.*

**TERRENCE BALDWIN, OZZIE JENKINS, ANGELA SLAUGHTER, MARY BORGES
ACCOUNTANTS JAMES HENDERSON, DON MORAGNE, DERI MITCHELL, CPA,
MIRROR ACCTG.SVCS., DESI SIMPSON, DANNY WILKERSON, CONSULTANT**
rozray160@gmail.com*** rrrlegal@gmail.com*** waltray33@gmail.com
202-722-7282/240-354-8624/240-353-2515

HOWARD UNIVERSITY SCHOOL OF LAW

MEN OF OMEGA PSI PHI FRATERNITY, INC.

MICHAEL A. BASKIN (Class of 1982)

DAVID BRANTLEY (Class of 1966)

STEVEN BRISTER (Class of 1982)

MALCOLM F. CUNNINGHAM (Class of 1980)

GEORGE W. DRAPER, III (Class of 1981)

DARRYL DYER (Class of 1973)

CLAYTON A. GRAHAM (Class of 1981)

RODERICK GRAHAM (Class of 1992)

MICHAEL A. HACKETT (Class of 1992)

EDWARD A. HAILES (Class of 1980)

LARRY R. HANDFIELD (Class of 1981)

KEITH C. HARVEST (Class of 1982)

JOHNNIE A. LANDON, JR. (Class of 1974)

JOHNNY L. LITMAN (Class of 1981)

GEORGE B. PEARSON (Class of 1982)

MARCEL A. PRATT, JR. (Class of 1983)

DONALD A. THIGPEN, JR. (Class of 1974)

WAYNE TONKINS (Class of 1980)

JEETTY L. VIOT III (Class of 1983)

JOHN M. YOUNGE (Class of 1981)

JUNIUS F. HICKS (decd.) (Class of 1980)

BRUCE F. WEEKS (decd.) (Class of 1971)

The abovementioned men of Omega Psi Phi, Fraternity Inc., who earned their scholarship from Howard University School of Law, proudly support the historic milestone and take part in uplifting the celebration of the National Bar Association's perseverance in reaching its Centennial Year (1925-2025). CONGRATULATIONS!!!

EGOS, Inc. Congratulates
the National Bar Association for 100 Years of Service

EGOS,

Education,
Goals,
Opportunities &
Sports

Enhancing the lives of our Youth through Education, Sports, and Community Service
Thanks, NBA, for mentoring so many of us and the young EGOS participants through the years.
Sincerely and with gratitude,

Walter I. Ray, III, J.D
PRESIDENT AND CO-FOUNDER

Beth Hodges, TGIF Owner
BOARD CHAIRMAN

Troy Hailey
Board Member

Keith Holman
BOARD MEMBER

Justin Kittrell
Board Member

Freddie Lewis, Indiana Pacers (Ret.)
Board Member

Dante Baldeh
Board Member

Accountants Don Moragne/ James Henderson
BOB COSTAS – CONSULTANT
ED HILL – CONSULTANT
RUSHION MCDONALD – CONSULTANT

Ricky Anderson, Esq. – Advisor
Rosalind R. Ray, Esq. – Advisor
Ozzie Jenkins – Administrator
Terrence Baldwin – Co-Administrator

Who We Are

E.G.O.S., Inc. is a 501 (c) 3 non-profit organization that empowers young people by enhancing their life skills via athletics, academics, mentoring and community involvement. We create, develop and manage a variety of educational, athletic and civic programs. While many EGOS participants are from disadvantaged backgrounds in the Washington DC Metropolitan Area, the organization reaches young people throughout the United States.

Our Goals

EGOS has identified four major strategic goals:

1) Strengthen and expand our scholarship and internship programs
2) Increase community service and social responsibility among our youth
3) Expand our health and wellness programs
4) Increase awareness of opportunities for youth in athletics, technology, science, mathematics and other professional careers.

EGOS, Inc.,
7826 Eastern Avenue, NW
Suite 209
Washington, DC 20012
Phone: (240) 353-2515
E-mail: waltray33@gmail.com

National Bar Association salutes the First Woman Vice President of the United States of America, Kamala

THE GATE CITY BAR ASSOCIATION
OF ATLANTA, GEORGIA

Congratulates the

NATIONAL BAR ASSOCIATION

on

100 YEARS OF

excellence, advocacy, and legacy

We celebrate your unwavering commitment to justice and the advancement of Black legal professionals

2025 EXECUTIVE BOARD

President: Christopher Bruce

President-Elect: Pierce Hand Seitz
Vice President: Cameron Hawkins
Immediate Past President: N. John Bey
Treasurer: Taylor A. Middleton
Secretary: Daedra Fenwick
Assistant Secretary: Brent Radcliff
Historian: Miguel Dominquez
Member At Large: Racquel McGee
Member At Large: William Boddie
Member At Large: Karlos Emmanuel
Member At Large: Shalamar Parham
Member At Large: Michelle Arrington

Congratulations to The National Bar Association - What an Accomplishment to reach a 100-year Milestone!

The NBA members and their families continue to make strides toward equality and democracy every day while setting great examples for our kids! We are so happy that we had an opportunity as a family to share so many memorable moments with so many of the NBA members over the years. We look forward to watching and sharing so many more occasions with the NBA as you embark upon meaningful impacts of civil justice for all!

Here's to Justice and not Just-Us!

Sincerely and with love,

Renae Brown & Genae Crump

And Brooklyn says "Me Too"

Hotel Sofitel
Chan Bryant Abney, Esq.
Salutes
the National Bar Association
on its 100th Anniversary
Igniting Justice for 100 Years
1645 Palm Beach Lakes Blvd, Suite 1200
West Palm Beach, FL 33401
NATIONAL BAR ASSOCIATION 100 YEARS
IGNITING JUSTICE FOR 100 YEARS
Licensed in Florida and Georgia

The **Wealth** Zone
UNIVERSITY

"CHANGE YOUR MIND ABOUT MONEY,
TO CHANGE YOUR FINANCIAL FUTURE"

$ THE FINANCIAL WELLNESS STRATEGY $

JUDGE ALICE A. BONNER, HOUSTON, TEXAS
SALUTES THE NATIONAL BAR ASSOCIATION 100 YEAR CELEBRATION

MEMBER FOR 55 YEARS 1970-2025 AND LIFE MEMBER

ATTENDED EVERY CONVENTION 1970-2025

BOARD MEMBER, 19972-1974

FOUNDING MEMBER, WOMEN'S DIVISION 1972

MEMBER JUDICIAL COUNCIL, NBA 1973

11TH CHAIR, JUDICIAL COUNCIL NBA 1981-1983

CHAIR, NBA (FRED GRAY) HALL OF FAME, 10 YEARS

GERTRUDE RUSH AND HEMAN SWEATT AWARDEE

Black America's Attorney General

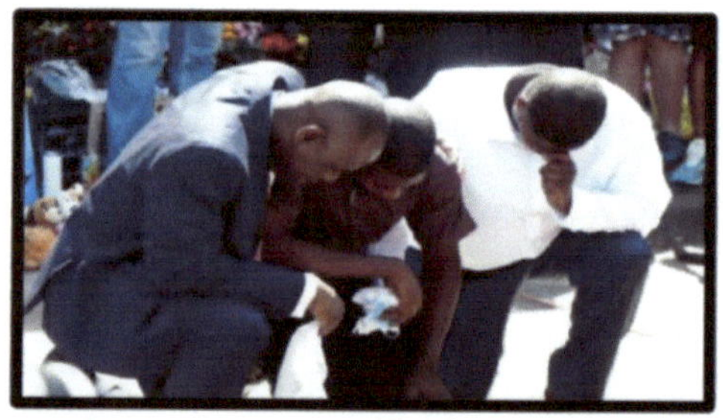

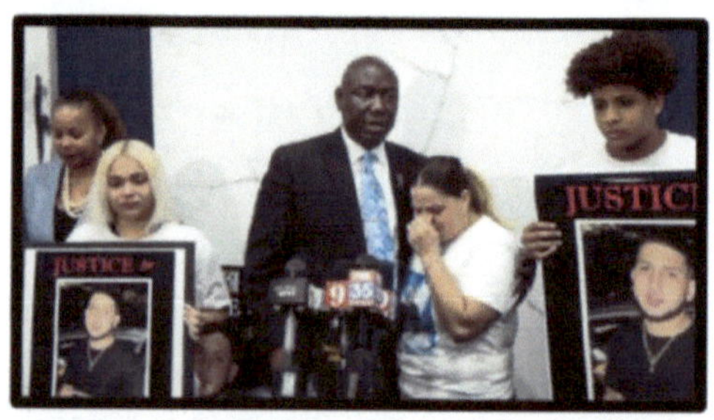

DreamFi
Empowering Futures, Transforming Lives

"Economic freedom makes personal freedom more than just a dream."
- Attorney Ben Crump

Build Lasting Financial Stability

DreamFi is not just a debit card but it is a membership[1] that provides access to powerful financial tools and resources. We're here to help you begin to close the wealth gap and build generational prosperity.

Cell Phone Plans

Access to affordable cell phones plans.

Life Insurance

Protect your family with life insurance. DreamFi account holders in eligible states will be able to obtain life insurance with our life insurance partner, subject to partner's approval.

Checking Accounts[2]

No minimum balance requirements. Access or deposit cash at over 40,000 Allpoint ATM locations in the US[3].

Prescription Savings

Compare major prescription savings programs- all in one place- to find the lowest cost at available pharmacies in your area.

Get Smart About Debt

Understand your loans and create payoff plans that fit your budget.

Coming Soon: Savings Accounts[2]

Build an emergency fund or make your money work harder for you by earning interest.

Join the movement at DreamFi.com

only **50%** of Americans are confident they can cover an unexpected $1,000 expense[4]

only **4/10** Black and Hispanic Americans are confident they can cover an unexpected $1,000 expense[4]

1.Fees may apply.
2.DreamFi is a financial technology company, not a bank. Banking services are provided by Finwise Bank, Member FDIC. Visa is a registered trademark of Visa USA, Inc. All other trademarks and service marks belong to their respective owners. The DreamFi Visa® Debit Card is issued by Finwise Bank, member FDIC pursuant to a license from Visa USA, Inc. Use of this card is subject to the terms and conditions of the cardholder agreement. Anticipated launch date summer 2025
3.To find a surcharge-free ATM in the Allpoint network visit allpointnetwork.com
4.DreamFi and Florida State Research, May 2025, n=1,500 US Adults.

Scan Now

DREAMFI.COM

CONGRATULATIONS
NATIONAL BAR ASSOCIATION
EST. 1925
100TH
Anniversary
FORREST B.
JOHNSON, ESQ.
National Bar Association's SFSPD Esquire Award
National Bar Association's Presidential Award for
Outstanding Service to the Association
National Bar Association's Presidential Award for
Exemplary Service to the Association
Gate City Bar Association
A.T. Walden Outstanding Lawyer Award
Gate City Bar Association
Hall of Fame Inductee
FBJ

Congratulations

to the

National Bar Association

on its

Centennial Anniversary

100 years of Social Justice, Bold Leadership, Advocacy, Empowerment, Service, Education and Mentorship

Belinda D. Stith, Esq.

Service to the National Bar since 1986:

Hall of Fame Inductee
Vice President (2 terms)
Board Member at Large
Region IX Director
Affiliate Representative on the Board
Board Member, National Bar Institute
Chair, Budget Committee
Chair, Elections Committee
Chair, Nominations and Elections Committee
Administration and Facilities Committee
Los Angeles Convention Committee
Women Lawyers Division Chair's Award
Presidential Award Recipient
Life Member, National Bar Association
Life Member, National Bar Institute

BDS

Congratulations to the National Bar Association from the Benjamin L. Crump College of Law as you make the 100-year mark!

Ben Crump Law PLLC
633 Pennsylvania Ave NW
Washington, D.C. 20004
(800) 688-7111
www.BenCrump.com

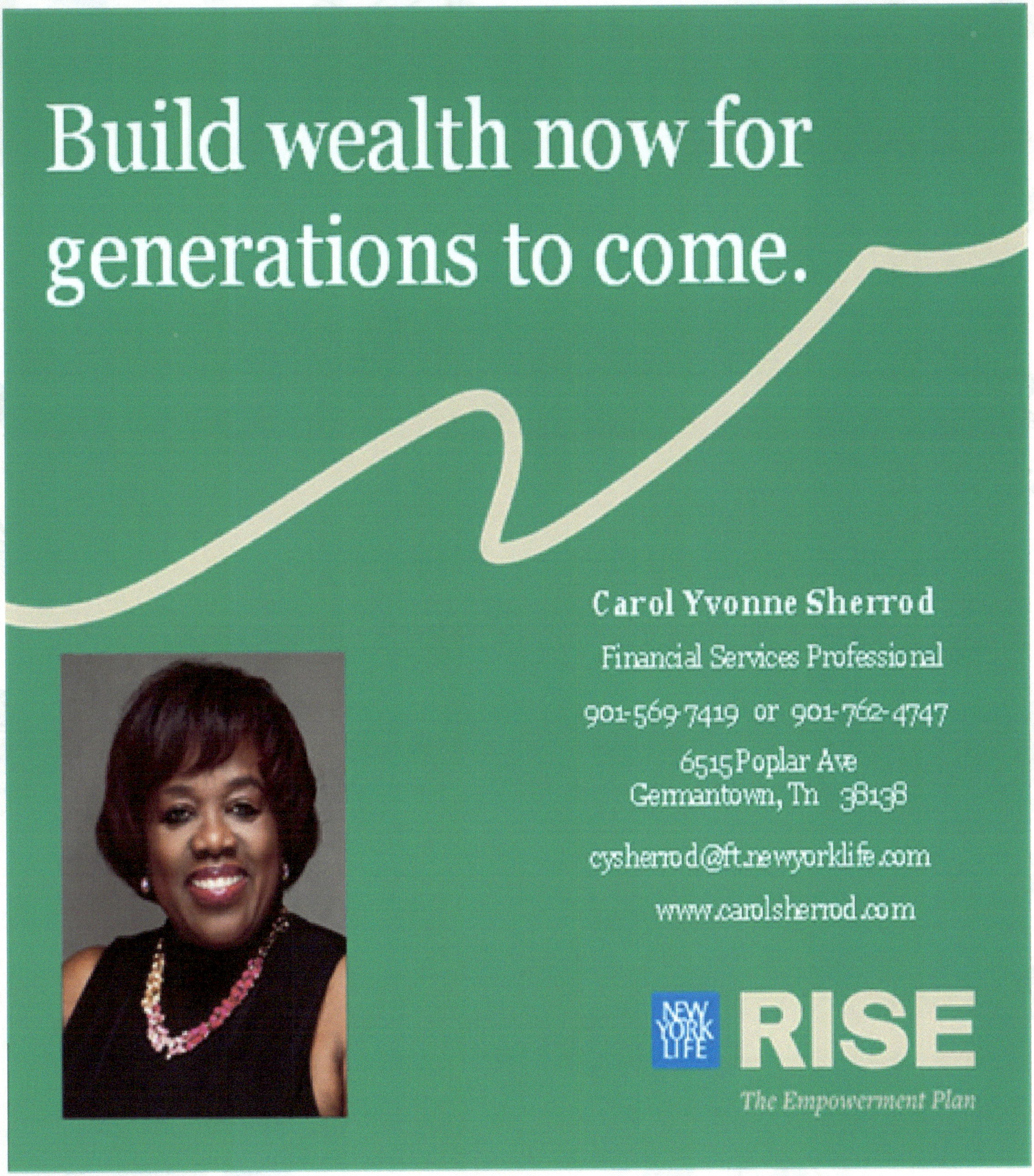
Build wealth now for generations to come.
Carol Yvonne Sherrod
Financial Services Professional
901-569-7419 or 901-762-4747
6515 Poplar Ave
Germantown, Tn 38138
cysherrod@ft.newyorklife.com
www.carolsherrod.com
NEW YORK LIFE
RISE
The Empowerment Plan

With pride and sisterhood, the
National Bar Association members of
Alpha Kappa Alpha Sorority, Incorporated® proudly celebrate
100 years of excellence, advocacy and igniting justice.

Congratulations

1925–2025

Carolyn House Stewart, Esq.

28th International President & CEO

Alpha Kappa Alpha Sorority, Inc.®
Tampa, FL

Dr. Glenda Baskin Glover

30th International President & CEO

Alpha Kappa Alpha Sorority, Inc.®
Nashville, TN

NBA Past Leaders & Members

Hon. Arnette R. Hubbard
39th President
Chicago, IL

Beverly McQueary Smith, Esq.
56th President
Kingwood, TX

Kim M. Keenan, Esq.
62nd President
Washington, D.C.

Vanita M. Banks, Esq.
65th President
Chicago, IL

Pamela J. Meanes, Esq.
72nd President
St. Louis, MO

Lonita K. Baker, Esq.
80th President
Louisville, KY

Justice Peggy A. Quince (Ret.)
38th Chair
Judicial Council
Tampa, FL

Hon. Denise Langford Morris (Ret.)
43rd Chair
Judicial Council
Detroit, MI

With pride and sisterhood, the
National Bar Association members of
Alpha Kappa Alpha Sorority, Incorporated® proudly celebrate
100 years of excellence, advocacy and igniting justice.

Congratulations

1925–2025

Hon. Randa M. Trapp (Ret.)
44th Chair
Judicial Council
Detroit, MI

Hon. Shauna Graves-Roberston
49th Chair
Judicial Council
Salt Lake City, UT

Hon. Kimberly M. Esmond Adams
52nd Chair
Judicial Council
Atlanta, GA

Hon. JaDawnya C. Baker
Atlanta, GA

Hon. Sonja N. Brown
Marietta, GA

Hon. Amanda N. Heath
Augusta, GA

Hon. Sandra Hemphill (Ret.)
Tampa, FL

Hon. Gina C. Higgins
Memphis, TN

Hon. Julie Harris Nelson
Miami, FL

Hon. Mitzi H. Pollard
Memphis, TN

Hon. Monica McCoy Purdy
Dallas, TX

Hon. Julie Simone Sneed
Orlando, FL

With pride and sisterhood, the
National Bar Association members of
Alpha Kappa Alpha Sorority, Incorporated® proudly celebrate
100 years of excellence, advocacy and igniting justice.

Congratulations

1925–2025

Hon. Alfreda Talton-Harris (Ret.)
Franklin, VA

Vicki D. Blanton, Esq.
Dallas Tx

Sharon F. Bridges, Esq.
Jackson, MS

Paulette Vance Burton, Esq.
Fredericksburg, VA

Cinnamon Butler, Esq.
Washington, D.C.

Brooke Cluse, Esq.
Houston, TX

Sonica R. Dixon, Esq.
Hackensack, NJ

Ellen E. Douglass, Esq.
Chicago, IL

Trina Alexander Eaddy, Esq.
Prince George's County, MD

Monique M. Edwards, Esq.
Baton Rouge, LA

DeMonica D. Gladney, Esq.
Houston, TX

Ava Danelle Green, Esq.
Charlotte, NC

With pride and sisterhood, the
National Bar Association members of
Alpha Kappa Alpha Sorority, Incorporated® proudly celebrate
100 years of excellence, advocacy and igniting justice.

Congratulations

1925–2025

Traci Williams Jones, Esq.
San Diego, CA

Danielle A. Pinkston, Esq.
Joliet, IL

Deborah Martin Owens, Esq.
New York, NY

Rosalind R. Ray, Esq.
Washington, D.C.

Valencia R. Rainey, Esq.
Washington, D.C.

Ebony R. Rivon, Esq.
Dallas, TX

Lani P. Shaw, Esq.
National Habor, MD

Charlyn Stanberry, Esq.
Washington, D.C.

Ellise M. Washington, Esq.
Birmingham, AL

Jordan M. Wellington, Esq.
El Paso, TX

Courtney White, Esq.
Dallas, TX

JUDGE DIANE M SHELLEY (ret.)

CONGRATULATES THE NATIONAL BAR ASSOCIATION ON IT'S 100th ANNIVERSARY OF FIGHTING FOR JUSTICE AND THE WILL TO FIGHT 100 MORE.

AND BEST WISHES TO THE INCOMING CHAIR OF THE JUDICIAL COUNCIL

JUSTICE FREDDRENNA M. LYLES

IN THE SPIRIT OF OUR ANCESTORS, BE STRONG, BE FEARLESS.

The CK Hoffler Firm
CONGRATULATES THE
NATIONAL BAR ASSOCIATION
100 Years of Service
The CK Hoffler Firm specializes in representing plaintiffs in trucking accidents, medical malpractice, wrongful death, catastrophic personal injury, civil rights litigation, commercial litigation, employment discrimination, opioid litigation, global commercial transactions, and Name, Image and Likeness. The law firm brings a high-calibered, multi-lingual team of professionals to the practice of law.
PRACTICE AREAS
CIVIL RIGHTS LITIGATION
MEDICAL NEGLIGENCE
TRUCKING ACCIDENTS
COMMERCIAL LITIGATION
EMPLOYMENT DISCRIMINATION
OPIOID LITIGATION
NAME, IMAGE, & LIKENESS ADVICE & COUNSEL
CATASTROPHIC PERSONAL INJURY
GLOBAL COMMERCIAL TRANSACTIONS
CONTACT US
www.ckhofflerfirm.com
(877) CKHOFFLER

NAME | IMAGE | LIKENESS
THE NIL LAW GROUP, LLC.

(877) CKHOFFLER
WWW.NILLAWGROUP.ORG

CONGRATULATES THE

NATIONAL BAR ASSOCIATION

100 Years of Service

ABOUT NIL LAW GROUP, LLC.

The NIL (Name, Image, & Likeness) Law Group is a national practice with six (6) powerhouse lawyers who specialize in counseling for athletes during NIL negotiations. Our firm has a proven track record of success both in and out of the courtroom. We pride ourselves on our trial lawyer instincts and negotiating experience to help our clients win on and off the field.

LEGAL TEAM

CK Hoffler
NIL Law Group, LLC., Managing Member

Latif Oduola-Owoo
NIL Law Group, LLC., Member

Michael E. Pérez
NIL Law Group, LLC., Member

Shannon A. Holmes
NIL Law Group, LLC., Member

Keith Lamar
NIL Law Group, LLC., Member

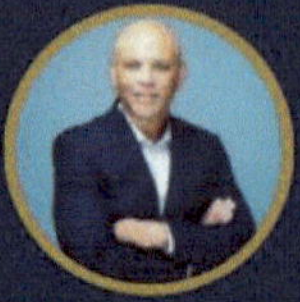

Robert Arrington
NIL Law Group, LLC., Member

Moorisha Bey-Taylor
NIL Law Group, LLC., Member

NEGOTIATE WITH A PURPOSE

Few people are as uniquely suited to take on Name, Image and Likeness (NIL) legal work as Tricia "CK" Hoffler. As one of the nation's leading trial lawyers for nearly four decades, Hoffler has fought fiercely and delivered exceptional results for clients during international business contract negotiations, serious personal injury cases, civil rights violations and more.

Hoffler also is passionate about working with young athletes. As the mother of two sons who are Division 1 college football players, Hoffler applies her personal perspective in helping athletes navigate NIL matters. She is dedicated to protecting athletes' interests just as much as she is to safeguarding her sons' rights.

These experiences prompted Hoffler to develop a thriving national practice with six powerhouse lawyers to counsel athletes during NIL negotiations. Hoffler's trial lawyer instincts, experience at the negotiating table and proven record in the courtroom help her clients win on and off the field.

Name, Image & Likeness (NIL) Contract Negotiations · Dispute Resolution · Litigation · Contract Drafting & Review · Risk Assessment & Mitigation · Personal Injury · Intellectual Property · Regulatory Compliance · Wrongful Death

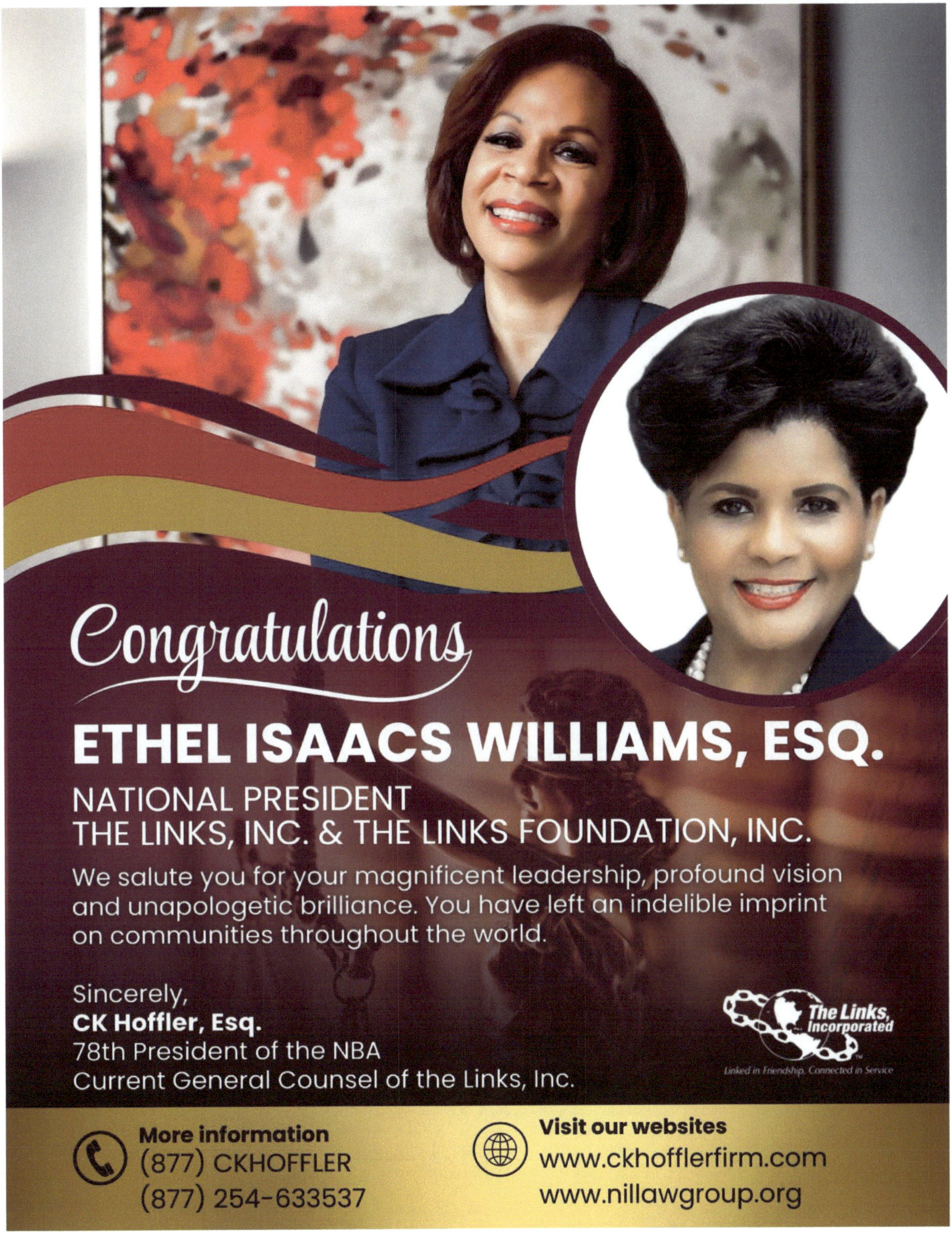
Congratulations
ETHEL ISAACS WILLIAMS, ESQ.
NATIONAL PRESIDENT
THE LINKS, INC. & THE LINKS FOUNDATION, INC.
We salute you for your magnificent leadership, profound vision and unapologetic brilliance. You have left an indelible imprint on communities throughout the world.
Sincerely,
CK Hoffler, Esq.
78th President of the NBA
Current General Counsel of the Links, Inc.
The Links, Incorporated
Linked in Friendship, Connected in Service
More information
(877) CKHOFFLER
(877) 254-633537
Visit our websites
www.ckhofflerfirm.com
www.nillawgroup.org

Congratulations
JOHNNIE COCHRAN
Honoring our legendary and legal powerhouse whose contributions will live on indefinitely, thank you for touching the lives of many in our profession. I had the honor of partnering with you and your team while working with legendary trial lawyer Willie Gary.
Sincerely,
CK Hoffler, Esq.
78th President of the NBA
More information
(877) CKHOFFLER
(877) 254-633537
Visit our websites
www.ckhofflerfirm.com
www.nillawgroup.org

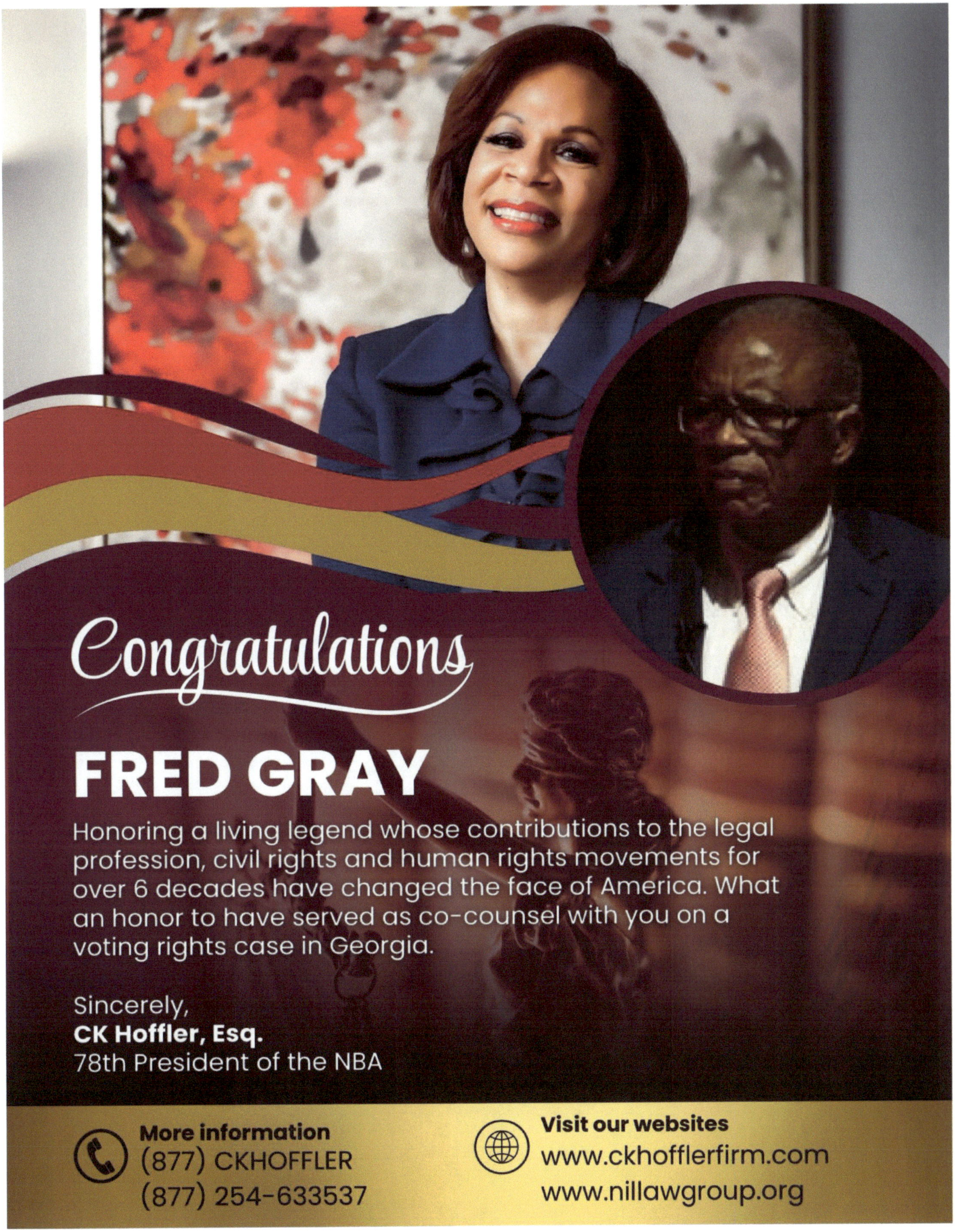
Congratulations
FRED GRAY
Honoring a living legend whose contributions to the legal profession, civil rights and human rights movements for over 6 decades have changed the face of America. What an honor to have served as co-counsel with you on a voting rights case in Georgia.
Sincerely,
CK Hoffler, Esq.
78th President of the NBA
More information
(877) CKHOFFLER
(877) 254-633537
Visit our websites
www.ckhofflerfirm.com
www.nillawgroup.org

Congratulations
WILLIE & GLORIA GARY
Honoring our living legends who built an unapologetic legal dynasty that trained and prepared generations of lawyers. Bravo for paving the way for NBA lawyers and honoring me with privilege of serving as one of your law partners. We salute you for your brilliance, philanthropy and for giving voice to the voiceless.
Sincerely,
CK Hoffler, Esq.
78th President of the NBA
More information
(877) CKHOFFLER
(877) 254-633537
Visit our websites
www.ckhofflerfirm.com
www.nillawgroup.org

Congratulations
REV. JESSE L. JACKSON, SR.
Honoring our living legend whose global impact on civil and human rights is unparalleled, thank you for granting me the privilege of serving as your legal counsel since 1988.
Sincerely,
CK Hoffler, Esq.
78th President of the NBA
More information
(877) CKHOFFLER
(877) 254-633537
Visit our websites
www.ckhofflerfirm.com
www.nillawgroup.org

Congratulations
LORENZO & JOVITA WILLIAMS
We salute you for helping to build a legal dynasty and for training generations of lawyers. Thank you for your leadership and for being a great role model to me as a trial lawyer and as a parent.
Sincerely,
CK Hoffler, Esq.
78th President of the NBA
More information
(877) CKHOFFLER
(877) 254-633537
Visit our websites
www.ckhofflerfirm.com
www.nillawgroup.org

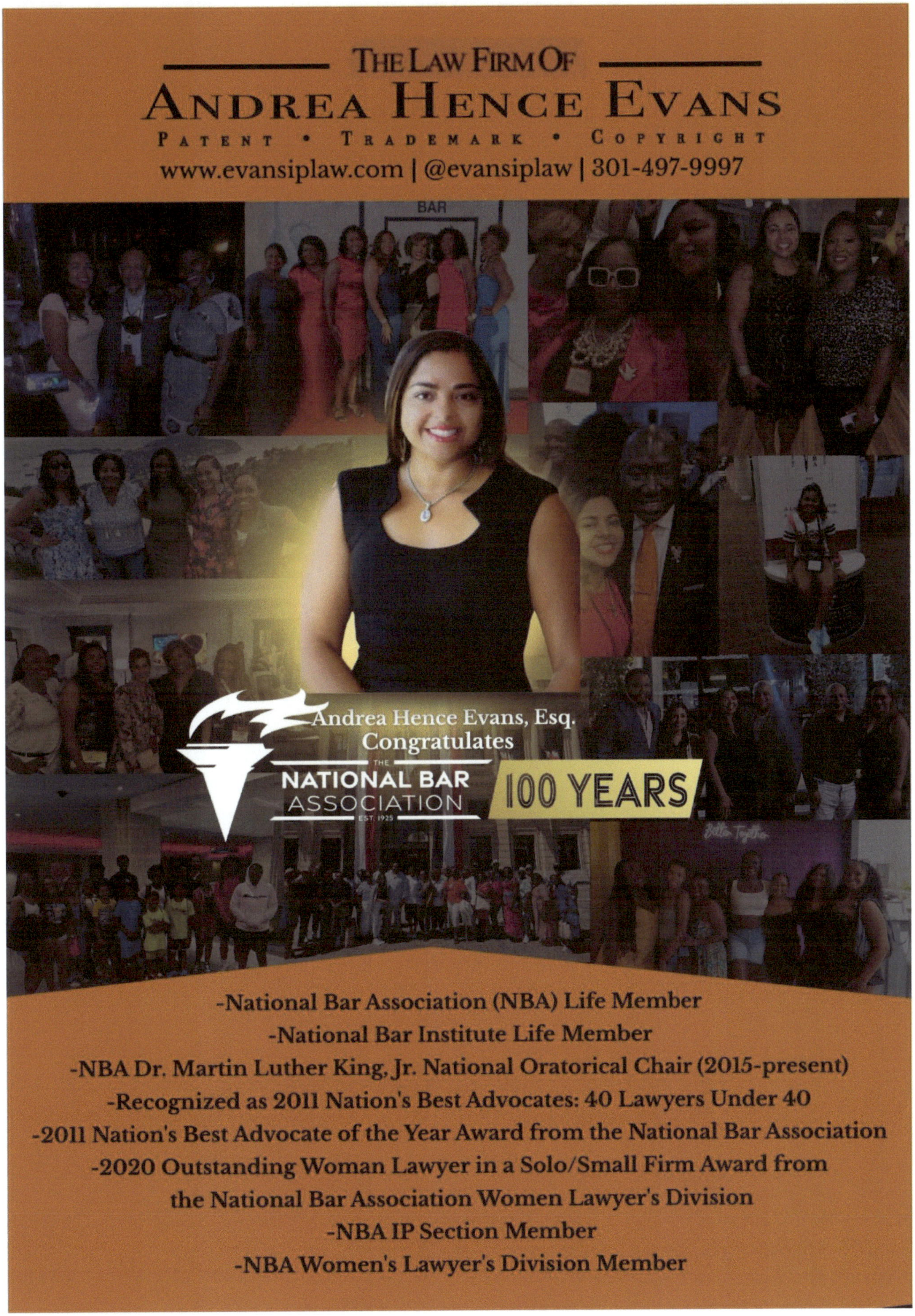
THE LAW FIRM OF
ANDREA HENCE EVANS
PATENT • TRADEMARK • COPYRIGHT
www.evansiplaw.com | @evansiplaw | 301-497-9997
BAR
Andrea Hence Evans, Esq.
Congratulates
THE
NATIONAL BAR
ASSOCIATION
EST. 1925
100 YEARS
-National Bar Association (NBA) Life Member
-National Bar Institute Life Member
-NBA Dr. Martin Luther King, Jr. National Oratorical Chair (2015-present)
-Recognized as 2011 Nation's Best Advocates: 40 Lawyers Under 40
-2011 Nation's Best Advocate of the Year Award from the National Bar Association
-2020 Outstanding Woman Lawyer in a Solo/Small Firm Award from
the National Bar Association Women Lawyer's Division
-NBA IP Section Member
-NBA Women's Lawyer's Division Member

Congratulations

THE NATIONAL BAR ASSOCIATION EST. 1925 **100 YEARS**

HONORABLE TANITA CAIN
District Court- Criminal Division
Birmingham, Alabama
NBA Judicial Council,
Asst. Parliamentarian

HONORABLE ERIC FANCHER
District Judge (Ret.)
Bessemer Division
Bessemer, Alabama

HONORABLE JACQUELYN GRANT JONES
District Judge
Birmingham, Alabama
NBA Judicial Council Member

HONORABLE DAVID J. HOBDY, JR.
Presiding Circuit Judge
(Bessemer Division)
Bessemer, Alabama
NBA Judicial Council, Historian

HONORABLE STEPHANIE HUNTER
District Court Judge
Bessemer, Alabama
NBA Judicial Council Member

HONORABLE AARON KILLINGS
Bessemer Municipal Judge
(Ret.)
Bessemer, Alabama

HONORABLE ADRIENNE MOFFETT POWELL
Circuit Court Judge
Domestic Relations Division
Birmingham, Alabama
NBA Judicial Council Member

HONORABLE KATRINA ROSS
Alabama District Court Judge
(Ret.)
Municipal Court Judge
Birmingham, Alabama

HONORABLE CAROLE SMITHERMAN
Circuit Court Judge (Ret)
Tenth Judicial Circuit Court
Birmingham, Alabama
NBA Judicial Council Member

HONORABLE PATRICIA STEPHENS
Presiding Judge Domestic
Relations Division
Birmingham, Alabama
NBA Judicial Council Member

HONORABLE THOMAS E. THRASH
Circuit Judge Jefferson County
Bessemer Division
Bessemer, Alabama
NBA Judicial Council Member

HONORABLE DEBRA WESTON – PICKENS
Presiding Judge , District Civil
Birmingham, Alabama
NBA Judicial Council Member

Honorable Brendette Brown Green
Circuit Judge
Jefferson County, Alabama
NBA Judicial Council, Chair
Birmingham, Alabama

MILES LAW SCHOOL
STRIVING TO BALANCE

NBA Links

With a sense of pride and unity, the members of the National Bar Association and The Links, Incorporated, come together to joyously commemorate 100 years of unparalleled excellence, unwavering advocacy, and the empowerment of justice.

Congratulations

Ethel Issacs Williams
National President
The Links, Incorporated
West Palm Beach, FL

Chan Abney
Stuart, FL

Arthenia Joyner
Tampa, FL

Sheree Davis Cunningham
West Palm Beach, FL

Patricia Moore Rosier
Bowie, MD

Kim M. Keenan
Washington, DC

Yolanda Cash Jackson
Miami, FL

Kimberly Esmond Adams
Atlanta, GA

Carla Pittman
Los Angeles, CA

Melissa Bondaldes
Brooklyn, NY

NBA Links

With a sense of pride and unity, the members of the National Bar Association and The Links, Incorporated, come together to joyously commemorate 100 years of unparalleled excellence, unwavering advocacy, and the empowerment of justice.

Congratulations

Sonya Hoskins
Dallas, TX

Andrea Evans
Laurel, MD

Rene Carter
New Orleans, LA

Daphne Forbes
Bowie, MD

Charlene Proctor
Bowie, MD

Linda Andrews
Bowie, MD

Belinda Stith
Los Angeles, CA

Denise Langford Morris
Detroit, MI

Trina Eaddy
Washington, DC

Vanita Banks
Chicago, IL

NBA Links

With a sense of pride and unity, the members of the National Bar Association and The Links, Incorporated, come together to joyously commemorate 100 years of unparalleled excellence, unwavering advocacy, and the empowerment of justice.

Congratulations

Algenita Scott Davis
Houston, TX

Sheila Tillerson Adams
Bowie, MD

Antoinette M. "Toni" Jackson
Houston, TX

Phyliss Gillespie
Stuart, FL

Dwinette Johnson Feemster
West Palm Beach , FL

Traci V. Bransford
Atlanta, GA

Danielle Carr
St. Louis, MO

Patrice Hinnant
Greensboro, NC

Irma Brown
Los Angeles, CA

Taylora Gary
Stuart, FL

NBA Links

With a sense of pride and unity, the members of the National Bar Association and The Links, Incorporated, come together to joyously commemorate 100 years of unparalleled excellence, unwavering advocacy, and the empowerment of justice.

Congratulations

Violet Travis Ricks
Atlanta, GA

Monica Harris
Atlanta, GA

Erica Williams
Tampa, FL

Anna-Marie Clark
St. Louis, MO

Gail Ash Dotson
Miami, FL

Ayanna Jenkins-Toney
Washington, DC

Kenya Johnson
Atlanta, GA

Congratulations to the National Bar Association 100 Years of Advocacy, Service, Empowerment and Education

My only Bar, the source of great friendships, networking and learning. To thine own self be true, wishing you 100 more!

DEBRA D. MATLOCK, Esq.

Serving the National Bar and its constituents since 1988:

Vice President
Member at Large
Chair, Women Lawyers Division
Chair, Corporate Law Section
Board Member, National Bar Institute
Life Member, National Bar Association
Life Member, National Bar Institute
Hall of Fame Inductee
Scroll of Distinguished NBA Women Lawyers
Chair, Elections Committee; Chair, Membership Committee; Chair, Administration & Facilities Committee; Chair, Constitution & Bylaws Committee; 1996 Chicago Convention Committee; Government Lawyers Section; Budget Committee; Convenor & Panelist, Transactional and Government law seminars.

Board Member, California Judges Association

Convener, First Secretary California Association Black Lawyers

Vice President John M. Langston Bar Association Convener and Founding Member of The Black Women Lawyers California (Los Angeles); second President and only two term President in the 50-year history of the organization.

Bernard M. Jefferson Judge of the Year, John M. Langston Bar Association

Judge of the Year Black Women Lawyers Association of Los Angeles

Black Women Lawyers Award for Judicial Excellence

Judge of the Year California Association of Black Lawyers

Black Prosecutors of Los Angeles County Association and Foundation Champion of Justice Award

Hall of FAME Inductee Langston Bar Association and National Bar Association

Convener, Founding Life Member Association of African American Judicial Officers of California

Judge Irma J. Brown, Superior Court of the State of California, County of Los Angeles (retired) 1982-2021

Loyola Law School, Los Angeles Black Law Students

Delegate to my first NBA Convention, 1971

Special Master for the Judicial Council of California,

National Bar Association

First Woman Judge appointed by the Governor of the State of California to the Compton Municipal Court (Challenged 9 days after appointment)

Retain Judge Irma J Brown Retention Campaign (Honorary Chair Stevie Wonder)

Presiding Judge of the Compton Municipal Court

Secretary, Municipal Court Judges Association of Los Angeles County

Chair of the California Center for Judicial Education and Research

In 1980, I proudly began my service as an Assistant United States Attorney in the Eastern District of Arkansas. In 1986, following my first National Bar Association Convention, I transferred to the District of Colorado, serving until 1996.

In 1993, I was honored to be elected President of the Sam Cary Bar Association, where I deepened my commitment to the NBA's mission.

Today, I humbly serve as a Circuit Court Judge for the First Judicial District of Arkansas, first elected in 2015 and re-elected in 2022.

I extend my deepest gratitude to my NBA mentors:
W. Harold "Sonny" Flowers, Jr., Esq. (Deceased), Judge Gary Jackson, and Judge Donald L. McCullin (Deceased), for their invaluable guidance during my service as Region IX Director and Civil Trial Advocacy Section Chair.

May God continue to bless the National Bar Association.

Judge Chalk S. Mitchell
Circuit Court Judge, First Judicial District of Arkansas

CONGRATULATIONS NATIONAL BAR ASSOCIATION ON ITS 100TH ANNIVERSARY

MLG THE MOORE LAW GROUP, LLC

PERSONAL INJURY • BANKRUPTCY LAW • COMMERCIAL LITIGATION

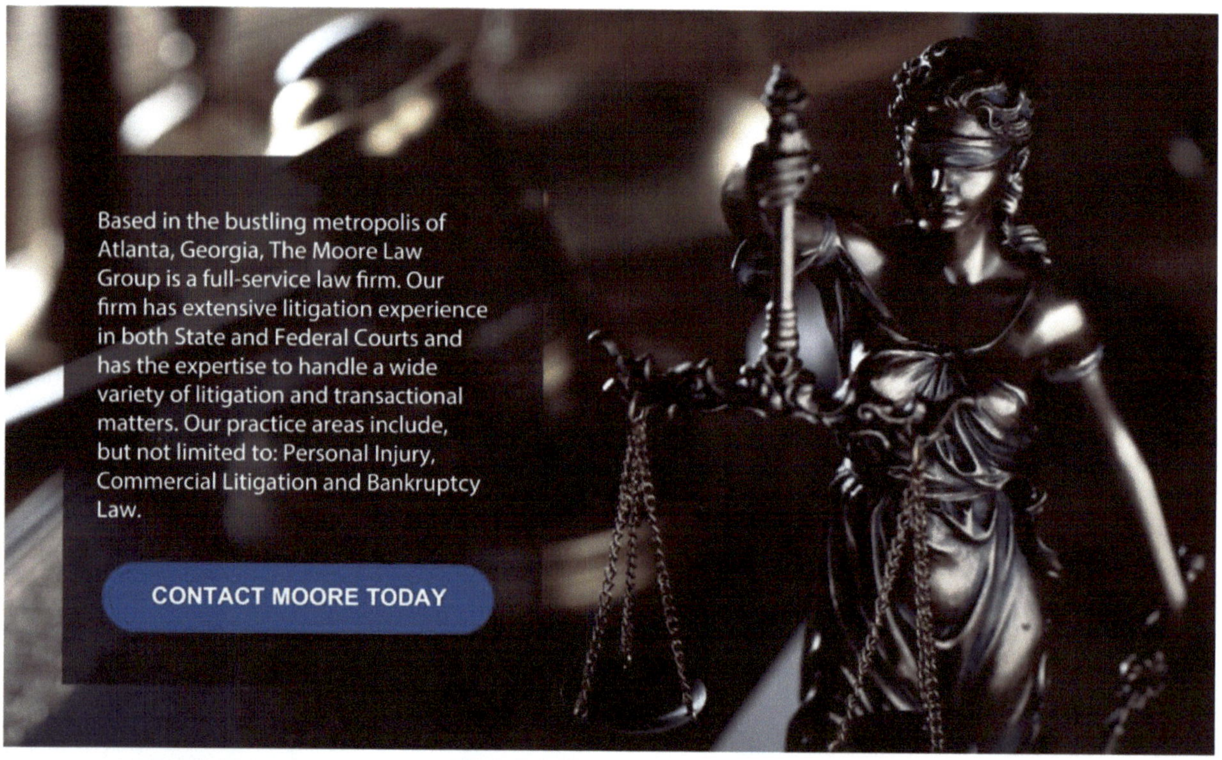

John A. Moore, Esq.
FIRM FOUNDER

ABOUT US

THE MOORE LAW GROUP

Our firm prides itself on offering "big firm experience" while providing "small firm values."

- Former Chair; NBA Small Firms and Solo Practitioner's Division;
- Former Chair; NBA Young Lawyer's Division;
- Former Chair; Law Student's Section

www.moorelawllc.com

Phone: 678.288.5600 • **Email:** jmoore@moorelawllc.com

1745 MARTIN LUTHER KING JR. DR., ATLANTA, GA 30314

The Cochran Firm is proud to celebrate 100 years of The National Bar Association and reflect on the important work of its leaders and members. For our firm, 2025 has also been a year of reflection on the legacy and responsibility left to us by our Founding Partner and prominent NBA supporter Johnnie L. Cochran, Jr. 20 years ago. The Cochran Firm looks forward to supporting the National Bar Association, its leadership, and members with the same enthusiasm as Mr. Cochran. Here's to the next 100 years!

THE COCHRAN FIRM

NBA Deltas

United in pride and solidarity, the esteemed members of the National Bar Association and Delta Sigma Theta Sorority, Incorporated, celebrate a century of unparalleled excellence, steadfast advocacy, and the empowerment of justice with jubilation.

Congratulations

Arthenia Joyner
Tampa, FL

Paulette Brown
Charleston, SC

Evett Simmons
Port St. Lucie, FL

Mavis Thompson
St. Louis, MO

Patricia Rosier
Bowie, MD

Ethel Issacs Williams
West Palm Beach, FL

Jasmine Crockett
Dallas, TX

Rene Carter
New Orleans, LA

Anne Marie-Clarke
St. Louis, MO

Chan Abney
West Palm Beach, FL

NBA Deltas

United in pride and solidarity, the esteemed members of the National Bar Association and Delta Sigma Theta Sorority, Incorporated, celebrate a century of unparalleled excellence, steadfast advocacy, and the empowerment of justice with jubilation.

Congratulations

Sheila Tillerson Adams
Bowie, MD

Cheryl Washington
Dayton, OH

Phyliss Gillespie
Stuart, FL

Antoinette Barksdale
Washington, DC

Chandra Holloway Walker
Silver Spring, MD

Sheree Davis Cunningham
West Palm Beach, FL

Sharon Strickland
Chicago, IL

Betty Hewlett
Bowie, MD

C. Hope Brown
Washington, DC

Andrea Evans
Laurel, MD

NBA Deltas

United in pride and solidarity, the esteemed members of the National Bar Association and Delta Sigma Theta Sorority, Incorporated, celebrate a century of unparalleled excellence, steadfast advocacy, and the empowerment of justice with jubilation.

Congratulations

Shelvin Hall
Chicago, IL

Valeria Obi
St. Petersburg, FL

Charlene Proctor
Bowie, MD

Nikki Simon
Pembroke Pines, FL

Toya Carmichael
Washington, DC

Valencia Tezino
Port Arthur, TX

Monica D. Abby
St. Louis, MO

Charis Lee
Flint, MI

Taylora Gary
Stuart, FL

Patricia Banks
Chicago, IL

NBA Deltas

United in pride and solidarity, the esteemed members of the National Bar Association and Delta Sigma Theta Sorority, Incorporated, celebrate a century of unparalleled excellence, steadfast advocacy, and the empowerment of justice with jubilation.

Congratulations

Yvette Alexander
Baton Rouge, LA

Kila Bobier
Dallas, TX

Deborah Henderson
Memphis, TN

Patrice Hinnant
Greensboro, NC

Miriam Perry
Ann Arbor, MI

Rachel Bell
Nashville, TN

Doreen Rachal
Washington, DC

Irma Brown
Los Angeles, CA

Iris Elijah
Tallahassee, FL

Danielle Carr
St. Louis, MO

NBA Deltas

United in pride and solidarity, the esteemed members of the National Bar Association and Delta Sigma Theta Sorority, Incorporated, celebrate a century of unparalleled excellence, steadfast advocacy, and the empowerment of justice with jubilation.

Congratulations

Gail Ash Dotson
Miami, FL

Tangela Barre
Atlanta, GA

Joretta Durant
Kinston, NC

Cheryl Gray Evans
Bristow, VA

Ernestine S. Gray
New Orleans, LA

Kristen McMullen
West Palm Beach, FL

Lynn Solomon
Ft. Laurderdale, FL

Eileen Olds
Virginia Beach, VA

Katri Kaye-Harris
Los Angeles, CA

Lanease Fuller
Houston, TX

NBA Deltas

United in pride and solidarity, the esteemed members of the National Bar Association and Delta Sigma Theta Sorority, Incorporated, celebrate a century of unparalleled excellence, steadfast advocacy, and the empowerment of justice with jubilation.

Congratulations

Yolanda Cash Jackson
Miami, FL

Charlene Honeywell
Tampa, FL

Ayanna Jenkins-Toney
Washington, DC

Rashinda MacMurray Abdullah
Washington, DC

Artis H. Cowan
Bowie, MD

Deidre L. Monroe
Gary, IN

Vicky Jones
Baton Rouge, LA

Anika Harmon
West Palm Beach, FL

Brendette Brown Green
Birmingham, AL

Nicole Lemon
District Heights, MD

NBA Deltas

United in pride and solidarity, the esteemed members of the National Bar Association and Delta Sigma Theta Sorority, Incorporated, celebrate a century of unparalleled excellence, steadfast advocacy, and the empowerment of justice with jubilation.

Congratulations

Elizabeth Winfield
Fayetteville, GA

Traci Woods
Baton Rouge, LA

Juanita Harris
Dallas, TX

Jacqueline Pierre
Houston, TX

Veronica James
Port St. Luce, FL

Erica K. Williams
Tampa, FL

Dwinette Johnson Feemster
West Palm Beach, FL

Salesia Smith Gordon
West Palm Beach, FL

Raqiyyah r. Pippins
Washington, DC

Ana Lisa Williams
Dayton, OH

Telsula Morgan
West Palm Beach, FL

CELEBRATING THE LEGACY OF

VIOLETTE N. ANDERSON, ESQ.

- 1st African American female attorney admitted to practice before the U.S. Supreme Court in 1926.
- 1st African American woman to graduate from Chicago Law School and only woman in her law school class
- 1st African American and 1st woman appointed as Assistant Prosecutor in Chicago

Triumphant Soror Violette N. Anderson, 8th Int'l President of Zeta Phi Beta Sorority, Incorporated served as a courtroom reporter for 15 years before attending Chicago Law School.

Triumphant Soror Anderson's commitment to law and justice broke barriers and opened doors for generations to follow.

WE HONOR HER LEGACY TODAY AND EVERY DAY

The National Bar Association Members of Phi Beta Sigma Fraternity, Incorporated and Zeta Phi Beta Sorority, Incorporated

To Connect with NBA members of the Blue and White family, please contact nbazetasandsigmas@gmail.com

NATIONAL BAR ASSOCIATION'S CHAPTER

NU BETA ALPHA

BROTHERS OF OMEGA PSI PHI FRATERNITY INC.

On behalf of the Brothers of Nu Beta Alpha Chapter of Omega Psi Phi, Fraternity Inc., house within the National Bar Association, we proudly support the historic milestone and take part in the celebration of the National Bar Association's Centennial Year!

1925-2025

CONGRATULATIONS!!!

O.T. WELLS, Basileus Emeritus "In Perpetuity" (decd.)
CLAYTON A. GRAHAM, Basileus
FRANK SEALES, JR., Keeper of Finance
STEVEN BRISTER, Keeper of Record and Seals

100th Years ANNIVERSARY
Congratulations to the
National Bar Association
on 100 Years of Excellence!
Honoring a Century of Justice.
Celebrating a Legacy of Leadership.
Congratulations to the National Bar Association on 100 years of championing justice, advancing civil rights, and empowering legal professionals across the nation.
For a century, the NBA has shaped the future of law, inspired generations, and stood as a beacon for equality and excellence.
Here's to 100 years of impact — and to the next 100 of bold progress.
Proud to celebrate this historic milestone with you.
GILLESPIE
LAW FIRM
Phyllis M. Gillespie, Esquire
Member since 1997
1 S.E. Ocean Blvd - Stuart, Florida 34994
Cell: 772-528-6666 - Office: 772-238-6388
www.gillespielawfirm.net

Congratulations to the National Bar Association on its 100 Year Anniversary and its continued commitment to promoting equal justice under the law
The Banks Law Firm provides counsel to corporate and municipal clients as they navigate today's complex and ever-changing environment. We strive to give every community what it deserves, and that is much more. That's building success.
• Affordable Housing and Community Economic Development
• Business and Corporations
• Cannabis
• Civil Litigation
• Education
• Estate Planning and Probate
• Labor and Employment
• New Market Tax Credits
• Commercial Real Estate
Antoinette M. "Toni" Jackson
Principal-in-Charge, Houston
NBA Life Member & NBI Life Member
tjackson@bankslawfirm.com
bankslawfirm.com
Durham Office:
919-474-9137
Houston Office:
832-954-2534
Atlanta Office:
404-689-6551
THE BANKS LAW FIRM P.A.
Building Success

"Congratulations to the National Bar Association on 100 years of stellar service."

SIA BAKER-BARNES

PRESIDENT OF
THE FLORIDA BAR

LIFE MEMBER OF
THE NATIONAL BAR
ASSOCIATION

We're proud to salute the

NATIONAL BAR
ASSOCIATION®
EST. 1925

**SEARCY
DENNEY
SCAROLA
BARNHART
& SHIPLEY** PA

ATTORNEYS AT LAW

AVIATION & RAILROAD DISASTERS • BOATING & WATERCRAFT INJURIES • VEHICLE ACCIDENTS • COMMERCIAL DISPUTES
CONSTRUCTION DEFECTS • DEFECTIVE DESIGN • INTELLECTUAL PROPERTIES • MASS TORTS • MEDICAL MALPRACTICE
PREMISES LIABILITY • PROFESSIONAL LIABILITY • TRUCKING ACCIDENTS • UNSAFE PRODUCTS • WILL AND TRUST DISPUTES

WEST PALM BEACH / TALLAHASSEE ◆ 800.780.8607 ◆ WWW.SEARCYLAW.COM

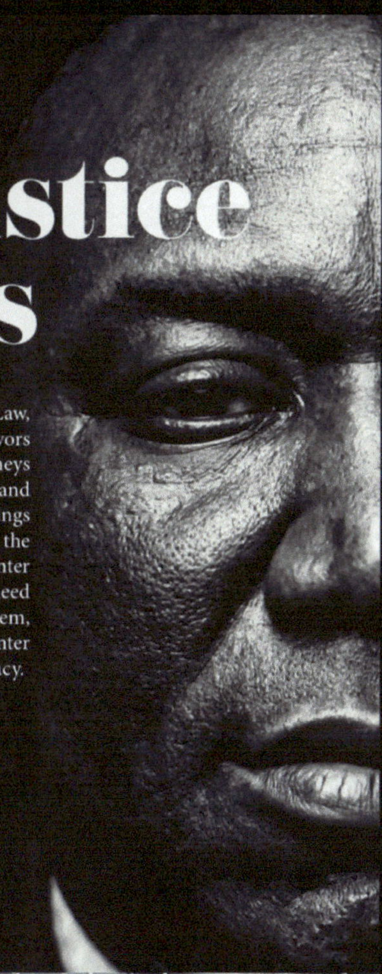

We Train Social Justice Engineers

Housed within the St. Thomas University College of Law, the Benjamin L. Crump Center for Social Justice endeavors to create an army of social justice engineers; future attorneys that will advocate for the marginalized, the victimized, and the disenfranchised. The Catholic church's social teachings emphasize that the dignity of the human person is the foundation of a moral vision for society. The Crump Center seeks to convene those aspects of society that are most in need of dialog: policy makers, law enforcement, the judicial system, and affected communities. The expressed function of the Center is the elimination of injustice through education and advocacy.

STU

College of Law
Benjamin L. Crump
Center for Social Justice

THE LAW OFFICE OF STEVEN E. BULLOCK PC CONGRATULATES

THE NATIONAL BAR ASSOCIATION 100 YEARS OF ADVOCACY, SERVICE, LEADERSHIP, EMPOWERMENT AND EDUCATION. THANK YOU.

CONTINUE TO FIGHT THE GOOD FIGHT!

THE NBA CONTINUES BE AN OUTSTANDING ORGANIZATION SERVING THOSE WHO MIGHT OTHERWISE BE WITHOUT OUTSTANDING COMPETENT LEGAL REPRESENTATION. THE NBA'S COMMITMENT TO BEING ON THE FOREFRONT ON THE LEGAL ISSUES OF THE DAY IS WHY I CONTINUE TO SUPPORT THE NBA. I AM VERY PROUD TO BE A LIFETIME MEMBER OF THE NBA. CONTINUED SUCCESS ON THE NEXT 100 YEARS.

The Hon. Anne-Marie Clarke (retired) St Louis, MO
NBA and NBI Life Member
47th Chair, Judicial Council (2017-2018)
Member, Centennial Commission

Even before I was a member of the Bar, I was aware of the National Bar. As a young child, our family's summer vacation was often to the site of the National Bar Annual Convention. This was back in the day when Black families had to choose the family vacation. The Clarke Family vacation was spent for my father, Atty. Thomas P. Clarke, to attend the National Bar Convention. When I got to Saint Louis University Law School, because of my father, I learned from Elmer Jackson, the NBA Executive Secretary, of a summer internship with the Joint Center for Political Studies at HUD. The Assistant Secretary was Samuel C. Jackson and, as a first year law student, I had the temerity to ask for time off from my internship to attend the NBA Convention! And Mr. Jackson gave me the time off—with pay!

It was the beginning of my NBA journey with my father. This was time we enjoyed together practically every summer. It was a family affair. My mom, Mary V Clarke, was active with the Bench & Bar Spouses (later NABBS). After I got married, my husband, Richard K. Gaines, got involved with NABBS. We were all present when my father was inducted into the Inaugural Class of the NBA Hall of Fame in 1986, exactly 40 years after he attended his first NBA Convention in Detroit. My last Convention with my father was 1997; he died in 1999.

Congratulations
to the National Bar Association's
Centennial (100th) Celebration
Serving the Community

BEVERLY F. DRUITT, ESQ.

RETIRED

NATIONAL LABOR RELATIONS BOARD

7935 LAKE PLEASANT DRIVE
SPRINGFIELD, VA 22153-2750

HOME: 703-912-6548 CELL: 703-342-2478

BFD605@VERIZON.NET

Zenobia Waters Jones, Esq.

With over three decades of Legal Excellence, Zenobia is a trailblazing Attorney, Political Strategist, and Mentor. Since launching her legal career in 1992. She has broken barriers as the First Attorney in Her Family and one of the few Black Women leading a successful Law Practice—The Waters Firm PC, founded in 1998. Her firm specializes in Personal Injury, Corporate, Government, and Entertainment Law.

Mentored by Legal Giants including Attorneys Willie E. Gary, Linnes Finney Jr., Yolvondra Martin-Brown, The Late Charles A. Mathis, and The Late Johnny Cochran, Zenobia's career is nothing short of extraordinary! She also serves as Of Counsel to Benjamin Crump. She is a passionate advocate for children, the elderly, and underserved communities, with extensive service with the National Bar Association for over Thirty Years. She serves on the Centennial Commission and Chairs the Torch Bearers Initiative for the NBA as well as services with the Georgia Association of Black Women Attorneys in Atlanta, Georgia.

Zenobia has also been a key figure in national and local politics, counseling elected officials, and also served as a surrogate speaker for Vice President Al Gore during his bid for the President of the United States. An Ordained Minister and Speaker, Zenobia extends her impact through Ministry, Film (trained by the great, double Emmy Winner, Greg Alan Williams), and Community Service—living her lifelong mission of Justice, Empowerment, and Service, all while being a devoted Wife, Mother, and Grandmother.

A Tribute to 100 Years of Excellence

I would like to take this opportunity to congratulate the National Bar Association on a historic and extraordinary milestone—100 years of excellence, advocacy, and empowerment.

For a full century, the National Bar Association has been an indispensable resource for African American lawyers, judges, and law students across this country. It has served not only as a professional home, but as a sanctuary—a place where we could be seen, heard, and supported.

I often reflect on my very first NBA Convention. I arrived as a small-town country lawyer, still wet behind the ears and unsure of what the future held. But when I walked into that room and saw a sea of Black excellence—brilliant minds, powerful voices, and proud traditions—I was inspired in a way I had never known. I discovered a network of individuals who understood the unique battles I faced and the burdens I carried. That experience was transformative.

The NBA became the soil in which I was planted and nurtured. Through mentorship, shared wisdom, and unwavering support, I was able to grow—not just as a lawyer, but as a leader, an advocate, and a believer in the boundless possibilities before me.

As minorities in a profession long dominated by the majority, we were often told—directly or indirectly—that we had to be twice as good to receive half the recognition. But the NBA taught us something different. The mindset was not merely to overcome—but to conquer. It instilled in us the power to defy limits, challenge systems, and change the face of the legal profession.

The NBA gave me—an HBCU graduate in both undergrad and law school—the confidence to stand tall in courtrooms across America. To know that I belonged, regardless of where others came from or what names were on their diplomas. I knew I had something just as valuable: the fire forged in community, resilience, and purpose.

And now, as we celebrate this centennial anniversary, I am filled with pride and gratitude to see the NBA continuing to pour into the next generation of Black legal minds—just as it did for me.

To the National Bar Association: thank you for 100 years of lifting as you climbed. May your next century be even more impactful.

Congratulations on 100 years of greatness.

Willie E. Gary, Esq.

THE LAW FIRM OF
GARY, WILLIAMS, PARENTI,
WATSON & GARY P.L.L.C.

100 YEARS OF POWER, PURPOSE, & PROGRESS

Honoring the National Bar Association's Centennial Legacy

The National Urban League proudly salutes the National Bar Association on 100 years of unwavering service, groundbreaking advocacy, and leadership in the fight for justice.

For a century, the NBA has been a pillar in the pursuit of civil rights, the advancement of Black legal professionals, and the protection of our communities through the rule of law.

As President and CEO of the National Urban League and a proud member of the National Bar Association, Marc H. Morial joins the Urban League Movement in celebrating this historic milestone. We look forward to the next century of continued partnership and a shared commitment to equity, empowerment, and justice for all.

Marc H. Morial
President &CEO,
National Urban League

JOIN THE MOVEMENT & STAY CONNECTED!

NUL.ORG

Follow us on social
@naturbanleague

National
Urban League

NEW DAY
PROMOTIONAL PRODUCTS
Creative Products For Your Business
Congratulations to
The National Bar Association On 100 Years
PROUD VENDOR AND SPONSOR OF
THE NATIONAL BAR ASSOCIATION SINCE 2014
TONS OF THANKS TO:
The National Office
Small Firms/Solo Practitioners' Division (SFSPD)
Women Lawyers Division (WLD)
Young Lawyers Division (YLD)
ADR Section
Civil Trial Advocacy Section
Washington Bar Association
an Affiliate of the National Bar Association
Through the years...
C. Francis Stradford Award
40 Under 40 AWARDS
Gertrude Rush AWARDS
Wiley Branton Awards
Here's to 100 more years of success!
LET'S GET YOUR BRAND OUT THERE!
Creative Products for your business or organization!
Awards • Trophies • Postcards • Programs
Graphic Design • Stationery • Brochures
T-Shirts • Booklets • Yard Signs • Buttons
Banners • Pens • Thousands of Products
(678) 551-5982
www.newdaypp.com
Find us on Facebook:
New Day Promotional Products
Find us on LinkedIn:
new-day-promotional-products
Yardyne Day
NBA Member, Brand Specialist & Author

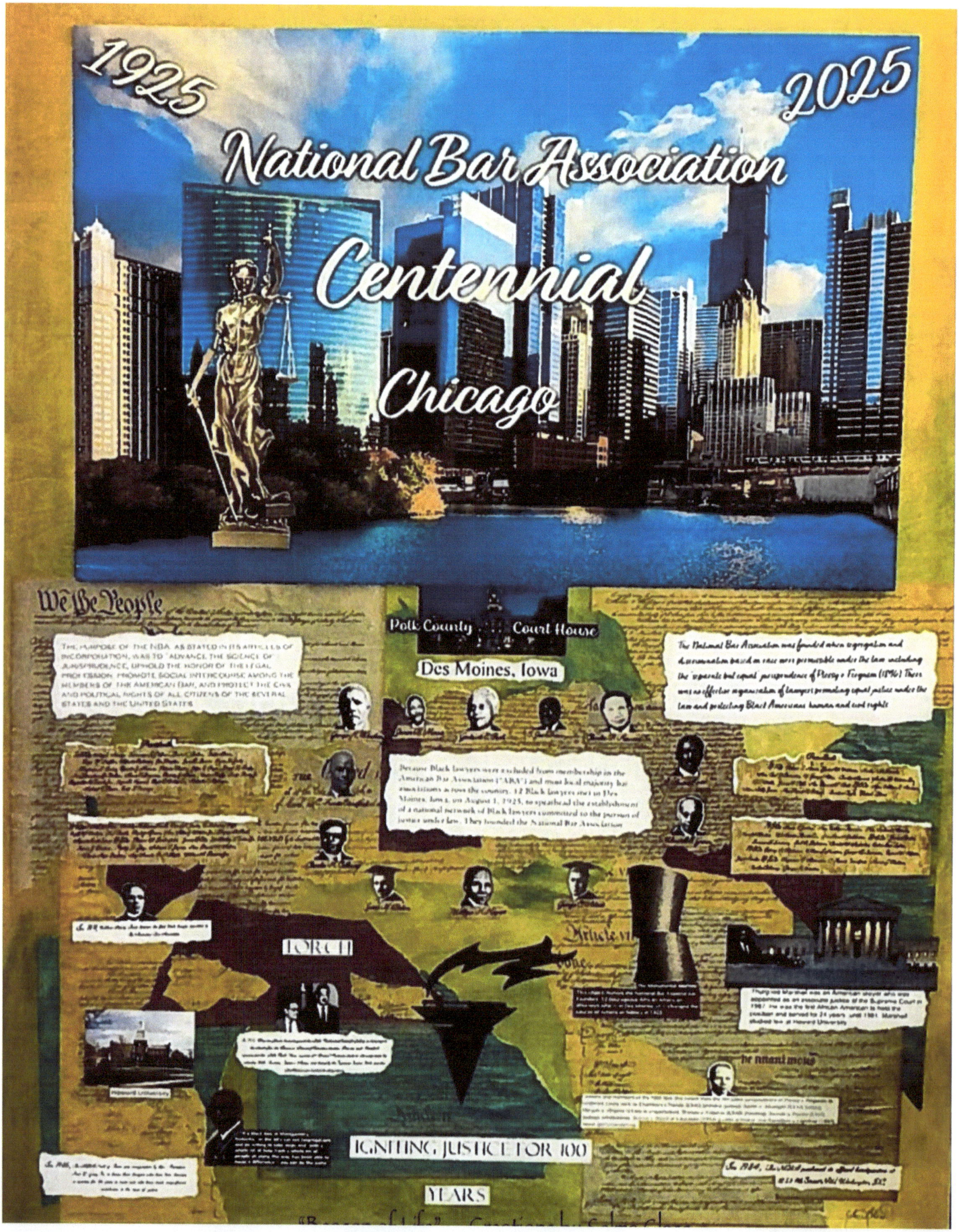
1925
2025
National Bar Association
Centennial
Chicago
We the People
Polk County Court House
Des Moines, Iowa
THE PURPOSE OF THE NBA, AS STATED IN ITS ARTICLES OF INCORPORATION, WAS TO "ADVANCE THE SCIENCE OF JURISPRUDENCE, UPHOLD THE HONOR OF THE LEGAL PROFESSION, PROMOTE SOCIAL INTERCOURSE AMONG THE MEMBERS OF THE AMERICAN BAR, AND PROTECT THE CIVIL AND POLITICAL RIGHTS OF ALL CITIZENS OF THE SEVERAL STATES AND THE UNITED STATES
The National Bar Association was founded when segregation and discrimination based on race were permissible under the law including the "separate but equal" jurisprudence of Plessy v Ferguson (1896) There was no effective organization of lawyers promoting equal justice under the law and protecting Black Americans human and civil rights
Because Black lawyers were excluded from membership in the American Bar Association ("ABA") and most local majority bar associations across the country, 12 Black lawyers met in Des Moines, Iowa, on August 1, 1925, to spearhead the establishment of a national network of Black lawyers committed to the pursuit of justice under law. They founded the National Bar Association
TORCH
Thurgood Marshall was an American lawyer who was appointed as an associate justice of the Supreme Court in 1967. He was the first African American to hold the position and served for 24 years until 1991. Marshall studied law at Howard University
Howard University
IGNITING JUSTICE FOR 100
YEARS

IN MEMORIUM

NATIONAL BAR ASSOCIATION
EST. 1925

MEMORIAL

When you think back about those NBA members you have crossed paths with in the national bar association, you now can reflect on their legacy.

Some spoke about freedom. some spoke about just....us which was really them saying no justice! some spoke about democracy! some spoke of demanding respect!

But one thing for sure they remain in your hearts and in your mind. this memorial section is a salute to those who made law enjoyable.

LEGACY
I write of Africa
I write of forest
I write of kings
I use a pen

MADE FROM ANGEL WINGS
I write of freedom
I write of famine
I write of floods
I use the ink

FROM THE PAGES IN MY MIND
I read what history will find
I read of apartheid
I read of hope I read of faith
I read of death

ON THIS 100TH ANNIVERSARY OF THE NATIONAL BAR ASSOCIATION, INC. WE SALUTE THE MANY LEGAL MINDS WHO HAVE SERVED US, TAUGHT US AND ENCOURAGED US TO BE THE BEST ADVOCATE FOR JUSTICE THAT WE COULD BE.

WHEN YOU THINK ABOUT MEMORIAMS, YOU THINK OF ONE'S LEGACY.

WE, THE MEMBERS OF THE NATIONAL BAR ASSOCIATION, INC. WILL ALWAYS PRESERVE THE MEMORY OF EACH AND EVERY SCHOLAR, HISTORICAL EVENT AND TRAGEDIES THAT HAVE COME TO PASS OVER THESE 100 YEARS AND ALWAYS REMEMBER THE SACRIFICES THOSE NBA MEMBERS BEFORE US MADE TO MAKE OUR JOURNEY JUST A TINY BIT EASIER WHILE REMINDING US THAT HARD WORK AND PERSEVERANCE MUST PREVAIL.

THE HISTORY AND SALUTES IN THIS JOURNAL COMMEMORATES THOSE TALENTED JURISTS, SOME WHO CHOSE TO NOT PRACTICE LAW BUT TO BE AN ADVOCATE FOR THE RIGHT LAWS ON CAPITAL HILL, AND SOME WHO TAUGHT THE BASICS OF THE LAW IN A COLLEGE OR UNIVERSITY SETTING SO THAT OTHERS COULD GO OUT AND ENFORCE THOSE RULES OF LAW WITH PRECISION.

100 Years!

Judge William S. "Turk" Thompson

When I think of a firm foundation, I think of my Mom and my Dad, Judge William S. "Turk" Thompson, a Past President of the National Bar Association. Judge Thompson laid the necessary groundwork, to ensure stability and success for those who came after him.

"Turk", as they called him, attended Howard University in Washington, DC, receiving his BS in 1934; He graduated from Robert H. Terrell Law School in Washington, DC in 1939. "Turk" went on to open his own Private Law Practice in Washington, DC. Later, Turk was a Washington, DC City Council Member. "Turk" then served at the DC Superior Court as an Associate Judge until his retirement.

"Turk" served as President of the National Bar Association, 1957-59; Secretary General of the World Peace Through Law Center, 1963-67 and 1972-89; President of the Washington Urban League Board, 1966-69; sat on the Advisory Board for the Jr. Citizen Corps Inc, 1976-; was Chairman of the NBA Judicial Council, 1989-90; and served as President of the Kiwanis Club-Georgetown in DC, 1990-91.

He was a trailblazer who clearly displayed the purpose of the National Bar Association through advancing the science of jurisprudence, upholding the honor of the legal profession, promoting social awareness among members of the bar, and protecting the civil and political rights of all citizens. On this 100th Year of Excellence of the National Bar Association, Inc. I salute my father, Judge William S. "Turk" Thompson.

Congratulations to the Members of the National Bar Association, Inc. as you celebrate 100 years! My father would be so proud of your continued strides toward justice and equality for all.

Sincerely,

Bill Thompson

Ozro Wells

WE SALUTE Ozro Thaddeus "O.T." Wells, Former National Bar Association President

"I am the Master of my fate; I am the captain of my soul"

(By: William Ernest Henley (Line from Invictus 1875)

Those who had the privilege of knowing 'OT" Wells are affectionately saying "That sounds like OT". Wells had a very colorful career, and he enjoyed every minute of it.

Let's take a look:

Served as NBA President from 1972-73.

Was a founding member of the National Negro Golf Association, the oldest African American golf association in the world.
**Was a proud member of the Omega Psi Phi Fraternity, Inc., standing by "Invictus" throughout his life.

Graduated from the public school system in Greensboro, North Carolina, received his Bachelor of Arts degree from Morehouse College in Atlanta (1953), and received his law degree from Boston University (1956).

His legal career began at the Wall Street law firm of Fink & Pavia, New York, NY, now Pavia & Harcourt LLP. In 1959, Mr. Wells was admitted to the New York Bar and joined with noted attorneys William C. Chance Jr. and Nathan Mitchell, which became Chance, Mitchell & Wells, one of the first minority law firms in the lower Manhattan court district, focusing on criminal defense.

Joined Attorney R. Franklin Brown to establish the firm of Wells & Brown which later became Wells, Brown, Mason, Bums & Hall, with a focus on criminal defense, personal injury cases, and other matters.

During the civil rights era, Wells was co-counsel with attorneys Percy Sutton and Mark Lane in the first sit-in cases in New York City.

As reported in 2018 in an article in The Washington Informer: Wells represented the civil rights organization, The Council for Racial Equality (CORE); represented attorneys, judges, elected officials, notorious Harlem underworld persons such as “Bumpy” Elsworth Johnson and “Red” Dillard Morrison; members of the clergy; members of the medical/dental professions; the Five Percenters, a splinter group of the Black Muslims; and represented extremists and various other so called radicals such as H. Rap Brown and his associates; and was counsel for the late great jazz trumpeter Miles Davis.

In the 70’s, Wells worked for the Department of Defense under President Richard Nixon and Nixon’s appointment gave him an equivalency of a major general. During that stint of his career, Wells investigated relations between Black United States military personnel and German nationals.

As NBA President, he became a member of the designated Attorney General Elliot Richardson’s five-man advisory group, which led to the selection of the first Watergate prosecutor, Archibald Cox.

As reported in 2018 by The Washington Informer article, Wells served as the Lead Trial Attorney for the historical litigation to resolve the leadership of The Church of God in Christ, the largest African American Pentecostal denomination in the world. He was subsequently instrumental in setting up the first constitutional convention for the Church, which resulted in establishing the offices of the General Board and presiding bishop. In addition, Wells has served as counsel to both the presiding bishop and the General Board of the Church of God in Christ.

Prior to his passing in 2018, Wells served as a guest faculty member in the “Trial Advocacy” program for the New York County District Attorney for two decades and “Of Counsel” to the prestigious Black-owned Law Firm of Donaldson & Chilliest, LLP.

In Memoriam: Honoring the Life and Legacy of

Clyde E. Bailey, Sr.

61st President of the NBA

A TRIBUTE TO A SCIENTIST, LAWYER, LEADER, ACTIVIST, CHAMPION, AND MENTOR

As the Centennial Journal of the National Bar Association commemorates a century of dedication to justice and service, we pause to honor the extraordinary life of Clyde E. Bailey, Sr.—a visionary whose multifaceted legacy has left an indelible mark on science, law, advocacy, and community.

Clyde E. Bailey, Sr. was a true Renaissance man, earning an impressive array of degrees: a Bachelor of Science in Mathematics, Master of Science in Physics, Master of Science in Material Science, Juris Doctor, Master of Law in Patent and Trade Registration Law, and completing an Executive Development Program. His relentless pursuit of knowledge exemplified a life committed to excellence and progress.

In the realm of science and engineering, Clyde distinguished himself as a Senior Engineer and Physicist at Xerox Corporation, a Technical Leader at General Electric, and an Adjunct Professor of Mathematics at Cuyahoga Community College. His pioneering work and dedication to advancing technological frontiers underscored his role as a trailblazer in his field.

As a seasoned attorney, Clyde's legal career spanned critical areas including intellectual property, space commercialization, and equal employment law—serving NASA with distinction and representing the interests of innovation and justice. His expertise as Patent Counsel at Eastman Kodak Company led him to prepare and prosecute over 500 patent applications worldwide, showcasing his mastery and commitment to protecting invention and creativity.

A dedicated leader and advocate, Clyde served as President of the National Bar Association and chaired the Board of Directors of the National Inventors Hall of Fame Foundation. His leadership extended globally through collaborations with international Bar Associations in Italy, South Africa, and across Southern Africa, championing shared resources, common interests, and the empowerment of African and African American communities. His voice resonated internationally as he spoke on cyber-terrorism, bridging borders and fostering global dialogue among justice and technology leaders from South Africa, the UK, Denmark, Australia, Lesotho, Canada, and Botswana.

Clyde's unwavering advocacy for African Americans and women reflected his deep commitment to equity and inclusion. His perspective on life was to confront every obstacle head-on, driven by a mindset to conquer. His unspoken confidence and positive outlook inspired all who knew him—encouraging others to strive for their best and own their greatness.

Today, we honor a man whose life was a testament to service, innovation, leadership, and advocacy. Clyde E. Bailey, Sr. exemplified what it means to serve well, lead with integrity, and uplift others. His legacy is a beacon guiding future generations toward justice, excellence, and the relentless pursuit of their dreams.

We salute his life—well served, deeply appreciated, and forever remembered.

Continue to Rest in Peace, Clyde E. Bailey, Sr. — a true pioneer and a cherished champion.

IN MEMORIAM:

JOSEPH H. HAIRSTON

(1922 – 2019)

DURING THE CENTENNIAL YEAR OF BOTH THE WASHINGTON BAR ASSOCIATION (WBA) AND THE NATIONAL BAR ASSOCIATION (NBA), WE PAUSE IN A CENTENNIAL SALUTE TO COMMEMORATE OUR BELOVED JOSEPH HENRY HAIRSTON FOR HIS EXEMPLARY LIFE, WORK AND MULTITUDINOUS CONTRIBUTIONS TO OUR NATION

AND

THE CAUSE OF EQUAL JUSTICE UNDER LAW

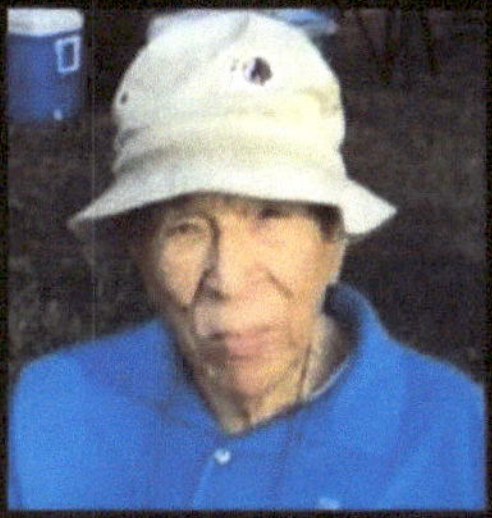

JOE'S BELOVED FRIENDS, COLLEAGUES AND MENTEES FROM THE NATION'S CAPITAL:

KEITH W. WATTERS, PAST PRESIDENT, NBA & WBA
KEVIN D. JUDD, PAST PRESIDENT, NBA & WBA
KAREN E. EVANS, PAST PRESIDENT, WBA
DONALD A. THIGPEN, JR., PAST PRESIDENT, WBA
FELICIA L. CHAMBERS, PAST PRESIDENT, WBA
ROBERT L. BELL, PAST PRESIDENT, WBA

In Loving Memory of The Honorable Morris L. Overstreet

"A Gentleman, an athlete and a scholar who gave out before he gave up."

- Life Member & Past Board Member, National Bar Association - Chair, NBA Judicial Council (1999-2000)
- Life Member, National Bar Institute
- Judge, Texas Court of Criminal Appeals (1990-1998) - First African American elected to statewide office in Texas state history

Honoring the Legacy of

John W. Davis, III, Esq.

A Keeper of Legacy, Love, and Light

September 19, 1947 – October 3, 1997

A man of boundless heart and integrity, John Whittaker Davis III, Esq., embodied what it meant to serve—with strength, grace, and unwavering commitment. Born and raised in Houston, he rose above every challenge, including the life-altering injury that never dimmed his spirit or purpose.

As a distinguished attorney, entrepreneur, and community advocate, John built more than a career—he built opportunity.Through his law practice and leadership in Bayou City Enterprises and Robinson and Davis, Attorneys at Law, he helped shape Houston's landscape and uplift its people.

John's dedication to the National Bar Association and Houston Lawyers Association was not just professional — it was personal. Whether hosting events, mentoring peers, or championing justice, he brought warmth, tradition, and vision into every room.

His faith anchored him. His actions inspired. And his legacy continues through the lives he touched—and through his beloved widow, **NBA Past President Algenita Scott Davis**, his daughter, Marthea Davis, and his son, John Whittaker Davis, IV.

With eternal reverence and respect,

The Davis Family

The Honorable Donald L. McCullin

When I think of the late judge Donald L. McCullin, I think of the movie, "An Officer and a Gentleman." No, Don wasn't in the military but he was always a Gentleman in the way he carried himself as an Officer of the Court.

Donald McCullin was a high school mathematics teacher who entered Saint Louis University Law School as a part time student. He completed Law School in 2-1/2 years. He was a partner at the firm of Wilson, Smith and McCullin before joining the United Auto Workers Legal Services as its managing attorney. His high school classmate and vice president at Anheuser-Busch, Wayman F. Smith, hired Don to join him as part of their Corporate Affairs Department where he was the Director of Diversity and Compliance. He served two non-consecutive terms as president of the Mound City Bar Association. He was a Regional Director of the National Bar Association.

He attended the NBA Annual Conventions faithfully. But he wanted to be a judge and after multiple times of applying, he was finally selected a Circuit Judge for the 22nd Circuit of Missouri in September 1999. He served 11-1/2 years and retired in 2011. But that began his next chapter as he served as a Hearing Officer for the City of St Louis Parking Commission. After the civil unrest in Ferguson MO, he sat as a Municipal Judge in Ferguson. Judge McCullin took seriously the importance of mentorship. He was willing to assist anyone and everyone. His mentees included children in grade school, high school and college and law school. He was loved and respected and is greatly missed since his passing on October 6, 2016.

Hon. Patricia Banks, Atty. Richard A Banks, Hon. Anne-Marie Clarke, Hon. Sandra Farragut Hemphill, Atty. Jerry M. Hunter, Hon. Michael Jamison, Hon. Chalk Mitchell, Atty. James Neely, Hon. Angela Turner Quigless, Atty. Daryl Savage and Atty. Dorothy White-Coleman

Judge Thelma Wyatt Cummings Moore

Past Judicial Council Chair

With deep sadness, I announce the transition of Judge Thelma Wyatt Cummings Moore, a trailblazing jurist, compassionate community leader, and former Chair of the National Bar Association's Judicial Council. Judge Moore passed away peacefully on October 9, 2024. Her remarkable life, filled with groundbreaking achievements and an unwavering dedication to justice, touched countless lives and set a profound example for generations to come.

Born in Amarillo, Texas on July 6, 1945, Judge Moore grew up with a strong sense of purpose and an unshakable belief in equality. She earned her law degree from the Emory University School of Law, breaking barriers as one of the few African American women in her field at the time. She was inducted into the Order of the Coif at Emory and honored with the Emory Medal. Her dedication to justice and fairness led her to become the first African American woman to serve as a judge on the Superior Court of Fulton County, where she would later become the Chief Judge, a position she held with distinction.

Judge Moore's judicial career was characterized by a commitment to protecting the rights of the most vulnerable, fostering accountability, and advancing equitable treatment under the law. Her landmark rulings and thoughtful approach to complex cases earned her respect and admiration across the legal profession and the communities she served. In recognition of her exemplary service, Judge Moore was elected as the Chair of the National Bar Association's Judicial Council, where she championed the causes of diversity and integrity within the judiciary. Judge Moore also chaired the American Bar Association's Judges' Advisory Committee on Ethics. She was a mentor to countless young lawyers and judges, always encouraging them to pursue justice with conviction and compassion.

Beyond the courtroom, Judge Moore was deeply involved in community service, advocating for education, civil rights, and the empowerment of underserved communities. Her legacy of service and dedication to equal justice under the law will live on through the many lives she touched and the barriers she helped dismantle.

A celebration of Judge Moore's extraordinary life and contributions to justice will be held on Friday, November 8, 2024, at Cascade United Methodist Church in Atlanta. In lieu of flowers, the family requests that donations be made to Dada Sisterhood Inc. to support the scholarship program in her honor.

Judge Moore's unwavering belief in justice and equality will remain an enduring light for all who seek to make the world a better place. She will be profoundly missed and lovingly remembered.

LETTER TO SARA SIMMONS

(September 23, 1945-December 13,2001)

My Dear Sister:

This is my final letter to you. I feel like I have been plucked from this earth, but you are the one who is making the journey. We were like one, but so different. You were my social director, my confidante, my mentor, my mother, my child, my Achilles heel, my joy, my spiritual advisor, my protector, my provider, and my responsibility. You did so much with me and wanted so much for me. I expected us to grow old together with you fussing over me.

I know you did not leave so unexpectedly on purpose. You were a joy to so many; but I also know of your pain and your exhaustion. I know of your pride and your desire to be the fine example that you were.

To say goodbye to you is so hard, but you are sitting at the foot stand of our Mama in the kingdom of God preparing a place for your family, including me. Your Life was short but full. God can truly say, "Well done good and faithful servant, well done."

When I see the brightest star in the sky, I will know it is you. When I see the most perfect flower with the boldest colors, I will be reminded of you. When I see the finest things in life and witness the kindest of deeds, I will think of you.

You had the touch - you called, you wrote, you gave gifts, and you gave you. Our time was your time. You are okay, and I need you to help those who love you and are left behind to be okay.

I ask the Lard why? And I wait for an answer. I hear nothing but then I wonder is it because you had done all you wanted to do down here and would only be here to help the rest of us? Is it because Mama wanted one of us with her in heaven and chose you to go first because you were her "Sweets'"? Is it because it was your time, a time none of us can change?

I read in Ecclesiastes that there is a time for everything under the sun - - a time to be born and a time to die. Yet you will never die as long as l live or anyone whose life you touched lives.

There is a saying that whenever one hears a bell ring, another angel gets her wings. I hear the bell. I hear the bell, and the sound is painful to me but a jay to you. Good night my sister, my mother, my friend, until we meet again and tell one another "Good Morning".

All my love,

Your Baby Sister, Evett

WAYMAN FLYNN SMITH III

WAYMAN FLYNN SMITH III was responsible for providing corporate sponsorship for a number of National Bar Association events, and bringing numerous new members to the NBA.

Wayman graduated from Howard Law School in 1965 – a graduating class of ten. The friendships that Wayman made at Howard include Atty. Cornell Moore, Atty. Warren Hope Dawson, Matthew Whitehead, Atty. Renee Brooks, Hon. Gabrielle McDonald, Hon. Ricardo Richardson, which friendships lasted throughout his entire life, and who were also members of the National Bar Association.

Wayman partnered with Atty. Margaret Bush Wilson in St. Louis and they specialized in civil and civil rights litigation, until he joined the executive staff of Anheuser Busch in 1980. Prior to that, in 1970, Wayman was appointed a City Court Judge, serving until 1975. Smith served on the St. Louis Board of Aldermen from 1975 to 1987 and was once president of the council's Black Caucus.

Wayman was initially hired as a consultant with Anheuser-Busch. But as a result of pressure on Anheuser-Busch by Rev. Jesse Jackson, Sr.'s Operation PUSH, Wayman was given the position of the first Black member and Vice President of Anheuser Busch's Corporate Affairs Department. Wayman eventually became a member of the policy board of Anheuser Busch, Inc.

During his twenty years with Anheuser Busch, Wayman designed several programs to raise the profile of Black professionals and create opportunities for Black youths. Wayman was an active member of the National Bar Association, Inc., and was also instrumental in establishing the National Council of Minority Bar Participants. Wayman also served on the Board of Directors of the Congressional Black Caucus Foundation, Inc.

Wayman served as a member of the Harris-Stowe State University Board of Regents for twenty-one years, and as chairman for twelve of those years (1989-2010). Wayman also served as a member of the board of directors of Howard University from 1989, and was chairman from 1991-1995. Wayman remained on Howard's Board of Directors throughout his lifetime, eventually becoming Chairman Emeritus. Upon his retirement, Chairman Wayman F. Smith III was presented Honorary Doctorate Degrees by both Harris-Stowe State University Board of Regents and the Howard University Board of Directors.

Wayman's only child, Kymberly, is also an attorney, and now teaches law in the state of Maryland.

Thank you!
Sheila
JACKSON LEE
CONGRESSWOMAN TEXAS' 18TH DISTRICT

DID YOU KNOW
NATIONAL BAR ASSOCIATION®
EST. 1925

Founder Gertrude Rush became a member of Delta Sigma Theta Sorority, Incorporated in 1919.

That NBA member and Past President CK Hoffler competed in Slalom ski competitions as a child.

That NBA member and Past President CK Hoffler was trilingual by the time she was 10 and she and NBA member Rosalind R. Ray, Esq. who speaks French assisted as translators during the NBA members trip to Morocco in 2014.

That NBA member and Past President CK Hoffler went to boarding school in foreign countries for her entire academic career prior to going to college in the U.S.

That NBA member and Past President CK Hoffler's children have played college football at Power 5 programs and are the inspiration behind her NIL practice.

That NBA member and Past President CK Hoffler's parents were once the largest chicken producers in Virginia.

That NBA member Ricky Anderson, Esq. authored an Entertainment & Sports two volume series titled Entertainment Law (2015) and Music Industry Contracts (2017) that is used for teaching at Thurgood Marshall School of Law, UCLA and many other Law Schools to teach the dynamics of law in those areas of law.

That NBA member Ricky Anderson Esq.'s daughter Alysia followed in her father's footsteps and practices Entertainment law in Los Angeles, California.

That NBA member Judge Greg Mathis wrote a book with Blair S. Walker titled Inner City Miracle giving a candid view of his life and journey to Judge.

That NBA members James L. Bearden, Esq., Arnold Gaines, Esq., Rosalind R. Ray, Esq. And Fred Samuels, Esq. Successfully represented the International Recording Artists, The O'Jays in their royalty case against Philadelphia International Records and Gamble & Huff in Philadelphia, PA.

That NBA member Rosalind R. Ray, Esq. wrote a book titled "Don't Let The High Heels Fool You".

That NBA member Shannon Holmes, Esq. Penned a book titled "Chief Executive Athlete" which talks about how to run your sports career like a fortune 500 company.

That NBA member Shannon Holmes' son Bryce played Marlon Jackson in The Michael Jackson Broadway play.

That NBA member Rosalind R. Ray Co-managed The International Recording Artists Eddie Levert, Sr. ,Walter Williams, Sr. And Eric Nolan Grant, THE O'JAYS for a decade including in 2004 co-producing as Associate Producer their O'Jays album with Mathew Knowles titled "IMAGINATION"and still remains as an advisor on special projects.

That in 2009 NBA member Rosalind R. Ray, Esq. Was an Associate-Producer on Walter Williams, Sr. 's solo album titled "Exposed" and distributed by Ray and Williams company WE-TWO MUSIC, INC. and featured one of Ray's Father's tunes written by Walter I. Ray, Jr. and Unifics lead singer Al Johnson titled "It's Raining Outside"

That NBA member Rosalind R. Ray, Esq. was the Mid-Atlantic Editor for Black Radio Exclusive Magazine (BRE) a trade magazine covering DC, MD, VA, DE and The Carolinas for over 25 years.

That in 2021 NBA member Lita Rosario Richardson was before the Supreme Court of The United States and co-wrote The Brief of Public Knowledge, Lita Rosario-Richarson, Esq., Library Futures Institute, and Fight for the Future as Amici Curiae in Support of the Petition which raised issues for Recording Artists such as termination rights.

That NBA member Kamala D. Harris was a member of Alpha Kappa Alpha Sorority, Inc. and before becoming the First Female African American Vice President of the United States she was The Deputy DA of the Alameda County District Attorney's Office in Oakland, California

That NBA member Jack H. Olender provided scholarships Earl B. Davis Awards every year for many years to deserving students at UDC and Howard University. Olender hosted a Christmas Party every year for all who wanted to join him during the holiday celebration.

That NBA member Attorney Michele Obama was the First Lady of the United States of America during her Husband's stint as President of The United States. Michelle attended Harvard Law School.

That NBA member Attorney Barack Obama was the 44th President of the United States and the First African American President. Barack attended Harvard Law School.

That Congresswoman Jasmine Crockett was a law student of NBA member Ricky Anderson, Esq. Crockett coined the phrase "Bleached Blond Bad Built Butch Body" when it was necessary for her to put her boots on the ground. Crockett serves as the U.S. Representative for Texas's 30th Congressional District since January of 2023.

That NBA member Professor Henry "Hank" Jones taught Civil Procedure at Howard University School of Law to many members of the NBA.

That NBA member Jimmy Cobb had a son who also practiced law named Charles Cobb who worked for the Department of Justice in Washington, DC.

That NBA member Judge Paul Webber was a Judge on the DC Superior Court. In 1996 Webber was rated "One of the Best Trial Justices in the Washington Metropolitan Area" by Washington Magazine".

That NBA member Beverly Perry was at PEPCO serving as Senior Vice President and Special Advisor to the Chairman of Pepco Holdings, Inc. (PHI) in Washington, DC and now Serves as Senior Advisor to Mayor Muriel Bowser in Washington, DC

That NBA member Alexis Herman was Secretary of Labor during President Bill Clinton's Administration. She was the first Black American to hold that position. She was Assistant to the President and Director of the White House Office of Public Engagement prior to that appointment.

That NBA member Billy Murphy was one of the attorneys in the Raphael Edmonds Case with NBA Member Professor J.R. Robertson of Howard University School of Law

*That NBA Member Maxine Waters was a Congresswomen who we affectionately call "Auntie Maxine". She has served as the U.S. Representative for California's 43rd Congressional District since 1991.

That Barbara Lee was the 52nd Mayor of Oakland and assumed office on May 20, 2025. For 27 years she represented California's 12th Congressional District and she served in both houses of the California State Legislature from 1990 to 1998.

That NBA Member Fred David Gray was one of the first Black State Legislators in Alabama in the 20th century along with Thomas Reed, both from Tuskegee. He was also elected as the first African-American President of the Alabama State Bar.

That Carol Moseley Braun was the first African-American woman elected to the U.S. Senate, the first African-American U.S. Senator from the Democratic Party and the first female U.S. Senator from Illinois. She received her law degree from The University of Chicago.

That NBA member Barbara Jordan was the first African American elected to the Texas Senate since Reconstruction, the first southern African American woman elected to the U.S. House of Representatives and one of the first two African Americans elected to the U.S. House from the former Confederacy since 1901, alongside Andrew Young of Georgia.

That NBA member Congressman Al Green serves in Houston, Texas and was censored in 2025 when he spoke out on Capitol Hill as he continues to fight for democracy.

That NBA member Sheila Jackson Lee was a Congresswoman and ran for Mayor of Houston, Texas She was also co-dean of Texas's congressional delegation. When she moved to Houston in 1987 she was appointed as a municipal Judge for the city by Kathy Whitmire.

That NBA member Johnnie Cochran sang with The Temptations at one of our our Annual Conventions and he coined the phrase 'IF IT DOESN'T FIT, YOU MUST ACQUIT".

That NBA member Cora Thomasina Walker was one of the first Black Women to practice law in New York. After having difficulty finding work, in 1947 after being admitted to the New York State Bar she started her own law practice in Harlem. She established a law firm with her son from 1976 to 1999 called Walker & Bailey. Walker became the first female president of The Harlem Lawyers Association sometime between the 1950's and 60's. In 1988 Walker was the Chair of the Commercial Law Section of the National Bar Association. She founded the Corporate Counsel Conference to connect corporations with the counsel of African American Attorneys.

That NBA member Marc Morial served as the youngest Mayor of New Orleans from 1994 to 2002 (59th Mayor of New Orleans) and is now the President of the National Urban League

That Honorable Floyd Flake was the 18th President of Wilberforce University and a minister in New York City.

That Honorable Bennie Thompson was the first Democrat and the first African American to chair the Committee on Homeland Security from 2007 to 2011 and 2019 to 2023 in that order. Since 2011 Thompson has been the only Democrat in Mississippi's Congressional Delegation.

That NBA member Congressman Hakeem Sekou Jeffries is a lawyer and went to school with The View's Sunny Hostin. Jeffries has served as House Minority Leader and leader of the House Democratic Caucus since 2023. Jeffries is in his 7th term as of 2025 and has been the U.S. Representative for New York's 8th Congressional District since 2013. He has served three terms in the New York State Assembly from 2007 to 2012.

That NBA member Attorney Sunny Hostin was a prosecutor and now an on air personality on THE VIEW. She is a Senior Legal Advisor for ABC News and Host and Executive Producer of Investigation Discovery's true crime series Truth About Murder with Sunny Hostin.

That NBA member Judge Mablean Ephriam is a former Los Angeles Prosecuting Attorney. She had her own court TV show Divorce Court for seven seasons from 1999 to 2006. She also was a judge in some of Tyler Perry's Madea films.

That Judge Lynn Toler replaced Judge Mablean during the 2006-2007 season. With her 14 seasons on the Divorce Court from 2006 to 2020, Toler is the longest reigning arbitrator on that series. She was a Republican until 2016 and became an Independent in 2016

That NBA member Judge Damon Keith has a nephew serving as a Judge in Detroit, Michigan named Judge Terrence Keith. Judge Keith was appointed to the bench by President Lyndon B. Johnson. Received an Honorary Degree in law from Harvard University in 2008 and was a member of Alpha Phi Alpha Fraternity.

That NBA member TV Judge Joseph Blakeney Brown, Jr. aka Judge Joe Brown was a former Shelby County, Tennessee Criminal Court Judge and former arbiter of the arbitration based reality court show Judge Joe Brown.

That NBA member Judge Greg Mathis had his very own court TV show for 24 seasons. Judge Mathis is the second longest-serving television arbitrator ever, behind only Judith Sheindlin of the Judge Judy show by three seasons. Mathis has a star on the Hollywood Walk of Fame. His is a member of Alpha Phi Alpha Fraternity.

That NBA member Honorable Angela Alsobrooks served from 2018 to 2024 as County Executive of Prince George's County, Maryland and 2011 to 2018 as the County's State's Attorney. She is the first female County Executive of Prince George's County and the first Black female County Executive in Maryland History.

That NBA member Judge Alexander Williams taught at Howard University School of Law prior to being a United States Circuit Court Judge

That NBA member Honorable William "Lacy" Clay served as a Congressman for Missouri following in the footsteps of his father The Honorable Bill Clay

That NBA member Yusef Jackson had a distributorship with Anheuser Busch, Inc.in Chicago and is the son of Rev. Jesse L. Jackson

That President Richard M. Nixon appointed Judge William S. Thompson to the D.C. Superior court Bench in 1969

That Judge William S. Thompson was a bench member of the 1st appointed City Council in the days before home rule

That NBA member James "Jimmy" Cobb, Esq. owned his own law firm and that his son is an attorney;

That NBA member Stacey Stafford is an attorney and the daughter of the husband and wife legal team who owned and operated their law firm in Virginia;

That NBA member Cheryl Chapman Henderson's father was NBA Member Attorney Clint Chapman, a well known practitioner in the District of Columbia;

That NBA member Jock Smith Esq. who practiced alongside Johnnie Cochran for many years before his passing, his daughter is an Attorney who followed in her father's footsteps;

That Past Presidents Patricia and Micheal Rosier's son, John Moore is also a lawyer who has been a leader in the NBA and a member of the Board of Governors as Chair of the Law Student, Young Lawyers and Small Firms & Solo Practitioners Divisions.

That Past Presidents Patricia and Michael Rosier were the first husband and wife team to serve as Presidents of the National Bar Association

That NBA member Judge Damon Keith's nephew is Judge Terrance A. Keith and he serves in the Probate Court for The State of Michigan, County of Wayne

That Executive Director, Emeritus John Crump's son Jason Crump is a practicing Attorney in the DMV.

That NBA member Lorenzo Williams has three children who are Attorneys. His son Amar Williams actually practices law at his father's firm, his daughter Ayanna Williams and son Akeem Williams, not to mention that Akeem's wife is also an attorney. Now that is a family affair.

That Past President Kim Keenan worked at the NAACP as their general counsel

That Past President and member of Omega Psi Phi Fraternity, Member O.T. Wells son is an attorney in New York

Carolyn Y. Howard, together with Frank Seales, Jr., drafted the Constitution and Bylaws of the National Bar Association and the Bylaws of the National Bar Institute.

Golden Elizabeth Johnson (1944–2010) was a trailblazing legal figure and advocate for racial and gender equity in the legal profession. She co-founded the Women's Legal Defense Fund (WLD), the Association of Black Women Lawyers of New Jersey, and played a key role in establishing the Garden State Bar Association. In 1974, she made history as the first Black woman appointed as a municipal judge in Newark, New Jersey, appointed by the city's first Black mayor, Kenneth A. Gibson. Johnson held a degree in microbiology from Douglass College of Rutgers University and earned her Juris Doctorate from Rutgers Law School.

Renee Jones Weeks made history as the first Black woman—and the first Black person—to preside in New Jersey's General Equity and Probate Court. In recognition of her groundbreaking achievements, she was honored by the U.S. Congress in 2009 through a tribute by Representative Donald M. Payne (155 Cong. Rec. E2398).

Eartha Jean Johnson married her childhood sweetheart, Lonnie Johnson, and together they have three children: Teiva Bell, Tiera Johnson Williams, and Antuan Johnson. Remarkably, Eartha, Lonnie, and all three of their children are attorneys, making law a true family legacy.

That NBA member Eric Holder has had a groundbreaking and historic legal career. In 1988, he was appointed as a judge of the Superior Court of the District of Columbia by President Ronald Reagan. He became the U.S. Attorney for the District of Columbia in 1993 under President Bill Clinton, and in 1997, he was nominated as Deputy Attorney General under Janet Reno. In 2001, he served as Acting Attorney General under President George W. Bush until John Ashcroft was confirmed.

From 2009 to 2015, Holder served as the 82nd U.S. Attorney General under President Barack Obama, becoming the first African American to hold the position.

In 1990, Holder married Dr. Sharon Malone, a prominent physician and the sister of Vivian Malone, one of the first two Black students to enroll at the University of Alabama in 1963, and its first Black graduate in 1965.

The Annual Awards Banquet is the premier event of the National Bar Association's annual convention, serving as the culmination of the week's activities. This elegant evening features the installation of new NBA officers and the presentation of some of the Association's highest honors. What makes the banquet especially meaningful is the opportunity for members to celebrate alongside their friends and family.

Over the years, distinguished keynote speakers have included President Bill Clinton, Secretary Rodney Slater, The Reverend Jesse L. Jackson, Judge Joe Brown, and Attorney General Janet Reno.

The convention kicks off in grand fashion with the Opening Concert & Awards, where the recipient of the prestigious SANKOFA Award is announced. This honor recognizes an individual who has empowered future generations through tireless efforts to make quality education accessible to all. Following the award presentation, attendees enjoy a lively concert. Past performances have featured legendary artists such as Gladys Knight, The Temptations, Will Downing, Joe Sample, The Four Tops, Roy Ayers, and Babyface.

The first annual 20 Millennials Raising The Bar program was held in 2014 in Atlanta, Georgia under Past President Patricia M. Rosier. The 20 Millennials Raising the Bar experience provides an opportunity for young NBA members to strategically connect with key leaders and decision makers across multiple disciplines. The NBA's distinguished corps of Past Presidents serve as the bridge between the past and the future.

John N. Johnson, a proud NBA member, holds the historic distinction of being Texas' first civil rights lawyer, blazing a trail for justice and equity in the legal profession.

For many years, the National Medical Association (NMA) and the National Bar Association (NBA) have shared a strong bond, exemplified by the tradition of holding their conventions in the same city and coming together in fellowship and mutual support.

The National Bar Association maintains a longstanding relationship with the Coalition of Bar Associations of Color (CBAC), convening annually to tackle critical issues affecting communities of color, such as judicial diversity, criminal justice reform, and immigration policy. These meetings have led to impactful dialogue with U.S. Senators, their staff, the Department of Homeland Security, and the White House Office of Public Engagement. Over the years, NBA representatives in these meetings have included notable leaders such as Past Presidents Benjamin Crump and Kevin Judd, Legislative Committee Co-Chairs, Stephanie Mickle, Chief of Operations Twanda Turner Hawkins, and Resolutions Chair Norma Hutcheson.

Each year, during the NBA's Annual Day on the Hill, members of the National Bar Association convene in Washington, D.C., to meet with Senators and White House officials. Representing nearly 67,000 African American lawyers, judges, and law students, these advocates address some of the nation's most pressing legal and social issues, such as voting rights, police brutality, and judicial nominations, in strategic meetings held at the White House and the Russell Senate Office Building.

The National Bar Association also honors the legal profession's highest traditions by gathering at the Supreme Court annually to witness the swearing-in of distinguished NBA attorneys. These ceremonies mark a significant milestone in their careers and symbolize their readiness to advocate before the highest court in the land.

HAPPY
FEELINGS
NATIONAL BAR
ASSOCIATION
EST. 1925

100 YEARS OF THE NBA

1925-2025

Photos From Their Personal Collections Courtesy of:

Darryl Carter, Debra D. Matlock, Rosalind R. Ray, Pat M. Rosier, & Bobbie Edmonds

AL B. SURE

BENJAMIN L. CRUMP
COLLEGE OF LAW

JUSTICE RUTH BADER GINSBURG

NATIONAL BAR
ASSOCIATION

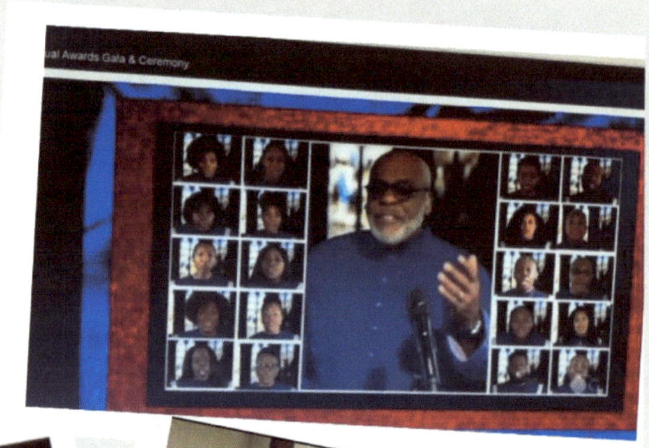

JUDGE GLENDA HATCHETT

VIRTUAL YEAR

LAWYER

LEGALIZED
GENOCIDE
OF COLORED
PEOPLE
OPEN
SEASON
BEN
CRUMP

UNDAUNTED
NBA CLS

SECRETARY OF LABOR
ALEXIS HERMAN

JUSTICE SONIA
SOTOMAYOR

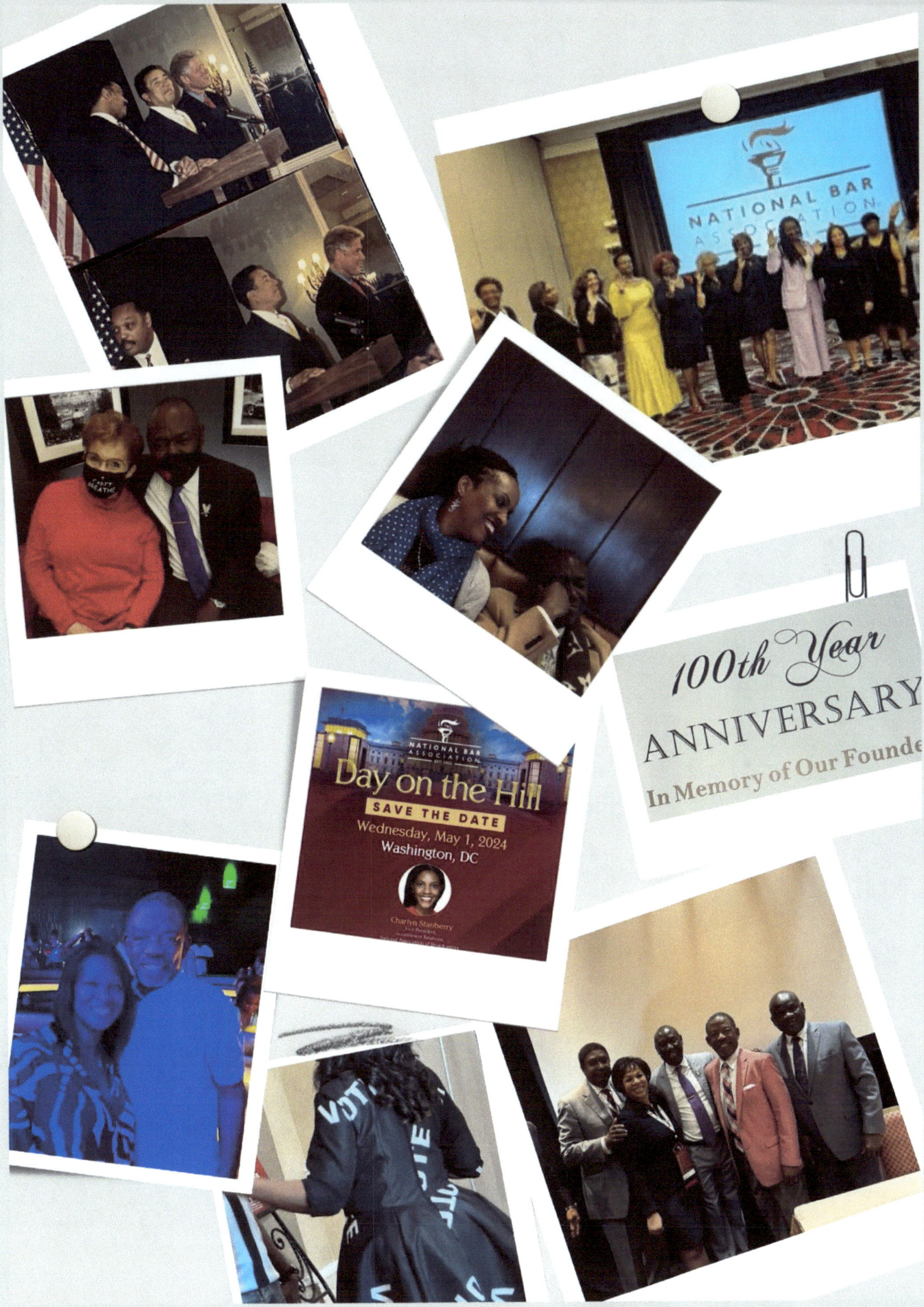
NATIONAL BAR
100th Year
ANNIVERSARY
In Memory of Our Founde
NATIONAL BAR ASSOCIATION
Day on the Hill
SAVE THE DATE
Wednesday, May 1, 2024
Washington, DC
Charlyn Stanberry

DEAN ROGER A. FAIRFAX, JR. (LEFT)

DR. DOROTHY HEIGHT

JUDGE
DAMON KEITH

JUSTICE KETANJI
BROWN JACKSON

SECRETARY OF STATE
COLIN POWELL

NATIONAL BAR ASSOCIATION

EST. 1925

UPDATE: Safety Warning

On August 1, the Federal Bureau of Investigation and the Minnesota Bureau of Criminal Apprehension notified the National Bar Association of a threat on Judges and Lawyers in the City of Minneapolis. Today, law enforcement updated NBA Leadership that the person who made the threat has been apprehended.

PRINCE'S PAISLEY PARK

BY CULTURE AND BY MERIT
AKA
AKA

Orpheum
NATIONAL BAR ASSOCIATION
GALA NIGHT

DECENT HOUSING NOW!

THE FOUR TOPS

OTIS WILLIAMS

PROFESSOR CHARLES L. OGLETREE, JR., ESQ (RIGHT)

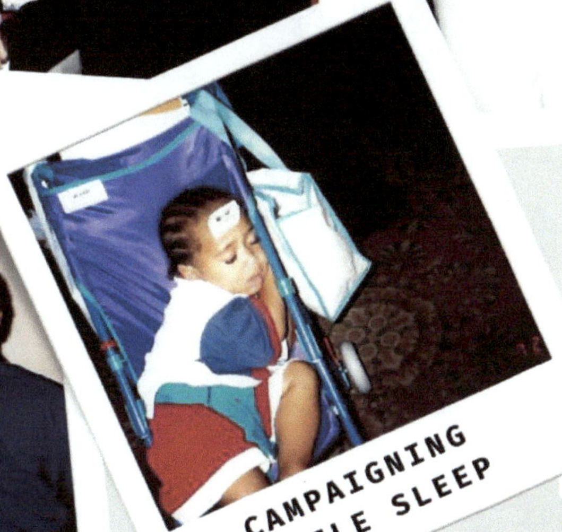

CAMPAIGNING WHILE SLEEP

BENJAMIN HOOKS (LEFT)

LORRAINE MOTEL

JUDGE JOHN YOUNG

JUDGE ARTHUR BURNETT

GLADYS KNIGHT

JOHNNY GILL

WALTER WILLIAMS (RIGHT)

1925
A Monumental Journey
SEE YOU NEXT YEAR IN
Chicago
2025
Honoring our Past,
while Preparing for our Future
NATIONAL BAR ASSOCIATION
NBA CBCF ALC
September 11-15, 2024
Washington, DC
35TH ANNUAL
WILEY A. BRANTON ISSUES SYMPOSIUM
October 17-October 20, 2024
Washington, DC
LABOR & EMPLOYMENT SECTION ANNUAL CONFERENCE 2024
October 17-October 20, 2024
Washington, DC
NATIONAL BAR ASSOCIATION
AWARDS GALA
March 20-23, 2025
Des Moines, IA
Spring 2025
Spring 2025

PRECIOUS MEMORIES

NATIONAL BAR ASSOCIATION®
EST. 1925

NOTES

NOTES

NOTES

Microsoft
Microsoft congratulates the National Bar Association on 100 years!
Because collaboration matters
LEARN MORE